THE ATTRIBUTES

THE

ATTRIBUTES

25 HIDDEN DRIVERS
OF OPTIMAL PERFORMANCE

RICH DIVINEY

RANDOM HOUSE

NEW YORK

Published in the United States by Random House, an imprint and division
of Penguin Random House LLC, New York.

RANDOM HOUSE and the HOUSE colophon are registered trademarks of
Penguin Random House LLC.

Library of Congress Cataloging-in-Publication Data
Names: Diviney, Rich, author.
Title: The attributes --:
25 hidden drivers of optimal performance / Rich Diviney.
Description: New York : Random House, [2021] | Includes index.
Identifiers: LCCN 2-020026664 (print) | LCCN 2020026665 (ebook) |
ISBN 9780593133941 (hardcover) | ISBN 9780593133958 (ebook)
Subjects: LCSH: Temperament. | Character. | Performance. | Success.
Classification: LCC BF801 .D58 2021 (print) |
LCC BF801 (ebook) | DDC 155.2/32—dc23
LC record available at https://lccn.loc.gov/2020026664
LC ebook record available at https://lccn.loc.gov/2020026665

Hardback ISBN 978-0-593-13394-1
International ISBN 978-0-593-24323-7
Ebook ISBN 978-0-593-13395-8

Printed in the United States of America on acid-free paper

randomhousebooks.com

2 4 6 8 9 7 5 3 1

First Edition

Book design by Edwin Vazquez

To Kristen, Connor & Josh.
For always encouraging me to lean out over my edges—
and always being on belay when I do.

This book, and all my life's endeavors,
are dedicated to you.

CONTENTS

1) Hidden Drivers   3
2) Surviving a Parachute Malfunction   16
3) The Dream Team Paradox   28

The Grit Attributes   45
4) Beware the Fearless Leader (Courage)   47
5) Fall Seven Times and Get Up Eight (Perseverance)   57
6) Be Like the Frog (Adaptability)   65
7) The Benefits of Little Tragedies (Resilience)   72
Grit Roll-up   84

The Mental Acuity Attributes   86
8) The Art of Vigilance (Situational Awareness)   89
9) Wired for Efficiency (Compartmentalization)   95
10) The Multitasking Myth (Task Switching)   100
11) Forged in Plastic (Learnability)   107
Mental Acuity Roll-up   115

The Drive Attributes   117
12) Mastering the Pivot (Self-efficacy)   119
13) The Self-disciplined Loser (Discipline)   127
14) A Fish Is the Last to Discover Water
(Open-mindedness)   132

15) The Princess and the Dragon (Cunning)   139
16) It's All About Me (Narcissism)   148
Drive Roll-up   156

The Leadership Attributes   158
17) No One Cares How *You* Feel (Empathy)   161
18) If It Doesn't Hurt, You're Doing It Wrong
(Selflessness)   170
19) You Can't Hide You (Authenticity)   175
20) Many a False Step Is Made by Standing Still
(Decisiveness)   182
21) Don't Be a Mediator (Accountability)   189
Leadership Roll-up   197

The Teamability Attributes   199
22) The Subjectivity of Right and Wrong (Integrity)   202
23) There's Always Something to Do
(Conscientiousness)   208
24) Play Black, Not Red (Humility)   213
25) Honor the Class Clown (Humor)   221

26) Dynamic Subordination   227
27) The Others   235
28) Decoding Your Palette   246
29) Go Perform Optimally   255

Acknowledgments   261

Appendix One: Life Plot   271

Appendix Two: List of Values   273

Index   277

THE ATTRIBUTES

CHAPTER ONE

HIDDEN DRIVERS

Y OU SAVED FOR YEARS for a trip to China and set aside a couple of days for a bus tour through the countryside. The scenery is spectacular, but the only stops are brief ones in remote villages miles from anywhere most tourists would see. In one especially tiny hamlet, the guide says you've got twenty minutes to look over a broad valley ribboned with late-afternoon shadows. You slip away from the group and follow a narrow path that winds up a small hill so you can get a better view in solitude. And it's spectacular. You lose yourself in the moment, and the next moments, too. You look at your watch: You've been enjoying that view for half an hour.

You sprint down the hill, but it's too late. The bus is gone, far down a sliver of dirt road so treacherous the driver couldn't turn around even if he realized you were missing. Your pockets are empty: You left your phone, your cash, and your passport on the bus because you didn't want to lose them. You look around. There are a half-dozen tiny houses, no vehicles, no power lines. An old woman gives you a curious look. You ask if she can help, but she can't even understand you: You don't speak Chinese and no one in the village speaks English. If you remember the itinerary correctly, the next stop is three hours away. It'll be dark in two.

What do you do?

How about this scenario: You take the family to New York City to see the sights. It's the first time the kids have been there, and they love it. You go to the Statue of Liberty and Times Square, and now you're all going to ride the subway up to the Museum of Natural History. Except you're on the wrong platform—this train is going downtown. You manage to corral two of the kids, but the five-year-old, too excited to hear you, slips through the crowd and onto the train by himself. The doors close and the train pulls away, then disappears into the tunnel with your child.

Now what?

One more: It's three months into a brand-new year. Things are going well. You've stuck to your resolutions, made progress on some long-term goals. Winter is beginning to wane and spring is on the horizon. Then a pandemic erupts across the globe. Seemingly overnight the entire nation shuts down, and the governor orders everyone to stay at home. The kids are out of school, you're not sure if you still have a job, stores are closing, and there's no toilet paper or hand sanitizer to be found. You're not sure how scared you should be because so much is unknown about the virus: You'd probably recover, but what about your aging parents? Worse, you have no idea how long this will last. A few weeks? A few months? Or has everything changed forever?

Did you have a plan for that?

No, of course you didn't. Those three scenarios have one thing in common: Each has plunged you into the depths of uncertainty, into a dark and unfamiliar place where panic rises with every heartbeat or confusion bleeds into fear. You can't practice for moments like those, can't learn any skills to navigate those first trembling moments. You pick up languages quickly? Not Chinese before nightfall. You've got big-city street smarts? Your five-year-old doesn't. Were you ready for the economy to grind to a halt, for a new normal of physical isolation? Was anybody?

But you still have to act. In such extreme situations, how you perform is much less about what you know than who you are.

Your *skills* aren't necessarily important.

What matters more are your *attributes*.

ATTRIBUTES ARE WIRED INTO our internal circuitry, always running in the background, dictating how we behave and react and perform. Think of them as the computer code behind an app on your phone. You tap an icon and a program opens, maybe your email or a game or the weather forecast. That's a visible behavior, an obvious and predictable cause and effect. Tap, open. For most people on most days, that's enough information to work with: If I touch this icon, a certain thing will happen, and if I touch this one, a different, yet still certain, thing will happen. Apply a skill and get a result.

What most people never consider, though, are the thousands of lines of code—the average iPhone app has fifty thousand—that determine how an app functions. Think of that code as a collection of attributes. Each app has its own unique combination, but there's usually no need to care about what it might be. If you want directions to the beach, you need to know which icon to tap for the GPS, not how to write code. Your home screen is neatly ordered, the apps are clearly identified, and you know what to expect when you click on any particular one.

But those little pictures don't actually do anything. What

you see—the icon that opens the app—doesn't drive performance. The code, the unseen programming, does that.

That code is pretty important.

Those attributes matter.

People are more complicated than apps, of course. None of us is siloed into a singular function, capable only of texting or posting Instagram stories. But the principle is the same: We all have an internal coding, a specific combination of attributes that guide our performance. Are you highly adaptable with a strong sense of humility but low accountability? You'll perform differently than someone who's cunning and disciplined and fears rejection. Neither is better or worse—for our purposes, consider attributes as neutral traits wired into us by both nature and nurture; they are neither moral failings nor superior accomplishments.

Nor should attributes be confused with personality traits. A personality is built from patterns of behavior that emerge over an extended period of time. It's an outward expression of all the things that make you *you*—your skills, habits, emotions, perspectives, and, yes, attributes, all blended together. A multitude of factors influence your personality, from genetics to upbringing to environment. Attributes are just one of those elemental ingredients.

But it's important to remember that attributes are always running in the background. Highly challenging situations, especially ones rife with uncertainty that force you to operate on instinct, will bring them to the forefront. But your levels of resilience and self-efficacy also influence how you perform every day; your authenticity and empathy impact how you treat others and how they perceive you. Attributes also affect how people—teams, managers, and subordinates, spouses, children, and friends—interact with one another; a dozen competent, skilled colleagues might be a disaster working together, while a collection of seemingly average individuals excel as a collective. Attributes can suggest who's an effective leader and who's a loyal follower.

While attributes are part of everyone's circuitry, they're not immutable. They can be tweaked and modified. Imagine that each attribute has its own sliding dimmer switch. If you have a very low level of, say, adaptability, the plastic slider will be set near the bottom; and if you have a high level of humility, that switch will be near the top. Those switches are pretty stubborn, too, because attributes tend to have natural set points in each of us. But they can be moved. With effort and practice, you can shift levels up or down, increase this trait and dampen that one, as you think is necessary.

You can't manipulate the attributes in other people. But you can learn to recognize them, which is extremely useful. If you want to understand human performance—yours and others'—the first step is to understand attributes.

I LEARNED ABOUT ATTRIBUTES the hard way, on the job and under pressure from the top.

In 2010, I was in charge of training for one of the premier special-operations units on the planet. Our command selected candidates from other spec-ops teams, men who already had proven themselves to be exceptionally skilled and committed. One Friday afternoon, I was sitting across a small table from one of those men, still sweaty in his fatigues from a long day of training. He was a Navy SEAL with eight years of experience behind him, a seasoned warrior who'd completed dozens of missions. His record was saturated with glowing reviews and recommendations from his superiors. He was also recognized as a mentor to younger, less experienced guys, and he'd been promoted at every available opportunity, often early.

On paper, he was perfect. But three weeks into a nine-month program, we already knew he wasn't going to make it.

The selection-and-training class had just finished a week of close-quarter combat exercises, or CQC. You've seen it in the movies and on TV, a SWAT team or a squad of soldiers busting into a building, staring down the barrels of weapons they're waving around, one of them shouting *clear!* every few seconds. The Hollywood version is much noisier and sloppier than reality, though. In real life, CQC is a complex sequence of movements, the exact order and timing of which have to be improvised in a fluid, high-stress environment where mistakes can be fatal. The lead man focuses only on the door and waits for a signal, a squeeze or a word, from the second man. Then he goes through the door and turns left or right, sweeping his sightline down the wall and ninety degrees toward the center of the room. The second man goes the opposite direction—left to the lead man's right, or vice versa—and does the same visual sweep. The third and fourth men keep alternating directions, each of them scanning the room for any bad guys who need to be neutralized or good guys who don't. All of that happens in a few heartbeats.

The guy sitting across from me had, in his career, cleared more rooms than he could likely remember. But each special-operations team has its own habits and techniques, and we needed him to learn our particular ones. We had precise rules about weapon control, when the safety was on or off, when a finger was on the trigger, even how far each man should be from the wall. Shedding habits is no easy task, but it was critical to our ability to train guys to do the exact same things, in the exact same way. Congruity of thought and action is essential in high-performing teams, especially when the environment is so dynamic and stakes are so high. At the beginning of CQC training, it's relatively easy: We start with two-man teams using dry pistols (without ammunition) clearing a couple of rooms. The program ramps up quickly from there. Two men become four, three rooms become eight, then ten, with hallways, L-shaped and T-shaped, added in. Dry-firing pistols are swapped out for rifles and live ammunition. The complexity increases by the day, and candidates are required to absorb and process more and more information at a rapid pace.

The candidate at the table had started strong, but after the first week or so, things began to get shaky. Little mistakes morphed into bigger ones, and his confidence was taking a hit. He knew he was falling behind, and he tried like hell to catch up. He stayed late, walking through scenarios, practicing techniques, asking instructors for feedback. None of it was working. One of the most highly trained warriors in the world, a man specifically recruited for this specialized unit, just couldn't keep up.

I wasn't happy that Friday afternoon, sitting at the table. This man's service record, all commendations and recommendations, was in front of me, and I leafed through it again. Everything in that file said he was a perfect fit for this unit; everything we'd seen in CQC told us he was not.

What was I supposed to tell him? That at least he wasn't the only one? That more than half—*half!*—of the candidates washed out, too? That wouldn't do: No matter how gently the words come out, *you're not good enough* is a hard blow to anyone's ego, let alone a guy of his caliber.

And then there were my superiors. There's a high attrition rate for candidates who want to get into special-operations units in the first place, and that is by design; about 85 percent of prospective candidates, for instance, don't complete basic SEAL training. But we were recruiting men who'd *already* proven themselves to be among the very best special operators. When only about 50 percent of those guys made it through our training, commanders farther up the chain understandably wanted to know why. If we couldn't give them an answer better than "They didn't cut it," sooner or later they would start to question the program itself—a program those of us at the unit knew was sound and had proven successful for decades. The questions, in fact, had already started coming: Before I took over training, my commanding officer had tasked me with taking a deeper look, to see if we could better articulate our process so that we could more accurately explain the failure, and success, of candidates.

On that day in 2010, though, I didn't have any satisfying answers. I told this highly experienced, highly decorated, and highly competent SEAL the only thing I could. "I'm sorry, you just didn't cut it."

He wasn't happy, either.

TO BEGIN FIGURING OUT a better way to explain why so many seemingly well-qualified candidates weren't cutting it, I decided that I needed to examine our roots. So I went back to the beginning, which was 1943.

Though World War II would rage almost two more years, it was a foregone conclusion that victory on the European front would require Allied boots on the ground. A limited number of paratroopers could be, and were being, dropped into enemy territory, but defeating the Axis armies would need to be done by many thousands of soldiers, an overwhelming force of men and matériel. Winning the war inevitably would require a massive amphibious invasion.

Allied forces had realized the same thing during the previous world war. The Gallipoli Campaign, in 1915, was planned as an amphibious landing followed by a ground assault to seize control of a key supply route. It was expected to be the beginning of the end of World War I. Instead, it was a disaster. Ottoman forces had crowded the straits with mines and underwater obstacles, and multiple ships, including two submarines, were sunk or damaged during the initial assault. The campaign slogged on for eight months and claimed half a million lives before the Allies withdrew.

The lessons of Gallipoli were not lost on Allied planners almost thirty years later. After a series of hazardous landing trials, commanders in the U.S. Navy realized a large-scale invasion would need to be preceded by a small group of infiltrators. Their mission would be to reconnoiter beaches, find and destroy obstacles, and guide landing forces ashore. Essentially, the success of D-Day, the largest seaborne invasion in human history, would rely on a handful of volunteers risking their lives to gather intelligence and clear a path.

Navy lieutenant commander Draper Kauffman was appointed to organize the new unit. More than a year earlier, he'd developed the U.S. Naval Bomb Disposal School, and many of his initial recruits—Seabees, Marines, Army combat engineers—already had demolition experience. The men in Kauffman's Naval Combat Demolition Units (NCDU), though, would be swimming into heavily defended enemy beaches wearing nothing but shorts, fins, and a mask, and armed only with a dive knife and whatever explosives they could carry. While holding their breath, these men would have to dive as deep as fifty feet, tie explosives to obstacles, locate and record mines, and take notes they could translate into a map for Allied invasion forces. In some cases, the NCDU teams would have to sneak ashore to identify and sabotage enemy positions. With nothing but a knife for self-defense, those men would certainly be killed or captured if they were discovered.

Kauffman understood, though, that being a strong swimmer who could sneak across a beach wasn't enough for his recruits. He needed men who could think on their feet. Men who could adapt and flex as fast as the environment did. Men who had the ability to be aware of multiple aspects of their surroundings, could work together as a team, and

learn new things quickly—and do so while under unfath-
omable stress.

Kauffman realized, in other words, that he wasn't looking for recruits who knew *how* to do the job but rather men
who *could* do the job.

The difference in that single word, between *how* and
could, is enormous. The required skills—diving, cartogra-
phy, demolition, and so on—could always be taught. What
Kauffman needed were men with certain innate attributes,
traits that are hardwired into each person's core.

These squads were needed as soon as possible, so Kauffman didn't have a lot of time to dither with selecting and
training his men. Instead of teasing out traits such as adaptability, compartmentalization, and resilience through months
of drills and practice runs, Kauffman had a flicker of unconscious genius: He would begin training with the most gru-
eling week he could imagine. Candidates were subjected to
intense physical activity, team challenges, combat simula-
tions, and problem-solving. They went nonstop for five
days, allowed to sleep for only three to four hours the entire
week—not each night, but for the entire week. Kauffman
conducted no exams or evaluations during that first week;
assuming an injury didn't prevent a man from continuing,
no one was forced out of the program. A candidate's ability
to make it through rested solely on that candidate. Was he
going to stay or was he going to quit?

Many quit. Most men, in fact, gave up by day two; the
attrition rate was about 90 percent. This did not matter to
Kauffman, however. Losing most of his recruits was basically
the point. The few who remained were the ones Kauffman—
and the Allied forces—needed. He knew that the handful of
men who made it through would be able to perform when
it was time for the real job, when things were guaranteed to
go sideways, when well-laid plans unraveled into infinite
complexity. Whether Kauffman consciously realized it or

not, the genius of that first week was that it mostly removed skills from consideration and instead revealed each man's hidden attributes. The ones who remained had the attributes required to push through and succeed, no matter how thoroughly circumstances deteriorated.

KAUFFMAN'S INITIAL WEEK OF misery was aptly nicknamed Hell Week. As the NCDUs over time morphed into the Underwater Demolition Teams (UDT) and eventually the Naval Special Warfare Sea, Air, and Land (SEAL) Teams, the necessary skills evolved and the training and selection course got longer and more complicated. What never changed, however, was the goal. Modern SEAL training—the Basic Underwater Demolition/SEAL (BUD/S) course—is primarily a selection program. It spans six months and Hell Week is now the fifth instead of the first, but the elemental objective is still the same: Does a candidate have the *attributes* the Navy is looking for?

That's exactly the question I returned to in 2010. In trying to explain why seasoned special operators were washing out, my colleagues and I were constraining ourselves by focusing on skills-based evaluations. That was the wrong metric. Yes, on a superficial level, a candidate might appear to fail because he couldn't perform one skill or another correctly or effectively. Yet we knew, as Kauffman did intuitively, that skills can be taught. What mattered was *why* those candidates stumbled. In much the same way Hell Week stripped recruits to their core attributes, so did our training program. And that environment highlighted how we were really assessing candidates, which was on the basis of their innate attributes.

Once we understood that, we set about asking ourselves the more difficult question: What attributes, exactly, were we looking for? We put together small groups at the unit to

generate separate lists of what attributes made a great operator. We were careful not to conflate skills with attributes, a
mistake which often happens. Things like "great shot" or
"excellent breacher" were discarded. We then compared all
of those lists to distill them into a single one.

Ultimately, we landed on a list of thirty-six attributes,
and it changed the game for us in terms of understanding
our process and explaining the results. We could now articulate, to ourselves and to candidates, what we were looking for and why. During training exercises, we could see in
real time what attributes a candidate did or didn't have. If a
guy was consistently unable to recognize which direction to
turn and what angles to take while entering a room, that
told us about his level of situational awareness and adaptability. When a candidate quickly absorbed new rules and techniques that were being thrown at him, it spoke to his
learnability. And if a candidate was consistently screwing up
and, rather than bouncing back, began to spiral downward,
it showed us how resilient he was. This allowed us to more
effectively, and more constructively, explain dismissals to the
candidates, the leadership, and ourselves. Now we could
show candidates, based on the master list, which attributes
they had more of, which ones they had less of, and, most
important, how that translated into their performance.

There was a positive collateral effect, too. Once we separated skill competence from attribute possession, we were
able to spot the dark horses early, the guys who might not
have been the most technically proficient but had all of the
attributes we were looking for. Those too often were the
guys we'd been dismissing because we weren't seeing their
potential when it was right in front of us. And we didn't see
it because we weren't looking with the right set of eyes.

Shifting our focus to include attributes made all the difference. Yes, skills will always matter. But once we figured
out what *informed* those skills—that is, what attributes were

hiding in plain sight—we were able to better articulate our selection criteria; explain why some candidates made it and others didn't in concrete, constructive terms; and, most important, assemble the best possible team of special-warfare operators.

Military training, especially among elite combat units, is a perfect crucible for separating attributes from skills, and working with sec-ops teams gave me the rare and valuable opportunity to observe and understand the differences. Yet those same principles apply just as readily in the civilian world as they do in the military. Want to understand why you just can't seem to prioritize and focus? Why do you always feel tense when circumstances change? Why can't you just get started on that goal of yours, or take it to the finish line once you do? Attributes are the place to start. Wherever and whenever people need to work cohesively, identifying and understanding attributes—in yourself and in others—is critical to performing at the optimal level.

CHAPTER TWO

SURVIVING A PARACHUTE MALFUNCTION

I HATE HEIGHTS.

Flying doesn't bother me. In fact, I love it. My dad had a pilot's license when I was a kid, and he would take my brothers, my sister, and me flying in a single-engine plane on weekends. We took turns sitting up front next to him, the coveted position, and every once in a while he would give us the controls so we could experience firsthand driving in three dimensions. My twin brother and I were sold right away: From the time we were ten years old, we had our sights set on becoming Navy fighter pilots. We lived and breathed aviation. We covered our bedroom walls with posters of military aircraft, and we memorized the specs—max altitude, top speed, mission—of each one. We both attended aviation colleges for a year after high school before landing at Purdue University with hopes for Navy ROTC scholarships. For the most part, we were successful. My brother didn't stick with ROTC, but he found his way into the Marine Corps and flew the AV-8B Harrier—the jump jets that can take off and land vertically—for twenty years. I was able to earn a scholarship and, when I graduated in

1996, was commissioned as an ensign in the Navy. By then, though, my goals had changed.

Shortly after the first Gulf War in 1991, I happened upon a *Newsweek* magazine that, on the cover, had a soldier with an expertly camouflaged face. The headline for the main story was "Secret Warriors," and it was about the special-operations units in each branch of the armed forces—the Army's Green Berets, Rangers, and helicopter pilots; the Air Force's Combat Controllers and Pararescue; the Marine Corps's Force Reconnaissance; and, of course, the Navy's SEALs. The article was illustrated with pictures of soldiers in different environments—in the snow and the jungle, underwater and in the sky. It was cool to see the different gear and uniforms guys needed to operate in those conditions, but I was struck by two other things. One was that out of thirty or so photos, probably twenty-five of them were of SEALs. The Navy special-ops guys worked in all those environments. That there were these kinds of men, able to do the job anywhere and everywhere, was inspiring; my childhood fantasies of being James Bond started to seem within reach.

The second thing that struck me was their specialty on, in, and under the water. Growing up near the ocean in New England, I had been a water rat since birth. But while the ocean is certainly fun to sit beside and play around in, it's also incredibly hostile to humans. The lack of oxygen, extreme temperatures, and bone-crushing pressures all explain why human beings are land dwellers. But SEALs made this environment their safe place. A mantra for them was that the enemy will never be brave enough or stupid enough to follow you into the water. When in doubt, go there. I loved that idea, the audacity of making a hostile place your refuge.

And then there was the exclusivity. The selection and training is widely renowned as some of the toughest military training in the world, with only about 15 percent of candidates succeeding. I was sure I could become a fighter pilot, but could I be a SEAL? Was I strong enough, smart enough, tough enough? I pictured myself in my fighter jet someday looking over a bunch of guys from a SEAL team, wondering if I could have made it. I knew I'd always wonder. So I made my decision.

That's how I found myself, ten years later, in a C-130 lumbering through the sky at twenty thousand feet one late spring night. When you're inside an airplane or helicopter, the sensation of height is muted: as far as the physical senses are concerned, you might as well be standing in a small wobbly room or sitting in an uncomfortable chair. But once we reached the right altitude, I was in the tail, standing on an open ramp, staring into a pitch-black abyss and getting ready to throw myself into it.

Did I mention that I hate heights?

The fear response is an interesting thing. There are some basic physiological reactions common to most people—an increase in pulse and respiration, dilation of the pupils—but others are idiosyncratic. Mine? I yawn. I know, it sounds weird, and I used to think it was, too. But what I now know is that yawning is just my body's way of trying to reregulate my breathing, take in more oxygen, and access my parasympathetic nervous system through my trigeminal nerve (don't worry, I'll explain all of that later). Of course, the outward appearance of this suggests the complete opposite of fear, which is handy when you don't want people to know that you're nervous.

But I was. I was nervous every time I got ready to jump.

THE NAVY HAD US jumping out of planes pretty early on. Back then, your first stop after graduating from BUD/S was the Army's static-line parachute course. A static line is a cord with one end attached to the parachute and the other hooked inside the aircraft. As the jumper exits the plane at about twelve hundred feet, the static line pulls open the parachute and the jumper floats down to the ground. There is no freefall in those jumps, and the big, round parachutes have almost zero forward motion, which means there is no "flying" of the parachute required. You just hope the spotter releases you over a good target, because you have no real control over where you land. At the Airborne course, we spent three weeks learning how to fling ourselves out of an airplane and float to the ground, which we did a total of five times. (Yep, three entire weeks for five jumps. After the intensity of SEAL training, many of us had real trouble with that pace.)

Following the static-line jumps was the freefall qualification. That was another four-week course to learn how to skydive from twelve *thousand* feet, ten times higher than the static line jumps: Freefall for several seconds, pull your ripcord, and, with a square chute that has a forward motion of about twenty-five miles per hour, pilot your parachute to the ground. The jump training became incrementally more complex until, ten years and countless jumps later, I was practicing the most difficult level of skydiving—high altitude, high opening, or HAHO. You jump from around twenty thousand feet, count to four, then pull the cord. The parachute opens at about nineteen thousand feet, which means there is a long flight to a distant landing zone. This training is done during the day and at night, with nighttime proficiency being the goal, which is why I was standing at the back of that C-130, yawning at the black sky.

Several things make jumping from that height more difficult. One is how cold it is up there. Average air-temperature differentials are approximately three degrees per thousand feet. This means that if it's a reasonable sixty degrees when you board the aircraft, you can expect the air to be a bone-chilling subzero temperature when you jump out. There's also very little oxygen at that height. At sea level, the air is almost 21 percent oxygen; at twenty thousand feet, it plummets to less than 10 percent. With air that thin, you're at risk of altitude sickness, which includes a myriad of symptoms ranging from dizziness, fatigue, and headache to massive confusion, shortness of breath, and complete loss of consciousness. This means that you have to jump with an oxygen canister and mask—and that's on top of full combat gear, a ballistic helmet, and, because it's pitch-dark, night-vision goggles.

That's a lot of equipment to juggle, which only adds to the list of skills needed to survive a HAHO. A jumper leaves the plane traveling at over a hundred miles per hour. At that speed, an improperly placed rucksack will catch air and drastically affect your ability to get into a stable falling position. Loose, unsecured gear could break off and harmlessly fall to the earth, in which case you'll be ill-equipped once you land. Or it could get snagged in parachute lines and cause an unrecoverable malfunction. So the first skill is making sure everything is where it belongs.

The second-most-important skill is getting out of the aircraft and into the correct position. Whether diving out (hands and head first) or exiting prone (hopping off backward), the goal is to get your body into a stable, straight down freefall as soon as possible. Parachutes perform optimally when a jumper is lying flat—chest and torso horizontal and level, giving the parachute on his back clean and unimpeded air to deploy into. Body position is critical—straight but not stiff, back arched, head up, arms and legs evenly spaced. Legs that are too straight will cause rapid forward horizontal motion; too bent, the more common problem for beginners, and you'll move rapidly backward, what's called backsliding. Lateral movement is extremely hard to be aware of, since you are so high up, yet it can drastically affect the proper deployment of a parachute, throwing it back or forward on a body, where there are things it can get tangled on. All of that is difficult enough in daylight, but at night the points of reference are almost nonexistent.

I'd mastered all of those skills. I'd made dozens of HAHO jumps. Yet my nerves quickened every time I stood at that open ramp. And none of those skills mattered if I couldn't force myself out the damn door. In times of high stress and great discomfort, skills aren't enough.

That's where attributes come in.

SKILLS AND ATTRIBUTES GET conflated all the time, yet they are inherently different things.

Consider a professional athlete. When New Orleans Saints quarterback Drew Brees, for example, floats a perfectly timed pass down the sideline and over the shoulder of a sprinting receiver, it's obvious that he is tremendously skilled. It's easy to assume, then, that Brees's success—Super Bowl MVP, future Hall of Famer, holder of almost every passing record in the National Football League—is built solely on those skills.

It isn't.

After all, many people can throw a football accurately at a moving target, and some might be as good at that particular, isolated task as Brees. But throwing a football is a skill, and skills alone aren't enough for optimal performance. To be able to do what he does, Brees also needs high levels of situational awareness, adaptability, decisiveness, and a whole host of things other than just skills.

What do I mean by *skills*?

First, skills are learned. They are not intrinsic to our nature. No one is born with the ability to throw or type or even walk. We learn to do those things either by being taught or by observing someone else. (There are numerous reports of feral children raised in the wild who didn't know how to walk upright because they'd never seen anyone do it.) Moreover, anyone can learn a skill, assuming they have the physical and mental capacity to do so. Competency and mastery will vary widely—most people will never be concert pianists, no matter how much they practice—but almost anyone can learn the fundamentals and improve with practice. Human brains are wired for acquiring skills.

Second, skills direct behavior. That is, skills tell us what to do in specific situations and environments. Wield a hammer, ride a bike, craft a note—each of those requires skills tailored to those tasks. The skills needed to ride a bike, for example, cannot be transferred to writing a proper thank-you note. In other words, a skill tells us how to behave to get certain things done.

Third, skills are easy to assess, measure, and test. We can see Brees throwing a football, hear the notes from a piano, taste what comes out of the chef's kitchen. Skills can be broken down into component parts and examined—the force of the backswing, the position of the hand, or the steadiness of the bow—and it's typically easy to see how well, or how poorly, a skill is executed. Most skills are never scored on a competitive level, but they're still observable. There's no trophy for driving safely to Target, but we can all spot the lousy driver in the parking lot.

To distill this concept of a skill to its simplest form, we can look at the earliest days of space exploration as an example. Engineers wanted to know if people would be able to function under the stress of liftoff, so they trained chimpanzees to push a lever in response to lights and sounds. In January 1961, a chimp named Ham successfully operated a lever in a capsule during a sixteen-minute, suborbital flight, proving it could be done. Four months later, Alan Shepard became the first American in space.

Ham learned a skill that directed his behavior—pulling a lever, which involved reaching and grasping in response to a light—and was easy to measure—either he pulled the lever or he didn't. Yet even if he'd been trained to push all the right buttons and pull all the right levers in the correct sequence, no one would consider Ham qualified to pilot a spacecraft to the moon. Even a person with those specific skills, who'd mastered them on the ground, wouldn't necessarily be the best choice, either. Space flight is complex and unpredictable. Things can and do go wrong. Such missions require something extra, what Tom Wolfe famously called "the right stuff."

BY "THE RIGHT STUFF," Wolfe basically meant the things hardwired into skilled pilots that allowed them to function at the highest level no matter how badly circumstances went sideways.

He meant, in those three words, attributes.

We all have attributes. They aren't magic powers reserved for astronauts and professional athletes and other high-performing people. Attributes are simply the innate traits that determine how an individual will absorb, process, and respond to the world around them. Depending on the situation, an attribute might give a person an advantage or disadvantage, but attributes themselves are neutral, neither positive nor negative. Patience is neither better nor worse than resilience or learnability. And because everyone has them, attributes are woven into life at all levels, from the business world to personal relationships, from the most mundane chores to the highest pinnacle of human achievement. Attributes are everywhere, in everyone, and yet largely unexamined. Your attributes are driving your behavior all the time, even now as you read this sentence.

Let's start by untangling attributes from skills.

First, attributes are elemental. We're born with them. Even infants can show varying levels of perseverance or adaptability. Some we have in abundance, and some we're a little short on. While attributes can be developed over time and with experience, they're not learned from other people in the same way as a skill. We can recognize certain traits in other people and try to emulate them, but often that requires overriding our defaults. A naturally impatient parent, for example, can practice patience with his children, but that will take time and diligence, and it may always require deliberate behavior rather than ever becoming a natural reaction. That parent might still be an impatient person who manages to mitigate it around his kids.

Second, attributes inform, rather than direct, behavior. While a skill might tell us what to do in a situation, attributes determine how we approach and handle that situation. Patience, open-mindedness, or resilience doesn't tell us how to ride a bike or craft a note, but each will affect how that note is written or how frustrated one gets falling off the bike a dozen times.

Third, attributes are difficult to assess, measure, and test. Given the implicit nature of attributes, they're hard to see. They are teased out in different environments and situations; because people are unique, the same situation likely will reveal different attributes in different people. Moreover, because attributes merely inform behavior, they're usually in the background, easy to overlook and to conflate with visible skills.

In fact, sometimes certain attributes are overlooked because we don't even know we have them. Those are what I call "dormant attributes." Typically, they emerge in environments that involve deep challenge, extreme stress, or both. Think of it as a Scrooge effect, where a night of haunting helps the self-proclaimed mean-spirited miser Ebenezer realize that he is, deep down, kind and empathetic. It's not likely that those attributes just appeared: They were tucked away, surfacing because the trauma of three ghosts tormenting him forced them out. Any story in your life that ends with the phrase "I didn't know I had it in me" is probably an example of dormant attributes rising to the surface.

FOR ME, HURLING MYSELF out of a perfectly good airplane required one of the most elemental attributes, courage. I'll talk more about that in Chapter Four, but for now know that courage involves the ability to manage your autonomic response in such a way that you can fully control your thoughts and actions during periods of high stress. More simply, it's the ability to not panic but to perform. It is obviously very useful, and fortunately something that we all possess to some degree.

Once I was out the door and freefalling, all sorts of things could go wrong. The joke in skydiving is that if you have a problem up there, don't worry—you have the rest of your life to figure it out. Depending on your altitude, that could be anywhere between five and forty seconds. That means that if something goes wrong you have forty seconds, tops, to cycle through five steps: assess the situation, decipher the problem, decide which skill is needed to solve it, implement that skill, then evaluate whether that solution worked. In the best case, it does work and you float to the ground. If it doesn't, you repeat the cycle, seconds ticking away. The last-ditch solution is called the cutaway, pulling one handle that releases the bad chute from the harness and then another that deploys a reserve parachute. The timing here matters, because when you're falling at terminal velocity, just the cutaway process can eat up between five hundred and a thousand feet. (This is why base jumpers often don't wear reserve parachutes. When you are jumping from only a thousand feet, there's no time. The main chute works, or your next experience is what we call *high-speed dirt*.)

Of those five steps, you might have noticed, only one

directly involves a skill. The other four steps require attributes. Surviving a malfunction while plummeting from the sky depends, in large part, on how deeply certain traits are wired into you.

Step one: Assess the situation. To do that while freefalling at 120 miles an hour, the ground rushing up at a frightening pace, you need a high degree of situational awareness (Chapter Eight). That means taking in as much information as possible about what's happening at that moment. What's my body position and altitude? The status of my parachute and its position? How am I currently moving through space? Am I spinning, stable, upside down? Situational awareness allows us to begin stacking certainty into a highly uncertain scene, to make sense of everything going on.

Step two: Identify the problem. That requires compartmentalization. I'll describe this in more detail later, but here I'll use the basic definition: It's the ability to process, prioritize, and then focus on the pertinent incoming information. Without that, you can't decide which skill needs to be applied to the current predicament. There are at least five types of major parachute malfunctions, and many variations from there. Each of those requires a different, specific solution to clear it out and not make things worse. Without compartmentalization, you can't process all of the information absorbed through your situational awareness, which means you can't figure out your options. And the ground is getting closer.

Step three: Decide which skill to use. Here we need another attribute, decisiveness. This is about as straightforward as it sounds, but the nuance is important. Optimal performance requires action. Any action obviously needs to be thought out, but you have to avoid paralysis through analysis. Success in this scenario means deciding on an action, implementing that action, then assessing the result—quickly and confidently, because every second that ticks by means falling another couple of hundred feet.

Step four: Apply the skill. You've trained, you've practiced, you're proficient. Just do it.

Step five: Evaluate whether it solved the problem. For that, you need to rely on your situational awareness combined with another attribute, learnability. You have to reassess and decipher what is happening now and rapidly learn from whatever that is. Did that action work? If not, why not? What do I need to adjust or do differently?

And then the most important question: How much time do I have left?

PARACHUTE MALFUNCTIONS ARE PRETTY rare, and you haven't read this far just to find out if you have what it takes to survive one. (Though if you have, I trust this has been helpful. You're welcome.) But, as I've already explained, attributes aren't secret powers reserved only for exceptional performers, for astronauts and athletes or even skydiving spec-ops guys.

Granted, attributes are more readily revealed in extreme situations like Hell Week and HAHO jumps. But most of life isn't lived in extremes. What you want to know—what you *need* to know—is what this all looks like in everyday life, how skills and attributes play off one another when you interact with colleagues and loved ones, and how your own unique alchemy of nature and nurture informs the way you work, play, love, and live. Our attributes influence our performance each and every moment, in ways both positive and negative. How we behave, in turn, affects everyone around us, and vice versa. In order to understand this better, we need to start making the invisible visible and the intangible tangible.

CHAPTER THREE

THE DREAM TEAM PARADOX

JULIE WAS EXCITED. SHE'D just made partner and been promoted to director of her department, and her first assignment was a project for one of her company's biggest clients. It was a pressure-cooker job on a very tight schedule, but Julie had put together a team of top performers from across the company—the number one salesman, a brilliant IT manager, the brightest star in marketing, the best people from every department. At their first meeting, Julie looked around the table at the ten people she'd selected and felt unstoppable. This had to be the most capable lineup ever assembled at the company. She didn't really know any of them personally but their performance records were out of this world. This was the dream team of dream teams.

Julie briefed each member on their piece of the job and explained how all those pieces would come together over the next five weeks. For the most part, everyone could work independently as long as they kept one another in the loop, even if only through cc'd emails. Julie would be the liaison to the client, who was fussy and occasionally mercurial. *That shouldn't be a problem,* Julie thought. She had a team of pros.

They got to work, and for the first two weeks, everything went smoothly. No, better than that: Julie believed the job was going superbly. She was thrilled with her good fortune. Her first big assignment was not only going to be a smashing success but it was on track to be completed ahead of schedule.

Halfway into the third week, though, there was a hiccup. The client wanted changes to a couple of key components, one element scaled back, another reoriented. By themselves, the adjustments weren't difficult, but they affected every other aspect of the project. Still, Julie wasn't fazed. She had her dream team, after all. They could easily adjust. She figured she could call a quick meeting, explain the changes, and suggest that everyone start working together more closely. The extra time required meant the job wouldn't come in ahead of schedule, but Julie knew that they could still make the deadline.

Except the meeting did not go as she expected.

To her genuine surprise, a few of the team members were extremely upset. They refused to believe that what they had produced was not right. They were the best in the business—they knew what *right* looked like. Perhaps, they suggested, Julie should tell the client that the *changes* were wrong.

"No," Julie told them. She was shaken, off balance, but firm. "The customer is always right, and it's our job to adjust."

Two people scoffed at her. One waved his hand dismissively. Then the blaming started. The client must be unhappy because the marketing person was incompetent, someone said. No, legal screwed up, someone else said. The graphics are awful, a third person said. The meeting spiraled downward, voices rising, fingers pointing around the table.

The situation only got worse after that. Over the next few weeks, Julie found herself in constant damage-control mode—massaging hurt egos, demanding extra work, and acting as middleman between colleagues who refused to speak to each other. Even the client became agitated, since hiding the tension was impossible. The deadline came and went. It was only after dismissing a few members and taking on a bunch of the work herself that Julie was able to limp the project across the finish line.

She was upset, disappointed, and flabbergasted. How could this have happened? She had assembled the most capable team anyone had ever seen. How could it have gone so badly?

I MET JULIE ABOUT six months later, at a conference where I'd given a talk about high-performing teams. She had been able to recover professionally, and she'd gotten over the emotions of the ordeal. But she still had those unanswered questions. She pulled me aside after my talk and asked me where she'd gone wrong.

The answer was simple. "When you assembled your team," I told her, "you were looking at the wrong things."

In her quest to collect the "best" people, Julie focused on skills. But as I've already described, skills only tell us how well someone can do a specific thing—sell widgets, draft documents, or come up with marketing slogans. And that's not enough when you're assembling a team that has to function as a unit. If you were to take the best parts from each automobile on the market and mash them together, would you have the world's best automobile? Of course not. You wouldn't even have an automobile—because the pieces wouldn't fit together. "A system is never the sum of its parts," Russell Ackoff, an organizational theorist and a pioneer in the field of systems thinking and management science, famously said. "It's the product of their interaction."

The same goes for teams. Ideally, a team consists of members with complementary and occasionally overlapping skills that work toward the required objective. A football team, for example, has a quarterback, wide receivers, running backs, linemen, and so on, each of whom bring specific skills to the game. As any good coach will tell you, though, if the players can't interact with one another effectively, then none of those skills will matter. The team will lose.

But let's not be too hard on Julie. To the extent that she did anything wrong, it was only because she did what almost everyone else has always done.

In the long history of humanity, assessing skills has been the most obvious and efficient way for people to see and select talent. Many of those skills, in turn, were critical for basic survival, which for much of human existence required far more effort than it does today. A Paleolithic tribe stalking mastodons almost certainly didn't bother with nuanced personality evaluations when they put together a hunting party: They needed men who could run fast and hurl a stone-tipped spear with accuracy and force, specific skills that were both easy to observe and necessary for putting meat on the fire.

As societies evolved, new trades emerged, and as labor became more compartmentalized and specialized, so, too, did the necessary skills. Skills, remember, are by definition something that can be taught, and people most often acquired them through on-the-job training—think of a father, the village carpenter, teaching his son how to frame huts. The Babylonians and ancient Egyptians formalized that practice into apprenticeships, where master craftsmen passed their skills to novices. The Code of Hammurabi, in fact, required masters to train the next generation, thereby ensuring a steady pool of stonemasons and such. By the Middle Ages, a similar system spread across Europe, where a person, usually a child, would be selected for a certain trade and then study under an artisan for many years, typically even living with the master so as to absorb all of the relevant skills.

With the dawn of the Industrial Revolution, apprenticeships became too time-consuming to develop an expanding labor force. Factory owners, drawing on English philosopher and physician John Locke's theories on training, put workers into classrooms. Built within the walls of the factories, they were designed to teach large numbers of people how to operate complicated machinery in a fast and efficient, especially cost-efficient, manner.

Regardless of how skills were transferred from teacher to student, they have always been the primary metric by which performance is defined and measured. That's perfectly rational and, in most cases, entirely sufficient. Hunters needed spear-throwers and mills needed machinists, and whether one had a higher degree of resilience (Chapter Seven) or self-efficacy (Chapter Twelve) was largely irrelevant. Focusing on skills makes obvious sense, and so it continues today: If you're hiring a salesman, you look for the person with the best numbers; if you need a lawyer, you look for one with a winning record. None of this is wrong, which is why people have done it that way for centuries.

SO WHY DIDN'T IT work for Julie or for the countless other team leaders and business people I've spoken with?

It didn't work because while skills are perfect for telling us how a person will behave in a predictable, known environment, even if it's complicated, they can't tell us how people will react in unpredictable and complex situations. And human interaction, by its nature, is inherently complex.

Complex is not the same as *complicated*. Consider a Formula One (F1) race car, a precisely engineered machine made up of more than twenty-five thousand different parts. All of them—the engine (which has six thousand parts all by itself), transmission, steering column, exhaust, and so on—work together toward one goal: speed. The intricate interplay among those thousands of pieces is a *complicated* system. But while complicated systems are not simple, they are predictable. They are governed by known rules. A forty-five-degree turn at a certain speed will reduce friction between the tires and the ground by a certain percentage. Performance levels and tolerances are calibrated to decimal points, and pit crews, coaches, and drivers all know the data as well as the average person knows how to find his way around his own home. If the complicated F1 system encounters situations outside of those tolerances, the results are also predictable: The car will break down or crash. It takes a massive amount of skill to drive an F1 but, again, skills can be learned, practiced, and mastered by almost anyone with the will and determination. In a predictable system or environment, no matter how complicated, what worked before will work again. Therefore, our skills can always get us through—and they can get better over time.

Now consider the human body, also precisely engineered though made from many millions of parts, as opposed to mere thousands. Unlike an F1, however, the way a body will behave in different environments is not fully predictable. That makes the human body a *complex* system—it will react and adapt to different environments, often in ways that can't be known beforehand. While there are certainly known limits to the human system—if you jump into a volcano you will die—there are countless examples of the human body pushing beyond perceived boundaries in order to adjust and survive. Like deep-sea diver Chris Lemons, who in 2012 was under three hundred feet of water at the bottom of the North Sea when his umbilical cord—the lifeline that provides air, communication, and heat—was accidentally severed. Lemons had only five minutes of air in his reserve bottle, and it took his teammates more than thirty minutes to find him. Unconscious and unresponsive when he was dragged into the diving bell, Lemons suddenly came back after two breaths of mouth-to-mouth resuscitation—and was fully recovered within hours. Theories for his survival range from the nearly freezing water slowing his system to the fact that his cells were supersaturated with oxygen. Whatever the reason, his body behaved unpredictably, in this case to his great benefit. We also know that different human systems will react differently to the same stimulus: A medication that helps one patient might be ineffective in another; a temperature that's insufferably cold to some people will be perfectly tolerable to others; caffeine will keep some people up all night while others can have two cups of coffee before bed and sleep like a baby. Finally, we know that in certain cases the human body can even be hacked to adapt to toxic environments. In antiquity, a storied method known as *Antidotum Mithridatium* was named after the ruthless king Mithridates VI. According to legend, Mithridates was so fearful of being assassinated by poison that he regularly ingested sublethal doses of various toxins. His immunities became so robust, the story goes, that when he later decided to commit suicide via poison, he was unable to. Whether we believe that or not, the science behind the legend is called hormesis, and it's the same way that some modern vaccines work. Small doses of smallpox, flu, or even some allergens are introduced in order for the immune system to adjust and build up a tolerance. It's a wonderful example of the complex human system—one that reacts and adapts.

The complexity of our bodies notwithstanding, humans prefer predictability. Our brains are wired to make sense of the world through repeat experience. Picture yourself sitting in a restaurant. You see the waiter approaching. Sight is only one of the senses taking in information for your brain to process—you can also hear busboys clearing tables and feel the seat beneath you and smell bacon on the grill. Your brain is routing all that incoming information to the hippocampus, which is basically an immense catalog of everything we've seen, heard, touched, tasted, smelled, and otherwise experienced before. New data is compared to the old files, a sifting process that happens in milliseconds. Our brain does the calculus to recognize the environment, then looks to apply a known skill or behavior. Based on all of that, you can expect the waiter to bring a pitcher of water and pour you a glass, for which you will thank him before taking a sip. The situation is familiar, and therefore generally predictable. You might spill your water, but your brain probably has a file for that, too.

But not every environment is familiar. All of us will face periods of stress and uncertainty. At times, events will momentarily override our ability to make sense of them and short-circuit our rational decision-making process.

Picture yourself back in that same restaurant, only this time the waiter is *running* toward you, almost maniacally. He's not carrying a pitcher of water but a giant inflatable beach ball. You've never been in this situation, and there's nothing in your hippocampus from which your brain can draw clues. Your stress level increases and your autonomic nervous system begins to heat up. Your brain is sending signals to the amygdala, tickling the fight-or-flight response. You need to figure out how to respond. In this uncertainty, your brain doesn't know which skills to apply. You fall back on those traits that are inherent to you, and therefore automatic. You're now running on attributes.

That's an acute version of what happened to Julie's dream team. The client asking for changes was the waiter with the beach ball. Julie knew exactly how her team would perform when things were predictable. But Julie had no idea how those same people would function when the plan went out the window and the job went sideways. She didn't know how some of the top talent at her company would respond when their work was questioned, even mildly; she didn't know how highly skilled colleagues would turn on one another at the first hint of trouble. She didn't know any of that because she took no account of the inherent attributes underlying each person's impressive skills.

THE MILITARY HAS A saying: "Train for certainty, educate for uncertainty." That implies, correctly, that training and education are two entirely different things. Yet they get conflated all the time, in much the same way that skills and attributes get jumbled together. Training is about learning and practicing specific skills; education is about broadening knowledge, developing beliefs and values, gaining experience. It's not a subtle difference. Imagine how it would sound if someone told you, "I'm going to educate my dog today." That phrase wouldn't compute because we don't *educate* dogs—we train them. We teach Rover to sit and stay and roll over. We are not looking for him to deeply understand the various environments and situations in which we might ask him to do those things.

But that is the reason *people* educate themselves: All of us learn about our environment in order to more effectively function within it. For the purposes of this discussion, that's all that an education means. It does not require advanced degrees or even elementary school (which is a fairly recent invention anyway). Think of a toddler stuffing Play-Doh in his mouth and tugging the cat's tail—he's discovering that Play-Doh tastes terrible and the cat makes a scary hissing sound. He is being educated.

People do this instinctively. We're naturally curious animals, constantly exploring the world around us. From man's earliest days, education has been necessary for survival. Wander too close to a flame and you'd learn that fire was hot; get sick from a certain berry and you'd learn not to pick from that bush. Threats—animal, human, and environmental—lurked everywhere. Social relationships, the ability to get along with people in order to build groups and tribes, were paramount. Survival favored those who could figure these things out, which required qualities such as cunning, creativity, social intelligence, and resilience. Those are attributes, not skills, and those attributes are teased out and developed through education.

Let's go back to that Formula One car. Even though driving that complicated system is predictable, *racing* such a powerful car at the peak of its capabilities takes more than just skill. Usually, a successful F1 driver will start with kart racing, then progress through Formula Ford racing, GP3, Formula Three, and GP2 before finally graduating to the F1. Those are higher and higher categories of racing in faster and more powerful cars, which means a driver is repeatedly throwing himself into different environments, learning the subtleties of different tracks and conditions and performance limits. That process takes approximately twelve to fifteen years, and during that time the best drivers will also work the pits, hang out in the garages, and read up on the history of the sport. Additionally, drivers will often find schools that teach driving in foul weather and on bad roads or no roads.

An F1 driver will never race his car in the snow, so why bother? Because by practicing in diverse and uncertain environments, he is exercising attributes—humility, situational awareness, self-efficacy—that he needs to race at the F1 level. The more complete his understanding of cars—of the mechanics, the physics, the known variations and potential variables—the more successfully he can develop his talent as a racer. This idea applies to everyone. Education, accumulated through diverse experiences, loads up our hippocampus with data to draw upon later. Just as important, it forces us to lean on our attributes as we seek to make sense of and understand new situations.

Following that principle, it's very possible that a woman who backpacked through Asia and dug wells for villagers in Africa might be a more talented HR rep than a guy who worked at a major consulting firm for ten years. Talent, as we now know, is not just skill. It's a dynamic synchronization of attributes and skills. Talent is developed through both training and education.

The problem, though, is that true education is hard, whereas myopic, focused training is much easier. The more that we can stay in a predictable environment, however complicated, the more comfortable we humans tend to be. We *like* predictability, and our skills improve as they become routine. Realistically, not many people have the opportunity to backpack through Asia for the life experience. And even if they did, they might not want to. The hard truth is that education takes more than time and effort—it often involves a willingness to dive into uncertainty.

EVEN IF JULIE HAD known to search out attributes among the members of her dream team, she still would have faced a problem: How was she supposed to identify them in other people? Just as important—for Julie, for you, for all of us—how do we assess our own attributes, more fully develop the ones we have, or work on the ones we might not?

Admittedly, this is not an especially easy task. When life is calm and predictable—which most people prefer and indeed strive to achieve—attributes tend to be camouflaged, muddled together, and muted. You might notice that one person is an introvert and that another has a quick temper, but characteristics such as those only hint at underlying attributes. To more fully see them generally requires stress and uncertainty, and there is a direct correlation between the intensity of that stress and how purely attributes are displayed. Being lost in a foreign city with no money and unable to speak the language will expose far more attributes than getting confused in the aisles of an Ikea store.

The task is even more difficult because people are infinitely variable. Every person has a unique combination of attributes that will play off one another in different ways. My patience, for example, might positively affect my situational awareness. It might also negatively affect my decisiveness. Moreover, stress is subjective. Heights make me uncomfortable, but put me underwater at night, floating in the dark with unseen sea life teeming around me, and I'm incredibly relaxed. For someone else (most people, I imagine), that same environment would be wildly stressful.

What this all means is that when we try to assess or develop attributes, the environment matters. There is no universal template, no generic set of questions or role-playing scenarios. Creating conditions of extreme stress is often impractical, if not abusive, and possibly illegal. Julie could not have realistically or ethically auditioned team members by dumping them into the ocean at midnight. Then there's the question of relevance. Night diving will bring out attributes that suggest how well one will function as a Navy SEAL, but it's less clear how those same attributes would apply in, say, the business world. (They could be completely relevant but not obviously so.)

As you read on into the details of various attributes, you'll find some examples of different environments, situations, and scenarios to help you generate ideas. That said, you'll have to think about them in the context of your own performance—in your personal life, in business, with your team. Because performance, after all, is also subjective. Which begs the final question: How do we know what high performance actually looks like?

———

ONE OF THE THINGS people most often ask me about is peak performance. Individuals, teams, and businesses all want to figure out ways to perform at their absolute best. That's an excellent goal, but it's important to remember that peak performance is just that—a peak, an apex from which there is nowhere to go but down. Peak performance is also often conditional. It typically requires a predictable and familiar environment, much like the Formula One car needs a flat, dry track. It requires training, discipline, and preparation. A professional football player will design his entire week's schedule so that he can peak for three hours on Sunday.

I have always been fascinated by something different. When I was working with some of the most high-performing people on the planet, none of us defined ourselves as *peak* performers. We were all *optimal* performers. Optimal performance is about doing the very best that you can in the moment—whatever that moment might be. When I was lying in the frigid surf during my own SEAL Hell Week—an exercise called "surf torture" for a reason—there definitely was nothing "peak" about my performance. I was doing the best I could, which was to not quit. It was dirty, cold, uncertain, and dark. None of us shivering in the waves knew how long we would be there or what was coming next. None of us had trained in any specific skills to get us through surf torture, and I'm not sure there are any that would have helped. Many of the guys around us gave up. But those of us who didn't were simply leaning on the attributes we had brought to the game.

For me, lying in the surf, one of the main attributes I relied on was perseverance. That is part of who I am at my core. Most days, it's not crucial; you don't need a substantial amount of perseverance when everything is going according to plan. But with a frigid ocean washing over me for what seemed like hours, choking on salt water, shivering until my joints ached? Yeah, perseverance came in pretty handy.

That is optimal performance, the ability to do the best you can in any environment. Sometimes the best is your peak, and sometimes your best is just surviving. But always underlying that performance are those inherent attributes.

The primary question, then, is how much of each attribute do you have? You, your team, even your organization? Which ones do you have but don't know about yet? And which ones are you looking to develop?

This book can't answer those questions for you—every person, every team, is unique. Rather, it's designed to arm you with the ability to answer those questions for yourself.

The chapters that follow don't include all of the attributes we identified in our selection-and-training course. Not all of them would be relevant to anyone else: SEALs are a unique culture with a specific mission and, accordingly, a very specific set of attributes. A comprehensive list of attributes might look different for a businessperson, an athlete, a surgeon, or a comedian. But the twenty-five in this book are an indispensable foundation for any list.

The ones that follow are grouped into five categories: grit, mental acuity, drive, leadership, and teamability. That does not mean that any particular attribute is relevant in only one context. For instance, empathy and accountability are not reserved exclusively for those in positions of leadership, and open-mindedness certainly is useful regardless of whether one is especially driven. Rather, the attributes are organized on the page in a way similar to how they tend to cluster in real life. People we think of as gritty, for example, generally have healthy amounts of the four attributes in that category. But, again, this is simply an organizing tool—it is entirely possible to have a sizable amount of courage yet not have a notable amount of grit.

Very few of us can have a high degree of all of the attributes on this list, or any list. That should not be the goal. In any high-functioning team, there is always a fluid mixture of attributes. Members of high-performing teams understand their strengths and weaknesses, and that allows them to mesh effectively; like the teeth of a zipper, they're much more effective when they work together. An understanding of what you and your team possess will allow you to find the gaps—and then create processes to help you fill them.

Identifying all of the attributes you or your team need is a subjective task and you may discover there are some you need that aren't mentioned. But the twenty-five in this book are a very healthy start for any list. They are the most common and the most applicable to the broadest spectrum of optimal performance. Understanding what they are and which ones you or your team possess will illuminate internal strengths and weaknesses and will provide answers on how you can perform even better—in any situation.

THE
ATTRIBUTES

THE GRIT ATTRIBUTES

"You Navy SEALs probably have more grit than anyone on the planet."

I used to hear that fairly often when I was in the military. It felt good, too. What badass special-warfare operator wouldn't want to be gritty? What's the alternative? To be soft? Delicate? To be lazy and dainty and afraid of getting dirty and working hard? SEALs aren't any of those things. Hell Week alone is like a grit factory, vulcanizing men into hard, durable warriors. SEALs are the ultimate optimal performers, so to be one of them, I was sure, clearly required an extraordinary and inexhaustible supply of grit.

Now I know there's more to it.

Don't misunderstand: SEALs are definitely gritty. But so are many other people. And everyone has the potential to develop grittiness.

When I started trying to figure out why some guys made it through training and others didn't—that is, when I started digging into attributes—I had to reconsider what a word like *grit* really meant. What I realized is that grit is not an attribute at all, because it's not one thing. It's the result of several attributes, blended and catalyzed. It's the loaf of bread that comes out of the oven after the ingredients have been mixed and baked.

The more I dug into grit, the more obvious this became. It was also clear that this amalgam of attributes is indispensable. Optimal performers need grit, and grit is not a singular trait. It's about carrying on and pushing through, sometimes only in tiny increments, no matter how difficult or miserable the challenge.

Others have examined grit in great detail. Psychologist Angela Duckworth, for instance, in 2016 wrote a brilliant book on the subject, *Grit: The Power of Passion and Perseverance*. In the SEAL environment, though, I deconstructed grit into four component attributes: courage, perseverance, adaptability, and resilience. No one can make it through BUD/S without fairly high levels of all four.

But *life* also requires all four. Everyone will face terrible challenges—a bad diagnosis, a layoff, an economic downturn, the death of a loved one, a global pandemic like COVID-19—and those with more grit will be better able to push through them. Yet it's not only in crises that these attributes matter. Every day can bring frustration, aggravation, disruption, and disappointment. Sometimes, just the grind of getting through the week will require you to call up a reserve of grit.

And you have it. You have some amount of courage, of perseverance, of adaptability, of resilience, which means you also have grit. You *know* you do, because you've relied on it before.

Maybe you don't have as much as you'd like right now, but that's okay. With enough effort, each of these four attributes can be developed. You can be as gritty as you want to be.

CHAPTER FOUR

BEWARE THE FEARLESS LEADER

Courage: *The ability to manage fear in order to confront danger, difficulty, or pain*

THOUSANDS OF YEARS AGO, a group of people lived together at the edge of a forest. For many seasons, it was a fine place to be. There was fresh water from a stream that burbled out from the trees, berries to pick, and fat tubers to dig. Small game—rabbits and squirrels—was abundant, and shallow caves provided shelter.

But after one very dry summer, the stream slowed to a trickle. There were fewer animals to hunt and fewer berries to pick. Winter was coming, and the people worried that they wouldn't have enough food and water to make it until spring. Anxiety began to set in.

Perhaps there were more plentiful resources on the other side of the forest, or maybe over the mountains in the distance. But no one knew what lurked in the shadows beyond the tree line because there had never been a reason to find out. There were likely dangerous creatures in there, bears and wolves and venomous snakes. There might also be other people, maybe hostile, who would not take kindly to interlopers. The forest was a place of dark mystery and high uncertainty. The people knew what they needed to do, but when faced with doing it, something more than just anxiety began to show up.

Anxiety and uncertainty, when they are combined, create fear. Most of the people responded to that fear by retreating into their caves, hoping that the snows would be mild and that they could scrounge enough food to survive until spring. They might go hungry, they reasoned, but that was probably better than getting mauled by a bear.

A few of those people, however, did not hunker down for the winter. Instead, they marched off into the unknown. They did not do so recklessly—they'd gathered a few primitive weapons to fight off bears—and they were not unafraid. They were simply able to manage their fear enough to start walking. It does not matter, in this prehistoric parable, what happened to those hardy explorers. (Let's assume, though, that they made it across the forest and found a wondrous bounty, which is a much better ending than getting eaten by bears.) The point is, they displayed courage in its rawest, purest form.

Courage is not an absence of fear but rather an ability to function despite being afraid.

It's the ability to get out of the cave. To take that step toward the forest and not surrender to that internal voice telling you to hesitate. And because everyone is afraid of something at some point—because life is inherently full of scary things—courage is one of the most important attributes of optimal performance.

DR. ANDREW HUBERMAN IS a tenured professor of neurobiology and ophthalmology at Stanford University School of Medicine where, among other experiments in his lab, he scares people. His subjects suffer varying levels of fear, from mild anxiety to full-blown phobia. Because fear often manifests behaviorally in curious ways—remember me yawning?—

scientists have a difficult time studying it in the wild. In the lab, though, Andrew can use a variety of sensors to accurately measure the physiological and, more important, neurological responses to fear.

I met Andrew in 2017, shortly after I retired from the military, when we had both been invited to deliver a presentation on peak performance for C-suite executives. It was an impressive panel, including a nutritionist, an expert on flow states, another on breath, even an expert on energy healing. Andrew and I gravitated toward each other, though, because we were both interested in optimal, as opposed to peak, performance. How does someone effectively move through any situation, especially if it is dangerous, difficult, or unpleasant? In Andrew, I found someone who was actually studying the neuroscience behind that question; in me, Andrew found someone who came from a community of people who do it routinely and who was interested in explaining how.

One way Andrew does that is by scaring people in his lab. He and his staff put their subjects in a small, bare room that, through the wondrous technology of virtual reality goggles, can transport them into a scenario tailored to their anxieties and fears. In VR, they're suddenly walking a narrow beam between two skyscrapers or diving with great white sharks or being attacked by giant spiders. While the danger is virtual, the fear it creates is real, which allows Andrew and his staff to monitor how people react. For example, because the brain processes so much information through vision, it's useful to understand how people look at their surroundings when they're afraid. People who have high anxiety will scan their environment in a very erratic way, whereas people who have low levels of anxiety will do so in a more deliberate, methodical way.

Andrew isn't interested only in identifying the responses of the body and brain to fear. More important is how quickly and effectively his subjects can move through the three phases of fear. There are only three, each distinct and identifiable: fear prior to the event, fear during the event, and residual fear that lingers after the event, the worst case being post-traumatic stress disorder.

Each of those phases triggers different circuits in the brain, and while they all are important, the easiest to measure—and, fortunately, the one of most interest to Andrew—is the middle one, fear during the event. Specifically, how do people respond physiologically, neurologically, and behaviorally as they move through fear?

"FEAR COMES ONE HUNDRED percent from the brain," Andrew says. It's a state of mind, which is why people are afraid of different things. Heights might not bother you at all, but they make others uncomfortable. Or maybe you have a debilitating phobia of snakes or rats, both of which many people consider delightful pets.

That's not to say, however, that fear *stays* all in your head. "Fear is considered by neuroscientists to be the subjective label that is put on the stress response," Andrew says. "And stress is more than just a state of mind—it's a physiological response to our environment."

But fear does start in your head. It begins with your brain detecting a threat, a process which happens in the amygdala. In very simple terms, the amygdala is a sort of trip wire for sensing danger, assessing both the existence and the severity of a threat. Often, this threat detection is a largely conscious activity. "I'm in the back of a plane, there's an open ramp, and I'm supposed to jump"—I'm fully aware of those things. But then my amygdala kicks in, and I'm anxious. The details might differ—maybe your amygdala sparks in deep water or in the nighttime dark of your house—but it's perfectly normal. People are supposed to recognize things that could be detrimental to their well-being. If we don't assess threats properly, we're at terrible risk: Evolution programmed us to not get complacent around things like fire that will burn us and large animals that might eat us. "Beware the fearless leader," I was told when I was a young military officer. "He'll likely get you killed."

Once the amygdala is engaged, it sends signals to our sympathetic nervous system, which is part of our autonomic nervous system. Largely operating without our conscious control, the sympathetic system is designed for survival. Think of it as the action system. When it's turned on, it fires stimulating neurotransmitters and hormones through the endocrine system, pushing blood to the most necessary organs and muscles. Heart rate goes up, respiration quickens, sweating increases. The pupils dilate to encourage a more precise focus on the threat, which can also lead to a sense of tunnel vision. At the same time, the sympathetic system slows or stops any functions that aren't immediately required, like digestion or nail growth or the production of saliva. You don't need saliva when you're fighting for survival, which is why your mouth goes dry when you're anxious or stressed.

All of this, of course, usually happens in reasonable proportion to the perceived threat. You might get dry mouth if you're nervous about a presentation, but your nails will still grow and your pulse shouldn't peak into the cardio zone. Meanwhile, the sympathetic system is balanced by the parasympathetic, which is responsible for the calming and restorative functions. Digestion speeds up, the salivary glands restart, stress hormones are purged, breathing slows. Also, our field of vision returns, the periphery comes back into view, and we're more aware of our surrounding environment. Remember my quirk of yawning when I'm anxious?

Yawning expands the diaphragm and stretches the trigeminal nerve, which triggers the vagus nerve—the one directly linked to parasympathetic stimulation.

Once we're in a fear state, however, our autonomic system gives us three, and only three, options. You probably know what they are already.

1. Fight, which means moving toward the threat or the source of stress.
2. Flight, which means retreating.
3. Freeze, which is actually a rapid oscillation between fight and flight.

In his research, Andrew has discovered that there are distinct neural circuits for each of those responses. If we choose flight, one part of the brain lights up. If we choose fight, a different set of neurons are engaged. And it doesn't matter why we're afraid—as far as the brain is concerned, what's important is how we respond.

"Nature doesn't care about the source of your stress," Andrew says. "It doesn't care about your hard-to-handle boss, the traffic you're sitting in, the sickness you're dealing with, or the ramp you're about to jump off of at twenty thousand feet. All it cares about is: Are you moving forward, are you pausing, or are you retreating? And when you physically move forward while in a state of stress or fear, you engage a specific circuit in your brain. That is courage."

That's not a metaphor, either. The reason Andrew calls that particular neurological reaction the *courage circuit* is because it encourages us, by evolutionary design, to engage the fear. Doing so is not always easy: Evolution, to say nothing of common sense, also has taught us to run from danger, and some threats are so unfamiliar or overwhelming that freezing can seem like a completely involuntary response.

But once we decide to fight, to move through stress and fear, our system rewards us with a jolt of dopamine.

Dopamine is a neurotransmitter and one of the most powerful chemicals known to man. It's not a direct source of pleasure but rather tells us when something else is pleasurable. The reason certain other chemicals can be addictive—opiates, nicotine, alcohol, and so on—is because they stimulate the release of dopamine. That, in turn, motivates the brain to seek out those same triggers, an effect so powerful that it can override a rational fear of lung cancer or a ruined liver.

Courage, it turns out, is one of those dopamine triggers. For those people living by the forest with winter looming, wandering into the unknown required an enormous amount of courage. When those few brave souls started walking, they were rewarded with a shot of dopamine. Keep in mind that the dopamine wasn't delivered only after they'd crossed the forest and found a safe haven. It was released as they were confronting their fear, a reward for simply making progress. Their brains were telling them, *Yes, this is good! Keep moving!*

That is courage, physiologically and neurologically defined.

This definition also makes two things apparent. The first is that courage cannot exist in the absence of fear. If something doesn't trigger fear, you won't have access to the courage circuit. A professional skydiver with thousands of jumps under his belt, for example, probably doesn't need courage when he leaps off the ramp. In fact, repeating a process or event that causes us anxiety can, over time, be an effective inoculation. I used to do that with my fear of heights. Every SEAL base has an obstacle course with a variety of climbing and jumping stations, one of which was a sixty-five-foot cargo net. It was very simple to navigate—climb to the top, hoist yourself over, and climb down the other side. I hated it. But every day, I planned my run to go past that net just so I could climb it. I would pause at the top, feel the wind and the unsteadiness of the ropes, let the fear in. Every day, I got that dopamine reward, until I got so comfortable up there that I was no longer afraid. I didn't need courage anymore—and I didn't get my dopamine hit, either.

Which leads us to the second thing: Because courage is required to receive the dopamine reward, people often seek out more difficult challenges in search of that jolt. That same pro skydiver will need to be brave when he switches to base jumping, and then brave again when he moves to flying a wingsuit. Those are all progressions in search of the dopamine reward.

EVEN THOUGH THE FEAR response can be unconscious and automatic, courage is largely a choice, a decision we make for which we are rewarded. Yet the ease with which each of us can make that decision is to some extent hardwired.

We all show up with an autonomic set point. In other words, we all begin to register threats and trigger our sympathetic stress response at different points. Let's use water as an analogy. Many of us will begin to boil—that is, reach our autonomic set point—at 212 degrees. But there are some people who boil over much more quickly, at 200, or even 190 degrees. Conversely, maybe you know someone who's pretty hard to rattle, who has a set point of 225 degrees. That person typically won't need to decide to engage the courage circuit as often as someone with a lower set point.

Extremes in either direction can be bad. A person with a hyperactive amygdala might get stressed when the slightest things go awry. People diagnosed with generalized anxiety tip that way, and it can be debilitating. (That's not to be confused, though, with being easily startled. We're all programmed to jump at sudden loud noises, but that's a reflex, not a state of mind.) On the other hand, a hypoactive amygdala might leave you so chill that you don't see the urgency in getting out of bed in the morning.

Most of us, fortunately, fall in a range we can work with. You can probably get a decent feel for your set point just by comparing yourself to those around you. If your set point is on the low side, that's not necessarily a negative. You'll need to decide to engage the courage circuit more often, but that's all to the good: You'll be well-practiced and well-rewarded with dopamine. If you sense yours is higher than most, you might have to work harder to recognize legitimate threats. An underactive amygdala can lead to a bulldog approach, and running into threats without fully appreciating the danger is never a good thing.

Optimal performance lies in the ability to move up and down the active amygdala scale in order to register the appropriate amount of fear. That, in turn, allows us to manage our internal environment—our physiological response—in the appropriate way given the circumstances. Each time we can consciously choose to fight, rather than freeze or take flight, we'll engage the courage circuit and receive the dopamine reward, which provides the incentive for the cycle to repeat. The key is maintaining a healthy recognition of what's going on internally and what's required externally.

But what if you just can't work up the courage? What if giving that presentation, confronting that co-worker, even jumping out of that airplane, is just too scary? What if flight is easier?

First, remind yourself that neither freezing nor fleeing is easier. It may be necessary—you should definitely not fight bears—but that doesn't mean it's easier. Second, courage can be developed. Being courageous is something you can decide to do, and you'll get better with practice. Go do things that scare you. Fear is subjective, so you choose what to confront. Begin small. Start a conversation with a stranger.

Give a speech. It doesn't matter what it is, as long as it's an activity or situation that creates anxiety. Get through it, recognize how good it feels, then move on to something else.

Whatever you decide to practice with, just know that it doesn't have to be death defying—but it's okay if it feels that way. Jerry Seinfeld once joked that 73 percent of people fear public speaking more than death—which means that most people at a funeral would rather be in the casket than giving the eulogy. So go and explore your courage, wherever you might find it. Because I can say with confidence that the optimal performer in Jerry's joke is not the one in the casket.

CHAPTER FIVE

FALL SEVEN TIMES AND GET UP EIGHT

Perseverance: *Constancy in doing something despite difficulty or delay in achieving success*

I MET HANK IN EARLY 2007, when I was the OIC of a SEAL troop of about two dozen guys. In any military unit, there is an officer in charge—the OIC—and, in SEAL units, a senior enlisted adviser, who is the highest-ranking enlisted man in that particular unit. He's known as the troop chief and his role is to provide leadership and counsel to the enlisted men and to the OIC. He's typically older and more experienced than the OIC, and as such is a trusted sounding board. The joke is that the troop chief and OIC should be as tight as a married couple, but it's pretty much true. If there's a weak bond between those two, the team usually is doomed to be subpar at best.

My previous troop chief was retiring from the Navy, and Hank was assigned to replace him. We hit it off right away. And one of the things that I noticed immediately about Hank was his perseverance. I knew that he had overcome a few ups and downs in his career and had always come back stronger because of them. In fact, his greatest challenge had also been his most recent.

About a year earlier, Hank had been deployed as the chief

of another troop. While planning a mission one night, the commanding officer ordered the team to include a SEAL from another troop. "I fundamentally disagreed with the order because, at the time, I didn't think it was in the best interest of the mission." He protested but the decision was final. "At that point, I felt like I should make a stand," he says.

Hank left the guy off the mission.

"I realize now that I was too caught up in the situation to see any reasonable alternatives," Hank says. "I made a decision that was not consistent with a senior enlisted in the SEAL Teams."

Even at the time, Hank knew that his decision could have severe consequences. He was not wrong. What he did was insubordination, a serious offense no matter where you are but especially in a combat zone. He was immediately sent home, and a SEAL review board stuck him in an administrative job at command headquarters as his punishment. "Every enlisted SEAL dreams about being a troop chief and leading troops in combat," he says. "I had worked for almost twenty years to get to that point. To go from that apex to getting sent home from the war zone was the lowest of lows," he says. "The whole thing was so painful, and I constantly shifted between being embarrassed and depressed, with spurts of being infuriated at everyone and everything."

Hank could have simply retired and left the Navy entirely. He'd done his required time, and there was no point pushing paper indefinitely, stewing and humiliated. But Hank wanted to be a troop chief. It was what he had dedicated his life to. He was good at it. He was determined to persevere until he was assigned to a new troop—which, as it happened, was mine.

———

IF COURAGE IS THE ability to effectively move through fear, challenge, and discomfort, then perseverance is the ability to keep doing it over and over again.

To persevere, though, does not mean simply to endure. Every challenge, every uncomfortable situation and fearful episode, has its own contours. Some might require only stoicism, a quiet suffering until the moment passes. Others might call for an active, aggressive response. There's a nimbleness to effective perseverance. To understand what I mean, let's break down this attribute to the atomic level so we can study its base components. There are three ingredients in perseverance: equal parts persistence and tenacity, with fortitude thrown into the mix.

People often think of persistence and tenacity as the same thing, but they are not. *Persistence* is when someone comes up with a possible solution to a task or problem and then stubbornly sticks to that process, regardless of whether it's flawed or inefficient. There is an obstinance in persistence that can be detrimental if the solution is incorrect—a hammer is never going to be the correct answer to a dirty window—but otherwise advantageous. It's like the Stonecutter's Credo, as described by photographer and activist Jacob Riis as he contemplated the slow pace of social reform:

> When nothing seems to help, I go and look at a stonecutter hammering away at his rock perhaps a hundred times without as much as a crack showing in it. Yet at the hundred and first blow it will split in two, and I know it was not that blow that did it, but all that had gone before.

Persistence requires patience. Tenacity is different—it requires impatience.

Tenacity also means formulating a solution to a problem, but then constantly assessing its effectiveness. A mechanic diagnosing an unusual sound in an engine will use trial and error to figure out the cause. He'll check the belts, then the plugs, then the fuel pump, and so on until he can find the problem and fix it. That's tenacity. A *persistent* mechanic will check the belts . . . and then check the belts again, over and over and over, accomplishing nothing other than jacking up your bill.

With the mechanic, tenacity is required for success. With the stonecutter, tenacity would spell failure—he needs to be persistent. This is why persistence and tenacity aren't enough on their own: Each has notable pros and cons depending on the environment.

Perseverance, however, is a balance between the two. Perseverance allows an individual to be persistent (and patient) when needed, and then tenacious (and impatient) when needed. In the business world, this is obvious. There are times when an organization must take the stonecutter approach to its long-term goals—patiently waiting on an investment to pay off or implementing small changes in a product that need time to take hold. On the other hand, there are times when a business needs tenacity, especially when innovating: Try something new, see if it works, and, if not, change the approach and try again. Fail early and fail often, until you get the desired outcome.

Yet perseverance also requires those two—tenacity and persistence—to be reinforced by a third trait, fortitude. That's another word that gets tangled with the other three, but which has a distinct meaning. Fortitude is the mental or emotional strength, or both, that *allows* a person to persevere. If tenacity and persistence are the engines, then fortitude is the fuel. It's the stuff that allows us to endure, to power through, to conquer.

That's key. Fortitude requires a goal, an objective. We engage fortitude because there is something we want to accomplish. *What* we choose to endure or conquer is subjective—my momentous achievement might be your pointless drudgery—but fortitude is the base component of the mental toughness that allows us to do so.

That's our deep dive into the atomic structure of perseverance. Now let's put those pieces back together and see what perseverance looks like in real life.

When I was lying in the surf during SEAL training, the water was as painfully cold for me as it was for all of the guys around me, many of whom quit. Physiologically, our nervous systems absorbed external information, like a miserable water temperature, pretty similarly. The difference was my *perception* of that pain. For me, it was a test, an essential rite of passage, an uncomfortable means to a highly desired end. That perception allowed my innate fortitude to come to the fore, where it fostered a mental toughness that led to a physical toughness. By combining fortitude with persistence—staying put because I knew they couldn't keep us there forever—and tenacity—tensing random muscle groups to see if I could warm them up—I was able to persevere.

AFTER DISOBEYING THAT ORDER, Hank had been placed in a job that he absolutely dreaded going to every day. Eighty percent of his day was spent on email, and the rest in meetings that seemed to drone on for hours. But Hank knew that he had to show up every day, dedicated and engaged, no matter how mundane the meetings or the volume of inefficient email. He had to keep hitting that rock, like a stonecutter. He had to be persistent.

He needed tenacity, too. Hank understood that repairing his reputation required doing his rote administrative work differently. Instead of conducting business with endless email chains, Hank got out from behind his desk and cultivated as many face-to-face relationships as possible. He met people, learned about them, learned what they did in their departments, and learned about the different aspects of what they did for the Command. He gained perspective and empathy for the people who support SEALs overseas and in training. And he gained allies, people who knew him now as more than a name on an email header. "All of that effort allowed me to grow stronger in every area," he says. "A stronger leader, a stronger learner, a stronger troop chief."

And it took fortitude. In a tribal community like the SEALs, atoning for an indiscretion is not the same as being absolved. If the punishment involves being cast out, absolution is practically impossible, as it can only come from one's peers. For those who remain in the community, it's still difficult: Men who depend on one another for their lives are not quick to forgive those who step out of line, and some never do. For Hank, showing his teammates and peers that he was both accountable and committed to getting back to a troop required an enormous amount of mental strength. "I was really fortunate that the guys on my review board let me stay at the command and allow me to earn my rep back," he says. "My perception of the punishment turned into gratitude for the opportunity."

IF A HIGH LEVEL of perseverance isn't wired into you, developing it is difficult. But it *can* be done.

First, break it down into components. Are you persistent or just plain stubborn? Are you tenacious or just impatient? Understanding where you fall on each will highlight your ability to balance the two. If you refuse to ask for directions when you know you are lost, you may tend toward stubbornness. If you constantly switch lanes in traffic, you might be impatient. Fortitude might be a little more difficult to gauge, but developing it is simple: Do tough stuff. What those tough things are is completely subjective, but they need to involve a challenge over time. The more often you throw yourself into environments that require mental and emotional strength to get through, the more you'll hone your fortitude.

Hank, though, has always been high on the scale, which he realized when he played football in high school. His coach was a tyrant. "He was a guy that just rode us really, really hard," he says. "Every single little mistake he would yell, scream, and tell us how fucked up we were. At that age, I really felt like I was the only one he was yelling at, and took it personally. Every single practice day I asked myself why I didn't just quit."

He didn't quit—he decided to persevere—because he loved playing the game and loved the camaraderie with his teammates. "Every day I told myself, if I endure this Monday through Thursday, then I can make it to the game on Friday. The coach is not on the field during the game, it was just me and my teammates, and that's what I loved the most." For those few hours, he basked in every aspect of the experience—the brightness of the lights, the smell of the grass, the coolness of the air, the roar of the crowd. It was worth it every single week. Hank learned early on that perseverance pays off.

This all came in handy, of course, when Hank got to SEAL training. Upon arriving at BUD/S he believed he would do pretty well. Physically, certainly—he'd been an athlete his whole life, after all. But he, like many of us, did not know a lot about the actual program. BUD/S doesn't care what kind of athlete you are—the program is designed to strip you down to your core, to the point where you can draw only on your attributes. And one of the most important in that environment is perseverance.

"Having grown up in Louisiana, I had never even seen surf before," Hank says. "I was coming in almost last on every swim, falling short on the long runs in the sand, and I started looking around at some of the guys who looked like Olympic athletes and asking myself, *What am I doing here?*"

Then came Hell Week.

Hell Week begins on Sunday evening with what's known as Breakout, and it's pure mayhem. Students waiting patiently in tents on the beach are roused by blank machine-gun fire, smoke grenades, simulated bangs of real grenades. They're funneled into the PT area—physical training—where instructors grab them at random and order them to do push-ups or crawl in the sand, or just berate them. All of this happens under the constant, cold spray of fire hoses.

The senior officer in Hank's BUD/S class was what Hank describes as "the perfect future SEAL." A college grad who'd been a star athlete, tall, astonishingly fit—and he quit during the first hour. "When that guy quit, a guy I thought had everything necessary to make it, I realized that it wasn't about how many push-ups I could do or how fast I swam," Hank says. "It was about perseverance. I knew at that moment that I was going to make it and that I was supposed to be there." That BUD/S class started with 120 candidates. Six months later, Hank and 17 other guys finished. He was supposed to be there.

CHAPTER SIX

BE LIKE THE FROG

Adaptability: *The ability to quickly and calmly adjust to changing circumstances and situations*

IN THE FALL OF 1987, Tyrell Biggs was an underdog when he fought for the combined heavyweight title in Atlantic City. He was an excellent boxer, an Olympic gold medalist who was undefeated in fifteen professional fights, but the smart money expected him to lose because he was fighting Mike Tyson, the reigning world champion and possibly the hardest puncher to ever step into the ring. Tyson didn't box so much as brawl, a ferocious style that made him the youngest world champion in history the year before. He won his first nineteen fights by knockout, and most of those in the first round.

But Biggs had a plan. He was seven inches taller than Tyson and better on his feet, more agile. He would jab and move, move and jab, keep Tyson at a safe distance and off balance. He would use his natural advantages—height and agility—and his superior skills—footwork and mobility—to defeat a formidable opponent.

That worked pretty well for the first round. But in the second, Tyson connected with a right hook. That was part of Mike's strategy, which was no strategy at all, really. As

Tyson famously said before the fight: "Everybody has plans until they get hit for the first time."

You've probably seen that quote before, or a version of it. Maybe it ended more colorfully with *punched in the mouth,* or maybe it was attributed to another boxer, Joe Louis. It wasn't even an original thought: Military planners have for generations lived by the truism that "no plan survives first contact with the enemy," a pithier version of something a Prussian field marshal named Helmuth von Moltke explained in the nineteenth century. But the Tyson version gets recycled, and often in the context of learning better planning techniques, because it is indisputably, graphically true.

Tyrell Biggs did not appear to have a plan after he got hit. He survived, bleeding and wobbly, until the seventh round, when Tyson dropped him twice and the referee stopped the fight.

The lesson, though, isn't that Biggs had a bad plan. He'd had, in fact, a terrific plan. The problem was that he couldn't adapt once that plan began to falter. Tyson, by contrast, could adapt to his opponent's varying strategies (though in fairness, his adaptations were minimal because his plan was to hit his opponent as hard as humanly possible and then maybe a little harder).

Combat sports are an excellent metaphor for adaptability. Boxers, wrestlers, and mixed martial artists all drill incessantly, perfecting techniques and mastering skills. And while they can plan for a match, they can't be rigid in their execution because their opponent has their own plan. Every move must be countered, every strike blocked and thrust parried. Every match is an unending sequence of reacting and adapting.

And that is a condensed, kinetic representation of life in general. Everyone, metaphorically, gets hit. Everyone gets punched in the mouth. The enemy always makes first contact. How staggering those blows are depends largely on our level of adaptability.

We are all like Tyrell Biggs, optimizing our skills, developing our strategy. What sets challengers apart from champions, though, is what happens after we get hit.

SIXTY-SIX MILLION YEARS AGO, when dinosaurs dominated life on earth, an asteroid roughly six miles in diameter and traveling at forty thousand miles per hour struck the edge of the Yucatan Peninsula. The impact, paleontologists estimate, was two million times more powerful than the largest nuclear bomb ever detonated. Miles-high tsunamis scoured the edges of continents, and flaming debris ignited wildfires that spread across the planet. Dust clouded the skies, plunging the planet into a perpetual freezing darkness. Plant life quickly died, starving the herbivores, which died within weeks. Carnivores scavenged those carcasses and lasted a few months longer, but they, too, died off. In fact, the Cretaceous-Tertiary extinction wiped out more than 80 percent of all life on Earth.

Among the survivors, though, were small creatures called anura. We know them as frogs.

In fact, the anuras' ancestors had already survived four mass extinctions before the one that killed the dinosaurs (ichthyostega, the prehistoric predecessor to the modern frog, lived 370 million years ago during the Devonian period). And while there were only three families of anura, they diversified so rapidly after the asteroid impact that there are now almost five thousand known species.

So how did the ichthyostega become the anura and, eventually, an abundance of frogs?

Adaptability.

As amphibians, frogs are built to live a double life. If it isn't safe or suitable on land, they can hop into the water.

Nothing to eat in the pond? Wander out on land to grab a bite. Frogs have adapted to environments on every continent except Antarctica, from low-lying deserts to the slopes of mountains at fifteen thousand feet. In the Australian outback, the water-holding frog can wait up to seven years for rain. Thanks to their cold blood, frogs can change their body temperatures to adjust to the temperature of their surroundings. And their legs provide a mobility that is extremely advantageous, allowing them to leap up to twenty times their body length, which is the equivalent of a hundred feet or so for you and me.

The evolution of frogs, of course, is classic Darwinism. Survival doesn't necessarily favor the strongest—fat lot of good that did the T. rex—but rather those life-forms that are most adaptable. The same is true for us. We weren't the strongest species to evolve from *Homo habilis,* which appeared two and a half million years ago, but we had bigger brains than our closest rival, the Neanderthals. A bigger brain gave us the ability to think more deeply, more abstractly, which in turn allowed us to more effectively adapt.

BUT SINCE NONE OF us is going to noticeably evolve, in the Darwinian sense, in our lifetimes, what do I mean by adaptability? Legendary basketball coach John Wooden put it best:

"Adaptability is being able to adjust to any situation, at any given time."

The physiological adaptability of humans is obvious. If you travel from New York to Santa Fe, for example, you might feel pretty low for the first day or two because the atmosphere is thinner at seven thousand feet than it is at sea level. But your body will adapt by producing more hemoglobin, the protein in our blood that carries oxygen, to compensate, allowing you to function normally despite there being less oxygen in the air. Sometimes, that kind of physiological adaptation is necessary for optimal performance: No one would consider climbing Mount Everest without acclimating at a high-elevation camp before summiting. But that also takes time.

When we're talking about adaptability as an attribute, we're focusing on the mental aspect.

What I mean is, the ability to change tactics, expectations, and strategies as circumstances require. Whereas perseverance is the ability to proactively adjust tactics and behaviors in pursuit of an objective, adaptability is the ability to *reactively* shift in response to external changes. Most people would simplify that as the ability to go with the flow without getting rattled. The faster one can do that under stress, in an uncertain situation with no obvious outcome, the higher his or her level of adaptability.

Let's go back to combat sports, boxing and MMA and the like. A fighter might have a plan to control his opponent, perhaps even a detailed sequence of planned moves— *if I do A, he'll do B, then I'll do C.* But he can't guarantee that his opponent will actually do B. What if he does G? Or Q? Jab-and-move was a perfectly rational strategy against Mike Tyson, but only if Mike Tyson didn't punch you in the head really, really hard. What then?

Regular life is no different. Circumstances always change. Sometimes slowly, sometimes in a blink. Sometimes, we get hit with the equivalent of a right hook—an accident, a major illness, a business catastrophe. Mostly, though, those changes are the equivalent of jabs—a new manager shifts priorities in your department, a supplier raises prices, a critically important co-worker calls in sick. Environments, atmospheres, and attitudes can shift—the laid-back boss suddenly becomes stricter, or a formal dinner turns into casual drinks. Adapting doesn't have to be dramatic, just appropriate and proportional.

For instance, a couple of Army special-operations guys I knew had to come to headquarters from a remote combat outpost. Spec-ops guys usually need to blend in with the local population, which often isn't even close to Army standards for grooming and uniforms. In the case of those two, it meant long hair, full beards, and loose clothing. When they were summoned to brief the general, they could have arrived as scruffy as they were in the field. But they would have stood out at HQ, where everyone is in uniform, clean-shaven, with regulation haircuts; the attention would have been on their appearance, not on their briefing. The immediate mission—making their case to the general—was more important than their beards, and it was in their best interests to adapt.

That's a very simple story. In fact, if you read it in a different context you might not have even recognized it as an example of adaptability. If we weren't specifically discussing adaptability, it probably would be a mundane and passing detail: "They shaved, put on uniforms, and went to see the general." Kind of a commonsense thing. That's good! It suggests you already have a decent level of adaptability because you see such accommodations as ordinary. Optimal performance sometimes means nothing more than adjusting to one's surroundings.

How well an individual or a team recognizes and interprets a shifting environment or situation and makes the necessary adjustments suggests their level of adaptability. If they do so with speed and enthusiasm, they likely are pretty high on the scale. On the other hand, if you find yourself resisting, making changes more slowly and begrudgingly in uncomfortable and unpredictable situations, your innate adaptability probably registers on the low end of the scale. But there are other, less dramatic measures, too. Remaining easygoing with hard-to-handle team members, staying fluid with mercurial clients, even a willingness to approach problems from a fresh perspective would all indicate adaptability.

If you suspect you aren't particularly adaptable, that hardly means you are doomed to rigidity. It only suggests you'll have to be more deliberate in choosing to adapt. Because you might not instinctively bend and flex with external elements, you'll have to consciously *decide* to do so. That will almost certainly be uncomfortable, at least in the beginning, and it might never become a natural reflex. Low-adaptability folks can adapt; it just takes a lot of energy . . . and it's often painful. If you find yourself on the low end of adaptability, don't fret; there's nothing wrong with it. Just realize that everything in the known universe changes over time, with few exceptions. If you can't find periodic ways to adapt to a changing environment, you risk becoming a dinosaur—not a frog.

CHAPTER SEVEN

THE BENEFITS OF LITTLE TRAGEDIES

Resilience: *The ability to rapidly return to one's baseline emotional and mental state after a stressful, traumatic, or even triumphant event*

IN THE EARLY MORNING hours of October 22, 2015, Hank stepped on a land mine.

He was in Afghanistan, retired from the military but working as a contractor. He was with a couple dozen other guys taking a break from the long patrol on a mountainside, but spread out, a standard security tactic. With some distance between them, they could keep eyes on a wider area, watch for threats coming from any direction. And scattered positions make for smaller targets, which is safer than clustering together as one big bull's-eye.

Hank, who was one of the mission leaders, was walking to one of the groups on the perimeter to make sure they had everything they needed and were ready to move out.

He heard a soft click beneath his boot.

There are land mines buried all over Afghanistan. Some were laid during the twenty years that U.S. troops have been there, and many others are left over from the 1980s, when the Soviet Union occupied the country, and from the civil war that followed the Soviet withdrawal. Land mines can last for decades, camouflaged in the dirt and fully functional. More than a hundred million are strewn across the planet, and they kill about twenty-six thousand people every year.

The mine Hank stepped on threw him six feet into the air. It blew off both his legs, fractured his pelvis, and punctured his right lung.

Mines typically are laid in clusters, so Hank's teammates, already dazed by the concussion, had to clear a safe path to him. They moved as quickly as possible, then tied five tourniquets to stanch the bleeding. A casualty-evacuation helicopter was called in. The pilots landed close to Hank, a dangerous decision that exposed them to potential enemy fire but saved precious minutes: As soon as he got to the nearest trauma center, Hank coded, which meant he went into full cardiopulmonary arrest. The doctors resuscitated him, but Hank coded a few more times before he stabilized. He needed more than two dozen units of blood, the trauma unit's entire supply, to keep him alive.

Hank spent the next three days drifting in and out of consciousness. He would dream of playing with his daughters on a sunny beach, then wake up thrashing at the restraints holding him to the bed, convinced he'd been taken prisoner. He didn't know where he was or even that he'd been injured. It was as if he was caught in a nightmare that he couldn't escape. At times, he thought he might be dead and that this was what dead felt like.

When he was finally able to gain awareness of reality at the military hospital in Landstuhl, Germany, a nurse came into his room. "Hank," she told him, "you stepped on a land mine. Both of your legs were amputated, one above the knee and one below, and your pelvis is fractured." Her tone was gentle without being emotional. "You've got a long road ahead," she said. "But you're stable and your family's been notified."

Hank stared at her for a moment, not saying anything. He repeated her words in his head, tried to make sense of them.

He was in a hospital, and both of his legs were gone.

All right, he told himself. *I'm going to be fine. Grab the paper towels and get to work.*

IMAGINE YOUR LIFE REPRESENTED by a line plotted on a page. The line moves from left to right, from the past into the present, and it extends a little bit more with each passing day. If your life was uniformly calm and pleasant, neither aggravating nor exciting, that line would be flat and level. We'll call that your baseline, and it's where you're most comfortable emotionally, mentally, and physically.

But the line is rarely flat, of course. It undulates, rising and falling like an irregular wave to mirror the highs and lows of your life (see Appendix One for an example). There are minor squiggles all along the line because that's how life works: Traffic makes you late for an important meeting and the line drops a bit; the meeting goes better than expected and the line rebounds, maybe even bounces up a little. There are bigger swells and deeper troughs, too, successes and disappointments, some more intense than others. Occasionally the line spikes, representing your greatest achievements, and sometimes it plummets—maybe your spouse divorces you or maybe you get fired.

Maybe you step on a land mine.

It's difficult to function in either those deep troughs or at those dizzying peaks. What you want—what you *need*—is to return to that baseline, to that state of pleasant calm that is neither aggravating nor exciting. That's what it means to be resilient.

Resilience often is mistaken for durability. A person who

can suffer an endless series of misfortunes, endure a tremendous amount of abuse, and still get up in the morning with a smile often is said to be resilient. Maybe. But it's possible that person simply has a high capacity for suffering and enduring and pretending to be happy, which is not the same thing at all.

Highly resilient people are able to genuinely return to that baseline. They're able to heal the damage or process the change that those spikes and trenches represent. They tell themselves, and they *believe,* "I'm going to be fine—time to get to work." How quickly and efficiently they can do this is a measure of where they fall on the resilience gradient.

To illustrate this more clearly, let's shift our metaphor a little bit. Imagine that your baseline, your natural set point, is a spot on a thermostat. Let's say seventy-three degrees is where you're most comfortable. But then something bad happens and your temperature drops ten degrees. You'll almost certainly warm yourself back to seventy-three degrees eventually—it's called a set point for a reason, and research suggests that people tend to revert to their general state of happiness regardless of their circumstances. If you're high on the resilience scale, you'll do so rapidly and smoothly. If you're less resilient, it might take a while longer and maybe the thermostat will jerk back and forth, rising six degrees, dropping three, before finally settling back at seventy-three.

Someone who's very low on the gradient, however, might never fully recover, They might only rebound to seventy-one degrees. But a baseline almost two degrees cooler than it was will affect whatever comes next, whether that's a ten-degree high or an eight-degree low. Highs will be muted and lows will be amplified. If the baseline keeps dropping, it can lead to apathy and then depression.

It's important to note that the same principle applies in the other direction, too, that it's just as important to reset from the highs as the lows. Consider someone who just received a major promotion, an obvious cause to celebrate that spikes the thermostat fifteen degrees. But if that person, after acknowledging the success, can't return to his set point, he risks a dangerously skewed view of himself and his circumstances. Will he be overconfident, unable to understand the realities of his new position? Will he become lazily self-assured, resting on his laurels? These are the seeds of arrogance, and arrogance almost always leads to complacency.

One of my former commanding officers used to coach us all on the two-minute rule, which was something his grandfather had taught him. The rule was that whenever something positive happened, any kind of victory or success, you had two minutes to celebrate and enjoy the spoils. After those 120 seconds, you were to put that success aside and move on. Conversely, if something bad happened, you were allowed two minutes to wallow, complain, or feel sorry for yourself. And then you needed to return to baseline and move on.

That is the crux of resilience. Often it takes work, especially when we hit those lowest of lows.

HANK SPENT MORE THAN four months in the hospital, enduring multiple surgeries and fighting off infections. When his wounds had healed sufficiently that he could be fitted with prosthetic legs, he faced a new front in an ongoing battle: learning how to walk again.

A key element of resilience is what Hank calls "movement." This begins with accepting a situation for what it is, figuring out how to begin returning to that baseline, and then acting upon it. We know from the neurology of fear (Chapter Four) that getting moving is critical to success, and the process isn't much different here. Deliberate movement toward a goal is the critical first step that encourages all the steps that follow.

It helps to have a certain mindset, one calibrated to separate what *has* happened from what *can* happen. In Hank, that was forged early on. One of his earliest memories is sitting in the living room watching TV with his family. He was five years old, and he wanted some milk. "I just bought a new gallon," his mom told him. "It's in the refrigerator."

Hank made his way to the refrigerator, where he realized, with great pride, that he was just tall enough to reach the shelf with the milk. He was on his tiptoes, coaxing the gallon jug to the edge of the shelf with his fingertips until it was close enough to grab. But he missed. The milk nosedived through his hands and slammed to the floor. There was milk everywhere—floor, cabinets, walls, even a splash on the ceiling. Hank heard his mom's footsteps coming. A pit fell hard and heavy in his stomach. "As a five-year-old," he says, "I remember thinking my world was going to end."

Mom rounded the corner, stopped, surveyed the mess, then looked at him, the maker of the mess. Her face was red, filled with anger and disbelief. But within a few seconds, Hank could see her relax. She had her own, quicker version of the two-minute rule. "Go grab the paper towels," she said, and with no more urgency than when she'd told him to get the milk in the first place. She was calm, almost casual about it, and they both set about mopping up the mess.

"She never made it a big deal," Hank says. "She basically told me that when something bad happens, don't waste time crying over it. Get over it quickly and get to work on the things that you can control."

That stuck with Hank. He realized later that it was one of his core mantras, one that showed up everywhere, from home life to the battlefield to that hospital room in Germany. It was such a visceral memory, in fact, that it came to him in the moment after he was blown up in Afghanistan. He was on his back, dust and smoke above him. He couldn't really move and he didn't understand why. He thought, *Shit, I'm the jerk that just gave away our position.* He wished he could go back in time ten seconds, put his foot in a different spot, do anything differently. Anger, fear, and despair welled up. *This didn't happen. This couldn't happen. I want a do-over. Please, please, please tell me this didn't happen!* And then he remembered his mother. *Go grab the paper towels,* he could hear her saying. *Now get to work.*

And he did. Lying in the dirt, disoriented, and unable to move, he knew he needed to get to work if he was going to survive. The only thing he could control was his right hand, which he started waving, and his voice, which he used to guide his teammates to his position. The fact that they were able to get to him so quickly is the reason Hank didn't bleed to death on that mountainside.

HANK WAS FORTY-EIGHT YEARS old when he stepped on that mine, which means his formative memory, the root of his resilience, was planted more than four decades earlier. "Resilience is something that happens *before* a tragedy, not after," Hank says. It is also an attribute that improves with practice. The little boy whose mother taught him not to cry over spilled milk became, with time and similar situations, the man who could help save his own life.

Part of the cause and effect of practiced resilience, Hank says, is a positive attitude: *cause* because it helps you be resilient and *effect* because resilience reinforces that attitude. Granted, "positive attitude" is not a precise scientific term. It's not quite the same as "optimism." For simplicity's sake, think of it as consciously casting situations and circumstances into their best possible light. Norman Vincent Peale wrote about this basic idea back in 1952 in *The Power of Positive Thinking,* and there is science to back it up.

Remember the sympathetic and parasympathetic systems we discussed in Chapter Four? Both of those can be engaged in positive and negative ways. The sympathetic system kicks in when we're stressed, anxious, or fearful. But it also fires during times of exuberance, excitement, and passion. Sex, for example, is a sympathetic-heavy activity, as is joyful laughter or engaging conversation. The parasympathetic system works the same way from the other direction: depression, apathy, peacefulness, and contentment are all parasympathetic-heavy states.

Now let's examine a separate, but related, part of the human machine involved in optimal performance and, more specifically, resilience. That is the endocrine system, which generates and dispenses neurotransmitters and hormones. When we go into a sympathetic response, our body immediately creates a chemical called norepinephrine, or adrenaline, to get us ready for action. A parasympathetic engagement will result in acetylcholine, which, among other things, slows the heart rate and dilates blood vessels. Both norepinephrine and acetylcholine are important neurotransmitters.

Where we need to focus, though, is on hormones, and specifically the two big ones, cortisol and DHEA. When either the sympathetic or parasympathetic system is engaged in a negative response—anger or depression, for example—the body produces cortisol. Cortisol is a hormone to both love and hate. On the one hand, it's the main hormone behind the stress response, which is necessary for survival. On the other hand, it's the main hormone behind the stress response, which means it's activated far more often than is required for survival. It primes our bodies for survival by increasing the amount of glucose in the bloodstream as a ready source of energy, raising the heart rate and constricting arteries, which in turn raises blood pressure. All of that is designed to get more blood and more energy to the big muscle groups. At the same time, cortisol slows or even temporarily stops bodily systems not essential for survival. Remember how fear and stress will stop the production of saliva? Cortisol has a hand in that, as well as in slowing the reproductive and immune systems. It's also designed for the long haul—that quick shot of adrenaline that helps you run from a bear is short-lived, but cortisol lingers in the body. That's why an inability to reset from a negative event, to fully recover to the baseline, is self-reinforcing. When your body is chronically soaked in cortisol, it creates all manner of physiological and psychological problems, from apathy and depression to high blood pressure and heart disease.

In the positive states of sympathetic or parasympathetic response, our bodies make DHEA instead. That hormone, the precursor to testosterone and estrogen, helps rebuild and repair after cortisol has done its hard work on our bodies. DHEA helps get us back to normal.

What this tells us, then, is that our emotions matter— a lot. If we are consistently angry (sympathetic) or depressed (parasympathetic), we're flooding our systems with cortisol, hindering our ability to heal and recover. If we are joyful (sympathetic) or peaceful and content (parasympathetic), however, we're juicing ourselves with DHEA, rebuilding damaged cells and accelerating our recovery.

"Being positive is a conscious and deliberate choice," Hank says. "Make a vow to be positive. Make a commitment to fill your life with happiness and joy and not pain and misery."

That's not always easy, not by a long shot. But if you commit to doing your best, then you consciously assist in your resilience. How do you do it? Hank will tell you to start by focusing on the little things. Like the two things he could control, his hand and his voice, when he was on his back in the dirt, dazed and hemorrhaging. Months later, when he was fitted for prosthetic legs and felt a depression settling over him, Hank reframed his circumstances to a comical degree. *Wow,* he told himself, *I haven't weighed a hundred and sixty-five pounds since eighth grade. And I'll never get athlete's foot again, or have to clip my toenails.*

That's a positive attitude.

Finally, gratitude is an important emotion in building and maintaining a positive attitude, which makes it a huge part of resilience. Being truly grateful for something deflects emotional energy from resenting anything else. There is also a major chemical benefit: Expressing deep gratitude releases huge amounts of dopamine. We know how powerful dopamine is when we're embroiled in a challenge—and it's exactly what the body needs for the long climb back up to baseline.

ONE'S LEVEL OF RESILIENCE is affected by the interplay with several other attributes.

There's an obvious correlation with courage (Chapter Four) and the dopamine reward that comes from directly engaging a source of fear or anxiety. Perseverance (Chapter Five), which is the ability to keep pushing ahead despite any obstacles or setbacks, is also important. So is adaptability (Chapter Six), the degree to which one can recognize new environments and adjust accordingly. The higher one ranks on any or all of those suggests how resilient they'll be.

Hank says one more trait is essential to increasing resilience: humor. We'll go into that in more depth in Chapter Twenty-five, but for now think of it as another dopamine hack, and of dopamine as an effective tool to get back to baseline. When we laugh, just as when we're grateful, our system is inundated with dopamine, the feel-good neuro-transmitter. Sometimes our most vigorous efforts at positive thinking fall short. Sometimes a moment just sucks. That's when a well-timed laugh is invaluable. Laughter is an uncontrollable response, like sneezing. Once we start, we can't help but feel better—because our brain is soaking up dopamine. As I'll discuss later, that's why having a class clown on any team can come in handy. But at times, we need to be our own clowns, looking for humor in a movie, a stand-up comic, or even the situation itself—whatever else gets us laughing.

Hank, though, was fortunate in that he was surrounded by teammates who were wired for humor, who could inject some light into even the darkest situation. And the most important person in his life, his wife, is Hank's perfect class clown. She had to wait almost five days to see him, until he was flown from Landstuhl to Walter Reed Army Medical Center in Washington, D.C. It seemed miserably longer, though, because all she really knew was that her husband of twenty-five years, the father of their two children, the man she loved, had been horribly wounded. There was so much she wanted to say. But when she got to the hospital, she looked at him for a moment, not saying anything. When she finally spoke, it was in a dead-on Forrest Gump impression.

"Lieutenant Dad!" she barked. "You lost your legs!"

"This boosted me up in ways that are hard to describe," Hank says. "And I knew then that I had everything I needed to recover."

Which he did. Forty-five days after he was first fitted with his prostheses—forty-five days after he started learning to walk again—Hank completed eight miles of the Bataan Memorial Death March, a twenty-six-mile hike through the high desert of New Mexico. He did it all under his own power, with only two trekking sticks for assistance.

"Getting over the little tragedies in daily life is how you

get over the big tragedies," Hank says. "Getting stuck in traffic, being late for work, or spilling milk are all little tragedies. For me, resilience is that spilled milk: something that happened before I lost my legs, not after."

Start recognizing the little tragedies—they are for your benefit.

GRIT ROLL-UP

When people comment about how much grit Navy SEALs have, I suspect the main reason is because of BUD/S.

It's the one thing most people know for certain about SEALs—almost everything else spec-ops teams do is classified—and it's become a pop-culture trope. The image of exhausted, weary men getting pounded by cold surf to prove their worth as inexhaustible, unwearying warriors is like a condensed hero's journey. It's more of an anecdote than an epic, but the narrative arc is the same.

That's fitting, too, because when it comes to attributes, grit is less about long-term adventures than short-term challenges.

There's a truism in BUD/S classes about Hell Week: "If you think about Friday on Monday, you'll never make it." Graduating is the goal for every man in every class, and most of them pursue it with a deep passion. But there is nothing to be passionate about when you're lying in the surf zone or lugging a boat around for the fifth straight hour. If, on Monday, you dwell on all the miserable hours yet to come, the dread will be overwhelming. So you focus on the moment, and gut it out.

That's grit.

But, again, grit is hardly specific to SEALs. Think of a cancer patient enduring another round of chemotherapy—the goal is remission, but getting through each session of chemo takes grit. The challenges don't have to be enormous, either; microdoses of grit can get us through the more routine moments of life. The goal is to have your best sales quarter, but the immediate presentation to a demanding boss takes grit. The goal is to get in better shape, but getting up early every morning and grinding through that workout takes grit. Put simply, your ability and willingness to step outside your comfort zone is evidence of grit.

The four attributes I've put under the umbrella of grit— courage, perseverance, adaptability, and resilience—all are useful on their own and in other contexts. But each is an indispensable ingredient in grit. They play off one another well. The physiological rewards of courage promote perseverance. Perseverance helps adaptability and vice versa, by helping you respond to changing external cues. Finally, resilience enhances all of the others as it allows you to reset and charge forward anew.

Explore and develop your courage, perseverance, adaptability, and resilience—and take advantage of the grit that you already have.

THE MENTAL ACUITY ATTRIBUTES

The brain is what sets us humans apart from the other animals. Evolution didn't make us the strongest or the fastest or the furriest, but it did give us a big brain, one capable of reasoning and imagining, of thinking abstractly and rationally, of absorbing and sorting and editing an endless stream of incoming data. Our bodies make us *Homo sapiens,* but our minds make us truly human.

Mental acuity is basically a measure of how sharp the mind is. It has little to do with education, or even raw intelligence; it is not a matter of how well-read or quick-witted you are. Rather, we're focusing on the ability to effectively absorb and understand information, to concentrate, focus, and remember.

Working with Andrew Huberman, the Stanford neurobiologist, I've deconstructed mental acuity into four key attributes: situational awareness, compartmentalization, task switching, and learnability.

These capabilities are hardwired into our cognitive physiology. Like all attributes, we all have them in varying amounts, and we all have the ability to amplify them with enough effort.

Huberman's gift is explaining complex brain functions in relatively simple terms. So before we dive in, let's discuss a few terms you'll read repeatedly over the next four chapters.

- **SCRIPTS.** Think of these as lines of code your brain is constantly writing to make sense of the world. Most of the time, scripts are based on external information: I touched that stove and got burned; I jumped off that tree branch and fell to the ground; I pressed the accelerator and my car moved forward. A script could also be written from internal data: My bladder is full, so I need to use the bathroom.

- **PATTERNS.** These are collections of similar scripts that build familiarity and certainty in our environments: *Every time* I touch a hot stove, I get burned. Patterns are how we learn. They help us predict our near-future environment and experiences— *if* I touch the stove, I *will* get burned—which allows us to make rational decisions. Our brains love patterns. In fact, when we deliberately arrange information into a pattern, the brain more easily files it away into our memory. Remember the Alphabet Song? Of course you do. There's a reason children learn their ABCs in a six-note melody.

- **CATEGORIES.** The hippocampus, which is in charge of long-term memory, groups patterns into categories for easier retrieval: using a stove, climbing a tree, driving my car.

- **CONTEXTS.** These are broad versions of categories—cooking, climbing, driving—and they can be applied to a variety of environments. For example, if you jump on a tractor or slip into a go-kart or take the wheel of a boat, your brain will recognize the context as driving.

As you read through situational awareness, compartmentalization, task switching, and learnability, think about where you fall on the scale for each. Optimal performance begins in the brain. The mental acuity attributes are the foundation.

CHAPTER EIGHT

THE ART OF VIGILANCE

Situational Awareness: *The ability to absorb and process meaningful information about our current environment*

YOU ARE RIDING YOUR bicycle down a quiet country road on a spring afternoon. A few puffy white clouds hang in a crystal blue sky. The air is warm, but there's a soft breeze from the west that rustles the fields on either side. You can hear birdsong and, in the distance, the buzz of a small airplane as you pedal down a ribbon of blacktop.

Sounds pretty peaceful, right? A quiet, empty road with nothing to distract you because nothing is happening.

Except that birdsong is the sound of chickadees in a panic over a raptor circling overhead. That field of wheat, waving almost as if it's happy, is being ravaged by a disease called Cephalosporium stripe that will kill half of it. The breeze is the leading edge of a low-pressure system that will blow the gentle cumulus clouds away and replace them with thunderheads. The airplane is fine, though.

There are countless things happening at any given moment in almost any environment. And your senses are capable of taking in most of it. The eyes can absorb about ten million bits of information every second, the skin another million, the ears and nose a hundred thousand, the tongue another thousand. All of that information, more than eleven million bits each second, gets routed to the brain—which really has no need to process all of it. There's nothing you can do about the chickadee, even if you understood its song. The weather is perfect for the moment. You are not a botanist, so you have no way of knowing what those yellow stripes are and no reason to care. Our brains naturally ignore irrelevant data and filter out the distracting parts, which usually isn't a problem and is, when you're on a pleasant bike ride, quite nice.

But now you're in a New York City subway station, and your five-year-old has just slipped away on a downtown train. Suddenly all those extra millions of bits of data matter. Solving the immediate problem is going to be based on how much information you have at the moment you begin working toward a solution. The more you understand your environment, the more you can decipher what's happening and why, the more of a head start you'll have.

That's what situational awareness means, and it's directly correlated with optimal performance. The more you have of the former, the better you'll be at the latter.

ELEVEN MILLION BITS OF information every second is a daunting amount to process, even for our sophisticated brains. Fortunately, situational awareness isn't necessarily about how much data our senses gather. It's about how many patterns we recognize, catalog, and put into context. (Remember, patterns are collections of scripts, categories are how the brain sorts those patterns, and contexts are broader versions of categories.) For example, a few moments ago you saw a man in a uniform on the subway platform, which your brain immediately recognized as a person of authority who can help when your child goes off on a train by himself. There's no need to think through an overwhelming amount of information. It's a mental reflex: Uniform means authority means help.

That recognition happens in a specific part of the brain called the inferior temporal cortex. The IT cortex is constantly interacting with the hippocampus, where long-term memories are stored, and with the working memory in the forebrain. Think of that working memory as the RAM on your computer, keeping certain necessary information readily accessible. If you were almost out of gas, for example, the directions a passerby gave you to the nearest gas station—next left, two lights down, right on Elm—would be stored in your working memory, available for the short term but unnecessary for the long term.

Because it's interacting with both the short- and long-term memories, the IT cortex is the workhorse of situational awareness. It's in charge of matching incoming information and freshly written scripts (those lines of brain code) with familiar patterns and categories and contexts. The IT cortex is where the brain recognizes a context—*I'm outdoors*—that it links to a category—*there are dark clouds above*—and, finally, matches it to a pattern we can understand—*it's probably going to rain*.

Clearly, part of situational awareness involves predictions and projections. Those dark clouds are significant because you know they're associated with rain, and you can project yourself into a near future where you'll get wet if you don't get inside. We do this all the time without thinking, overlaying memories onto current circumstances to predict an outcome or alter our behavior. Traffic is stalled and you immediately recognize you'll be late for work. The sun is at high noon on a cloudless day, so you put some sunscreen on your nose.

Everyone's IT cortex is always working, just at different levels of intensity. Most people's brains are less concerned with decoding patterns on a leisurely bike ride, for instance, than when a child goes AWOL on the subway. So what's the difference between a person with high situational awareness and a person without as much?

In a word, vigilance. And that starts in the amygdala, the part of your brain associated with fear and the fight–flight–freeze response. "But the amygdala isn't just about fear," Andrew Huberman says. "It's for threat detection." A slightly tweaked amygdala, then, means a more finely tuned antenna for things that are out of place. There's an amygdala sweet spot: too relaxed and you are oblivious to threats, but too alert and you tip into stress; your sympathetic nervous system takes over and, among other symptoms, your brain is taking in *less* information because your field of vision narrows.

"Situational awareness has this vigilance component," Andrew says, "but we don't want to confuse it with being stressed. It's simply a way of looking for patterns. The difference with someone who is more vigilant is that they are constantly running scripts back and forth through the inferior temporal cortex, pattern-matching based on current context and updates." Someone who has less situational awareness, on the other hand, is probably just matching information with memory and bypassing the IT cortex. It's the difference between seeing a bunch of trees clumped together and understanding that you're looking at a forest.

SOME PEOPLE HAVE A propensity to engage their IT cortex more often and more intensely than others. They're the ones who walk down a city street and notice the oncoming traffic, the dark alleys, the pedestrians who drift a little too close. They're tuned in a bit more to the world around them, vigilantly scanning for threats both minor and major, or even things that just seem a little out of place. Others are set to a more relaxed state, barely noticing the gathering clouds, the agitated crowd, or any number of things going on around them. We all vacillate somewhat between those two states, our IT cortex more active in some situations, set to idle in others, but the level at which you generally function is the measure of your situational awareness.

As with any attribute, extremes can be detrimental. Too little situational awareness risks obliviousness to real danger. Too much, or hypervigilance, can wear out the nervous system and perhaps even mask an underlying paranoia. A constant state of fear keeps all of the sympathetic nervous system responses continually active, which is both exhausting and distracting.

If you typically operate closer to the oblivious side of the scale, though, it's possible to bring yourself closer to the optimal middle. Think of the IT cortex as a muscle that can be exercised: Deliberate vigilance practiced often enough eventually will become natural vigilance. Again, the brain likes to find patterns, and we often tell it what to look for. If you've ever bought a new car, you probably understand this. You hardly ever saw, say, a Mazda 3 on the road until you started driving one—and then suddenly it appears to be the most popular car ever made. The supply hasn't actually gone up, of course; you've just loaded a script into your brain that your IT cortex is tagging. When we focus on anything, we're telling our brain to pick that pattern out of those eleven million bits of information per second. With repetition, those patterns become ingrained.

To exercise your IT cortex, pull the headphones out of your ears, put away your smartphone, and start paying attention to the world around you. Do it right now, even. Put this book down for a moment and identify everything blue in your surroundings. Big things, little things, all the things—it doesn't matter. The next time you're outside, notice how many sedans drive by and how many hatchbacks. Yes, it sounds random and maybe even silly, because it is.

But this is how you develop situational awareness: through a deliberate practice of paying attention to the world around you, even if nothing particularly interesting is happening. The more new information you absorb, the more scripts and patterns your brain will create, which will allow you to be more comfortable, more aware, in more situations.

CHAPTER NINE

WIRED FOR EFFICIENCY

Compartmentalization: *The ability to effectively chunk an environment or situation into meaningful pieces, then focus on that which needs immediate attention*

THE BRAIN CAN GET tired. We've all been there. Flood the brain with new information and unfamiliar contexts, and you will feel mentally exhausted. The first day of a new job, when you're learning the office routines and wrestling with HR, can tire out the brain. So can landing in a foreign country or an overwhelming city. The brain is extremely efficient—it runs on about as much energy as a 40-watt lightbulb—but it can get weary if it works too hard for too long.

We already know some of the ways the brain saves effort and energy. Scripts and patterns and templates allow it to discard most of the eleven million bits of information streaming in every second. Still, there is usually an enormous amount of data that *isn't* discarded. It can't all be processed at once, so the brain has another trick: compartmentalization.

Psychologists use this term to describe a mental defense strategy where conflicting ideas, emotions, and memories are walled off from one another, often because of trauma or anxiety. We're applying a similar concept to a neurological, as opposed to emotional, level. Compartmentalization in this context isn't a defense mechanism but, at its best, a key to cognitive efficiency and, in turn, optimal performance.

The first thing to understand is that it isn't a singular activity—in other words, it's not a matter of *I don't like this so I'll block it out* or *I'll deal with this project now and that project later.* Those might be appropriate strategies for getting through the day or week or month. But we're focused on the brain and how it operates second to second. It is a dynamic, fluid process that, like situational awareness, involves the inferior temporal cortex, hippocampus, and the forebrain.

In very simple terms, your brain is constantly deciding which information is relevant and which is irrelevant, and shuffling those bits to their appropriate compartment. Yet the criteria constantly change; relevancy shifts with each update of the running script. How rapidly and efficiently this happens is a measure of your compartmentalization.

COMPARTMENTALIZATION IS A THREE-STEP process: assessment, prioritization, and focus. Let's take them one at a time with a simple example.

You're in a big, unfamiliar airport, and you're late for a connecting flight. Rows of shops and restaurants—Hudson News, Chili's, all the usual suspects—line wide corridors. A voice is making garbled announcements over the public-address system. To your left is an enormous screen scrolling through flights and gates and times. To your right, a bathroom that's closed for cleaning. Straight ahead is a long concourse with dozens of gates. Your boarding pass is on your smartphone, which is in your right hand.

Step One: Assessment. Your brain is running a simple script: Go to the gate. It scrolls through all of that information (and much more; we're just noting the big things here) and identifies what's most immediately relevant. Chili's, the bathroom, the magazine shop—those are slotted into categories and patterns that have nothing to do with getting on a plane, so those are set aside. The important things are your boarding pass, the gate numbers, and the concourse, all of which your brain recognizes as relevant to the script it's running.

Step Two: Prioritization. What gate are you trying to find? Obviously, that is the most important information. But remember: The script is constantly updating. Once you glance at your boarding pass and see the number—34, let's say—the script changes from finding your gate number on your phone to finding Gate 34. As you start down the concourse, your brain flags three things as possibly helpful: the airport map on your phone (but the signal is weak and, anyway, it's a straight concourse); the flight monitors (but you already passed one and the next one is a five-minute walk away); and large signs with bright, clear numbers on them marking each gate. The gate signs are prioritized.

Step Three: Focus. Engage the priority. Scan the gate signs; recognize that they line the concourse in ascending order, odd numbers to the left, even to the right. Your IT cortex and hippocampus recognize the pattern, and finding Gate 34 is at that point almost automatic.

THAT IS NOT AN endpoint, however. Even while you are focused on the current priority, you are still taking in information so that the script that you are running can be updated. An announcement says your flight is delayed three hours. Chili's is suddenly more relevant. The flight monitor says your gate has changed. Rescan the signs.

This is an endless process. Compartmentalization is not static, as if you silo your thoughts into a tight box and keep them there. It's ever-changing, the script constantly updating with information shuttling between the IT cortex, the

hippocampus, and the forebrain. Having this all happen efficiently, of course, assumes that you are alert and calm. If
you're stressed—maybe you're running because you believe
the plane already boarded—you might stay focused on the
gate numbers and miss the announcement or sprint right
past the monitor. And back to that mental exhaustion: In
unfamiliar settings, ones in which you don't have familiar
patterns and categories on which to rely, it can be a taxing
process under the calmest of circumstances.

Some people, particularly those who have high levels of
situational awareness, compartmentalize with ease. Others
might struggle a bit, which might affect their task-switching
ability (something we'll get into in the next chapter).
Whether you can update those scripts rapidly or not depends on the strength of your IT cortex—and, remember,
your IT cortex can be exercised.

As with situational awareness, compartmentalization can
be practiced. Under that constant bombardment of information that is life, start noticing what's being discarded.
Consciously assign relevance, prioritize, and focus. Even
better, put yourself in new and dynamic, but safe, situations
and environments to give your brain a workout. This is one
of the reasons I love riding the subway in New York City. I
don't get there very often and, frankly, I find the system
thoroughly confusing. When I'm down in the tunnels, I'm
forced to take in a bunch of information, assign relevance,
prioritize, and focus.

A good exercise for me is to start at Times Square, the
busiest station in the city, and pick some place, any place, to
go. Brooklyn, let's say, Jay Street. First I have to figure out
which of the dozen or so lines tangled under Midtown I
want to take. The map I downloaded to my phone tells me
the express A train is faster but since I'm not in a hurry I
decide to take the C. I focus on the signs. The A and C lines
are marked with blue circles, which means I can ignore the

red circles (1, 2, and 3 trains) and the yellow ones (N, Q, R, and W). I follow those toward the platforms, and then make sure I'm on the one for southbound trains and not the ones going uptown. I get to the correct platform, but there are tracks on both sides. I look for more signs—the subway is surprisingly well marked—and find out that the track on the left is for the express A. I want the right side. There's a train coming, but I can see the letter E on the front. That line doesn't go to Brooklyn. So I wait for the next train, which is southbound C. Once I'm on the train, I have to know when to get off. Jay Street is the tenth stop, just after High Street. If I can't understand the conductor announcing stops, I can keep count.

If I get it wrong? Well, I go down the track an extra stop or two. But as long as I'm not shuttling around an excitable five-year-old, I just have to allow some extra time and enjoy the brain development. And I'm getting pretty good at it.

CHAPTER TEN

THE MULTITASKING MYTH

Task Switching: *The ability to shift focus among tasks or contexts*

MOST PEOPLE BELIEVE THEY can multitask. Most people, in fact, believe they're very good at it. In one famous study from the University of Utah, a statistically absurd but remarkably confident 70 percent of participants thought they were above average in their ability to do multiple things at once.

They weren't, and you aren't, either. When people try to do several things at once, almost everyone—a full 98 percent, according to that Utah study—gets worse at each individual task. And another study, at Stanford, found that people who habitually multitask actually do *more* poorly over time. In other words, the more you practice texting and driving, the more of a menace you are on the road.

The idea that anyone can talk on the phone, answer emails, tidy their workspace, and think through the kids' after-school schedule *all at once* is enticing, but it's also cognitively impossible. The conscious mind simply isn't set up to focus on multiple things at the same time. Even that tiny minority in the Utah study, the 2 percent who didn't get worse or even improved—David Strayer, the cognitive neuroscientist who led the study, calls them "supertaskers"—weren't truly multitasking. They were task *switching* at an exceptionally rapid and efficient rate.

You almost certainly aren't, and will never be, a supertasker. (They appear to have a different neural architecture than the population at large.) But all of us task switch. As we discussed in compartmentalization, the brain is constantly loading information into the inferior temporal cortex. That means that even when we're focused on one thing, our brain is updating scripts for the next thing. As long as we're not in a state of deep stress, as long as we're calm and alert, we're cognitively prepared to shift priorities. How effectively and quickly we do that is a measure of task switching.

THERE ARE TWO WAYS that we task switch.

The first is when we switch focus inside the same context. When you are driving a car, for instance, one moment you are focused on pressing the accelerator, the next on checking your mirrors or using your turn signal, then on pressing the brake. Each of those is a task, and you can switch from one to the other seemingly without thinking because your brain is running a compartmentalization loop for you: rapidly taking in information, assessing relevance, prioritizing, and focusing—and doing it over and over. The script is being continuously updated within the context of driving.

The other way that we task switch is when we need to hop between contexts. This also happens repeatedly. When you get out of your car and are walking across the parking lot, that's a new context. Enter an office building, and that's another new context. To you, that might all be part of your routine commute, but to your brain each of those steps is a new context. The reason there's no cognitive challenge involved—that is, the reason you don't have to consciously think about it—is because the scripts and patterns and categories are familiar.

When you walk into a Target store, you know what to expect and so the hop to a new context is easy. But what if you walked into that Target and saw an Olympic-size swimming pool swarming with teenagers in the middle of a swim meet? You'd need to take a pause because the pattern for Target stored in your brain doesn't match what you're seeing.

Unexpected hops into contexts that we're not prepared for and to which we can't apply previous templates are where uncertainty comes from. This is you in that Chinese village after the bus drove away. You were in a lovely context, taking in a view and relaxing. Then suddenly you're shoved into a new and utterly unfamiliar context, and there is nothing in your memory banks to draw on. You have not effectively switched tasks. You're probably beginning to spiral into a deep stress, which has a negative effect on task switching, compartmentalization, and situational awareness (your lack of which got you into this jam to begin with). The stress response is designed to limit, if not shut down, any functions that don't focus on the perceived threat. This is by evolutionary design: In a crisis that might be immediately lethal—getting chased by a bear, for instance—you want all of your physical and mental resources concentrated on surviving. Getting stranded in a Chinese village won't kill you, but your physiological stress response isn't calibrated finely enough to recognize the difference.

It's quite a conundrum. In a situation where you most need mental clarity, it comes the least easily. That's why your attributes, the innate levels of task switching and such that are wired into you, matter. They will take over when your conscious mind is overwhelmed.

Think back to the spring of 2020, when the novel coronavirus pandemic forced hundreds of millions of people to stay home. Most of us had to exercise our task switching in new and difficult ways. We needed those new scripts to be written.

For example, I was writing this book. Every day I went to a small office that I rented and my wife went to work selling real estate. Our boys were in school from just after breakfast until late in the afternoon. We spent evenings together as a family. The next morning, we'd start over. It was a nice routine, comfortable without being monotonous.

But then all of those contexts were mushed together. In my office, I could switch quickly from writing to answering questions from my editor to researching neuroscience. My brain is used to those things happening in that context. At school, the boys could easily switch from algebra to social studies to English. But suddenly we were doing all of those things at home.

Suddenly, there was a swimming pool in Target.

All of our mental-acuity attributes got a workout, but especially task switching. I would be editing a chapter and then switch to helping with advanced algebra. A business call would interrupt algebra, and I'd have to pull out of that to make lunch for the boys. I'd switch back to writing and then switch to walking the dog.

You might have gone through something similar, and you might remember feeling a little foggy, maybe tired, possibly overwhelmed. It's not that any of those specific tasks is difficult—it's that switching among them in unfamiliar contexts was more difficult than you probably realized.

My wife had an easier time because she'd had more practice. She'd been home with two young boys when I was deployed for months at a time, and that's a crash course in task switching. Every parent who's been home with multiple kids can probably relate: One child is hungry, the other needs help in the bathroom, that mess in the bedroom still hasn't been picked up, and do I really have to make dinner again? It's impossible to focus on any one thing for too long. The exhaustion from tending to small kids often comes less from the physical activity than from the cognitive load that only stops when you sleep. That's assuming you get to sleep.

Task switching requires energy and, from a neurological standpoint, a lot of it.

MOST CONTEXT SHIFTING IS not disruptive. Moving from one to another to yet another is a normal part of any day. All of us move from one discrete task to the next, cognitively speaking, hundreds of times a day. How easily we can do so depends, in part, on how much top-down control we have, or, put another way, how readily the forebrain takes charge. We'll get into the way the limbic system and forebrain interact when we discuss empathy (Chapter Seventeen); for now, just know that if you are predisposed to have more top-down control, you will task switch more easily.

Regardless of where we sit on the scale, we can make intentional choices to switch tasks and focus. It's just hard. One problem is that most of us don't realize that we are debilitating our performance by deliberately shifting context more often than we should—and usually for no good reason. And yes, this is the part where we discuss the scourge of mobile phones.

Smartphones have no doubt enhanced our ability to communicate and, in some ways, the quality of our lives. But there are a lot of cons that come with those pros, including unnecessary context switching. Your phone is a massive collection of contexts. The Instagram posts, the Amazon shopping, the game app, the text threads. Your brain has scripts and patterns for all of those contexts, which is fine in isolation. But they rarely are isolated. You'll be in a real-world context—an important conversation with a friend or a meeting at work—and you'll hear that ping or buzz. Even if you think you're choosing to ignore it, your brain isn't.

Those alerts jar you out of your current context. And not gently, either. Neurologically, it's like being teleported from a bookstore to a soccer field. Your brain has to expend energy refreshing its understanding of the new context. Sure, we are designed to be able to do that—task switching is an attribute, after all—but your attention isn't fully engaged where it needs to be. You've hopped out. In fact, research shows that when we shift out of our current context by immediately attending to our little devices, it takes an average of twenty minutes to fully refocus on the task at hand.

It's not only technology—emotion also inhibits our ability to effectively task switch (or compartmentalize or be situationally aware, too). If you are upset or excited about something that previously happened, your brain is still running that script, which makes it difficult to fully indulge the script for the present moment. This isn't complicated: When you're upset, it's hard to focus. The ability to let go of past emotional states, to remain calm and alert, really does matter.

Task switching can be developed, though not as easily as compartmentalization or situational awareness. Getting better at it just requires making deliberate decisions.

First, figure out where you fall on the scale. Do you tend to start a bunch of different things but not really finish any of them? You might be a little high on the task-switching attribute (folks with ADHD are definitely on the far end of this scale). Or do you more often focus intensely on one project at the expense of other obligations? That suggests you're a bit low.

In either instance, you'll need to make conscious, intentional decisions to help calibrate your task switching. If you suspect you're on the high end, concentrate on completing the task at hand; if you're low, force yourself to disengage and move to something else. As with most attributes, though, don't expect a dramatic shift one way or the other. The key is to be aware of and understand your personal level so you adjust your behavior accordingly.

CHAPTER ELEVEN

FORGED IN PLASTIC

Learnability: *The ability to absorb, process, and apply new information to a current or future context*

Among the mental acuity attributes, the most important is learnability. It's a sort of catalyst that allows those other cognitive traits to be put to effective use. If we didn't have the ability to update and adjust the scripts our brains are constantly writing, or to apply and remember the appropriate patterns and templates—that is, to learn—then compartmentalization and task switching would only help us make the same mistakes more efficiently. Situational awareness wouldn't be especially valuable if we'd never learned from the things we were aware of in other situations. There's not much point in recognizing an approaching thunderstorm if you haven't learned to come in out of the rain.

All of us are able to learn, of course. The fact that you understand this sentence is proof: You learned how to read. We human beings, all of whom began as helpless, squawking infants, have a marvelous capacity to learn. Barring some cognitive impairment, in fact, almost everyone can learn pretty much anything with enough time and effort. Not master, necessarily, but understand the rudiments. Maybe you don't have the manual dexterity to be a concert pianist, but you can learn which keys make which sound and which notes make which chords; you might never be fluent in German, but you can study the vocabulary and grammar. Our brains are designed to absorb information.

As an attribute, though, learnability doesn't involve what you know. It's not about your education or your study habits (which are skills you've learned anyway). For our purposes, learnability is a measure of how quickly an individual can receive, process, and integrate new information into their cognitive system. Information is constantly looping between the sensory inputs, the hippocampus, and the inferior temporal cortex, and the brain needs to sort the new and important from the old and irrelevant. People with a higher level of learnability adapt quickly to new contexts, move on from mistakes, and are able to replace outdated data with more current material. Learnability also amplifies and enhances other qualities, such as resilience, flexibility, and self-efficacy by reinforcing known and dependable patterns.

ONE OF THE KEYS to learnability is a concept called plasticity. It's a term that refers to how easily something can be shaped or molded—how plastic it is. Brain plasticity, or neuroplasticity, refers to the brain's ability to change and adapt as a result of experience.

This is meant in a literal, physical sense. Our thoughts and feelings are, at an elemental level, a series of electrical impulses traveling through circuits of nerve fibers. Movements—a step forward, scratching your nose, sitting down—are also controlled and directed by those neural circuits. We're not born with a full set of circuits ready to be activated; rather, we develop them one by one. Every new

thought, feeling, and movement creates a new neural pathway. Our brains, in fact, are at their most plastic when we're
infants and rapidly learning all sorts of new things.

Once those circuits are created, there are three ways
they're reinforced. The first is through repetition. Much like
routinely lifting weights can increase muscle mass, repeating
the same neural activity over and over will increase the speed
with which the electrical signals travel the circuit. As Dan
Coyle explains in his book *The Talent Code,* this is because a
substance called myelin wraps itself around those nerve
pathways every time we repeat a behavior. Myelin works
like a lubricating insulator. The more reps, the more myelin
wraps, and the more myelin wraps, the faster and more efficiently signals travel that pathway. Consider walking.
When toddlers take their first steps, the effort is as much
mental as physical. It's a new experience, so the brain has to
build circuits to instruct specific muscles in a specific order.
But every step adds a new layer of myelin, which allows the
signals to travel faster, which makes walking easier and easier
until it happens without conscious thought at all. The brain
is by then sending impulses along a myelin superhighway
rather than a slow, unfamiliar trail that's just been freshly
blazed. The same thing happens with all of our scripts, patterns, and contexts; practice really does make our brains
proficient. (On the downside, this is why habits are so hard
to break, too. Myelin is resilient.)

The second way those circuits are reinforced is through
intensity. This is where the brain is more versatile than the
muscles. If you bench-press three hundred pounds one
time—a pretty intense weight for most of us—your pecto-
rals and deltoids won't get any stronger. But if you drop
those three hundred pounds on your chest, crack two ribs,
and half-suffocate before a proper bodybuilder rescues you,
your brain will create a well-developed neural circuit that

says *Don't try to lift an insane amount of weight.* Myelin production increases with intensity, and a humiliating near-death in the gym is a very intense experience indeed.

Intense, though, doesn't necessarily mean traumatic or even dramatic. Think of it more as information distilled to a more potent form. You can be told that a ghost pepper is insufferably hot, and that circuit—*ghost pepper hot*—will be roughed out in your brain. It might quickly fade, or it might be slowly reinforced if you keep hearing about ghost peppers. But bite into a ghost pepper and that circuit will be slathered in myelin. Like the old adage says, experience really is a good teacher.

The third way circuits are reinforced is through focus, which also increases myelin. When you focus on something, for whatever reason, that information slips out of the working memory and into long-term storage. Scripts are rapidly written.

This happens all the time. We tend to easily remember the highlights and lowlights of our daily experiences because those were the moments upon which we focused. It could be the pain of the beesting or the pride of a promotion. It could also be a small compliment or papercut. It's not about the size of the event but rather about the clarity of our focus. Usually, the greater the focus, the more details will stick. We'll remember colors, sizes, temperatures, feelings, even specific faces.

My wife was once visiting New York City with her mom, sister, and niece. At one point, they were walking down the street, talking and laughing, not really paying attention to anything, when a stranger approached them. "Excuse me," the lady said to my wife. "I just wanted to let you know that your fly is down."

"Oh my God," my wife said, instantly flush with a combination of mortification and gratitude. "Thank you so much. You're my hero!"

She's never forgotten that woman. She still remembers her face, what she was wearing, the sound of her voice—all because she was forced to focus on an anomaly in an otherwise routine experience. That's the forebrain saying, *This is a novelty. Let's make a note of it.* That's neural plasticity.

And here's the best part: Such focus does not have to be accidental. We can choose to take control, to deliberately burn a memory into our hippocampus. "It's scary how strong this is," says Huberman, the cognitive neuroscientist. "I've been taking snapshots with my eyes since I was a kid. I'll look at something and say to myself, 'I'm never going to forget this'—and that image will stay with me forever. I'll remember the color, shape, orientation. Even the feelings will come back if I include those in my snapshot."

Think about that for a moment. So often we feel as if we need to capture certain moments with cameras or videos. When I attended my sons' elementary school recitals, I often saw more people watching the event through their phone screens as they recorded instead of seeing it through their own eyes. I don't begrudge anyone a video record of their children's events, but no one should forget their own innate ability to keep a mental record, sometimes even more richly nuanced and detailed. Unlike a video you might never watch again, the recall from the hippocampus is always available—the images, the sounds, the smells, even the feelings of the moment, too. No high-end camera can capture all that.

THERE IS A REMARKABLE amount of efficiency built into learnability. Unless there is repetition, intensity, or deliberate focus involved, incoming information likely will be dumped from our working memory once it's no longer needed. This is a good thing. We don't want to waste neural real estate on tidbits we only need to get through the day.

The number on your deli ticket can be forgotten as soon as your sandwich is ready because you will literally never need that particular number in that context again. Learnability is about sorting and processing useful information, not stockpiling useless data.

As an attribute, the baseline level of learnability does not vary much from person to person. There are certainly outliers, savants who pick up things instantly on the one end, those with slower circuits on the other. Even those outliers are relative, though. The musical prodigy might be a horrible driver; your cubicle neighbor who can't seem to figure out the accounting system might be brilliant at navigating the shifting digital landscape. The majority of us fall in a midrange, comfortably building those new circuits as needed, accelerating the pace when we want to. That can be done deliberately, as with Huberman's snapshots, but it also happens naturally when we enjoy what we're doing. The IT expert at work who loves programming is going to pick up the intricacies of the new operating system much faster than the sales guy who can't find his way past the log-in. *Passion* in this context is synonymous with *intensity,* and when we're doing things about which we're passionate, we become myelin machines—which means we learn quickly.

Being able to raise your level of learnability, and identify it in others, is critical to optimal performance, especially in complex environments. The ability to learn means the ability to develop skills, which means that a high level of learnability can compensate for a lack of experience.

Most people can probably figure where they fall on the learnability scale, at least if they're being honest with themselves. Take me, for example: Among the mental acuity attributes, learnability is where I rank lowest. It usually takes me more time than I would like to pick up new skills and absorb lessons. But recognizing this allows me to address it. Because I typically need to repeat something two or three times before it's ingrained, I plan that extra time when I'm learning something new. During my own training in the Navy, I forced myself to study longer and practice harder. When I was learning close-quarter combat (CQC), I would often stay late, reviewing what we had learned that day and visualizing different scenarios that had given me trouble. Outside of formal learning, I sometimes have to figure out a way to compensate for my limitations. I can find my way around most of Manhattan, for instance, by remembering that the numbers on the streets and avenues go up as I head north and west, but I know I'll need a map in Greenwich Village.

If you suspect you're lower on the learnability scale, engage that attribute as often as possible. Exercise it by throwing yourself into situations that force learning, even fun ones. When we went to Scotland on a family vacation, I specifically requested a rental car with a manual transmission. I drive a stick shift almost every day at home, but in Scotland everything is on the opposite side. You drive on the left side of the road and the steering wheel is on the right side of the car; instead of shifting gears with the right hand, you have to shift with the left. It's all very unnatural—it took me ten damn minutes to get into reverse. But within a day or so, after I'd yelled at the kids a hundred times to keep quiet and my wife did 100 percent of the navigating, my brain had built new scripts and patterns and I was good to go. Other than that first day of driving, it was a wonderful vacation.

BUT HOW TO ASSESS it in others? The best way is to create an environment that requires a rapid learning progression, and then add some stress, a wrench thrown into the plan, or a time limit. The information that needs to be learned should be kept simple and clear, but stacked in a way that requires it to be absorbed and integrated before the next level can be introduced. CQC, progressing from dry weapons in one room to live ammunition in multiple rooms linked by hallways, was an ideal scenario to tease out learnability. Remember, though, that context matters. CQC training is perfect for SEALs because their job involves close-quarter combat. Putting prospective accountants through CQC, though, probably wouldn't tell us anything about their learnability in an accounting environment.

MENTAL ACUITY ROLL-UP

The attributes grouped together in the mental acuity category are listed in a specific order.

We started with situational awareness, which is the ability to absorb and process information from your surroundings, because that's the base upon which the other three attributes rely. This should be obvious: If you're not taking in information, there's nothing to compartmentalize and no cognitive tasks among which to switch.

Compartmentalization followed situational awareness because our brains can't process everything. We have to prioritize, focus, select, and deselect. Then, after all that happens, we can deliberately—or not so deliberately—task switch. That is, our brains can shift from one context or task to the next to allow us to move through the external dynamics of life.

The fourth attribute in this category, learnability, both influences and is influenced by the first three. The higher we are on the scales of situational awareness, compartmentalization, and task switching, the more effectively we're able to learn from that processed information; and the higher we are on the learnability scale, the more easily we can put that compartmentalized and task-switched material to good use.

Learnability is also the only one of the four working while we sleep. Our conscious minds are largely offline, but the brain is busy solidifying the patterns and scripts we created while awake. Memories are consolidated and neural connections are strengthened when we sleep. Neural plasticity relies on the waking mind shutting down to rest.

Topping the scale on all four of these attributes is unrealistic. But recognizing where you and other people fall on each can help explain everyday performance. If you have great situational awareness but are lousy at compartmentalizing, for example, you probably notice a bunch of things but might occasionally feel overwhelmed, especially when there is a lot going on around you. A person who's high on task switching but low on learnability likely moves quickly from one activity to another but repeatedly makes the same mistakes. Or someone can be terrific at compartmentalization but not very high on task switching—which can mean being able to deeply focus on one thing but at the expense of other priorities because of an inability to pull out of that focus.

In trying to develop any one of the mental acuity attributes, keep in mind that they are all inextricably linked. Attributes in the other categories are mostly severable; courage and perseverance complement each other, for instance, but you don't need to engage your courage circuit to bolster your level of perseverance. For mental acuity, all of the attributes are entwined. When I practice compartmentalizing in the New York City subway, I have to also engage my situational awareness—in order to have information to compartmentalize—and task switching—to move between those different categories or contexts. All three of those, meanwhile, tweak my learnability, which is running in the background enhancing the entire process.

Regardless of how strong you are in any one attribute, you can work on your gaps. Just remember that you have all of these; the fact that you are able to function in the world is proof.

THE DRIVE ATTRIBUTES

We all have needs, and drive is how we try to fulfill them. If you're hungry and thirsty, to use the easiest examples, you are *driven* to find food and water. Those are admittedly much easier tasks now that we can satisfy those needs by opening the refrigerator and turning on the tap. But for many millennia, eating and drinking required expending a considerable amount of time and energy. The more driven among our ancestors were the least hungry and thirsty.

There are two kinds of human needs, intrinsic and extrinsic. Intrinsic ones come from within and are usually physiologically based. The aforementioned hunger and thirst, as well as the need for air, are built into the human design. Others, such as drug addiction, are learned. The second broad category of needs is extrinsic—needs that are applied by outside forces. We need money, for instance, because we live in a world that requires buying stuff, and since we need money, we also need a job.

But because we are human, and humans are social, intelligent, and emotionally complex, there is a wide category of intrinsic needs that are created, influenced, and measured by *extrinsic* forces. Most people have, to varying degrees, needs for affection and knowledge and understanding, for achievement and recognition. Pressure from a co-worker is extrinsic, but it can trigger a need for acceptance and belonging, which is intrinsic.

This cause and effect matters. In his 2009 book *Drive: The Surprising Truth About What Motivates Us,* Daniel H. Pink explains how intrinsic needs are far more powerful motivators than extrinsic ones. Things like money, reward, and punishment hold little value when compared to what he labels the three elements of true motivation: autonomy, mastery, and purpose. Those are all intrinsic, all relative, and, in many ways, unique to each of us—my purpose, in other words, probably isn't the same as your purpose.

The ability to satisfy those needs depends in large part on how driven we are. And how driven we are can be determined by five main attributes: self-efficacy, discipline, open-mindedness, cunning, and narcissism. None of them creates drive. Rather, these are the attributes that *contribute* to drive, from getting started to following through.

We all know people who are extremely driven and others who can't ever seem to get started. We probably also know people who are fast off the starting line but never finish, while some others are unstoppable only after they get an initial push. The difference, at least some of it, can be found in these attributes.

It might seem odd that cunning and narcissism, two typically negative behavioral traits, are even on the list. Give them a chance. Some qualities that typically are considered pejorative are, in fact, simply human. It's time to maximize our humanness. That is, after all, what optimal performance is all about.

CHAPTER TWELVE

MASTERING THE PIVOT

Self-efficacy: *A belief in one's ability to achieve a goal, especially when the path is uncertain or unknown*

WHEN I WAS RETIRING from the Navy, I met a woman named Sandy Travis. She worked with The Honor Foundation, a nonprofit that helps special-operations personnel transition from the military to civilian life, a process which is more difficult than you might think. Combat deployments aside, there's an easy security to the military. Everything is regimented—there are rules and regulations and chains of command. Medical and dental care are readily available, and life insurance support for loved ones is automatic. There's no need to network or polish your résumé. Unless you really screw up, your job is guaranteed for as long as you want it, and promotions follow a clear, predictable path. Hell, you don't even really have to worry about what to wear: Check the calendar, throw on that season's designated uniform, and you're done.

The military does a fairly good job preparing soldiers and sailors for the civilian world. But organizations like The Honor Foundation are enormously helpful with job hunting, networking, and writing a résumé, as well as how to more effectively function in the working world.

Sandy was brilliant at it.

For more than thirty years, she'd worked all over the planet as an executive coach and organizational consultant. By the time I met her, Sandy was a gray-haired lady in her mid-sixties, lovely and sharp-witted. Sometimes she joked that her physical appearance camouflaged a "very resourceful, determined tough cookie." Her clients sometimes call her a "badass fairy godmother."

I liked her right away. We shared a passion for human performance and neuroscience, and the conversation during our coaching sessions would often take tangents into those topics. Sandy was always wonderfully optimistic.

But the most remarkable thing about Sandy was what I didn't know when I met her. While she was coaching me, she was being treated for a cruelly aggressive type of breast cancer. Except Sandy wasn't *battling* cancer. She wasn't *surviving* it or, even more optimistically, *living with* cancer. No, Sandy had chosen to *thrive*. She made the deliberate decision to see her surgery and chemotherapy not as a fight for survival but as an adventure, another challenge in her life to embrace.

Sandy is the kind of person who showed up proudly bald, having shaved off the hair that chemo hadn't forced out in clumps. She high-fived the spec-ops guys she was coaching, then took a poll about what color wig she should try. Red was the unanimous choice, so she showed up next time as a redhead. And then a brunette and a blonde, a rotating, playful palette of shades and styles.

I have never met a purer embodiment of self-efficacy than Sandy Travis.

LIKE SOME OTHER ATTRIBUTES, self-efficacy can be dissected into components. It's a combination of confidence, initiative, and optimism. It's not as simple as *I got this*. That's usually bravado. Self-efficacy is thoughtful and serious. It's "I know I can do this because I am willing to take the first step, and even though I don't yet know all the answers or how this will unfold, I'll continue until I am successful."

Let's start with confidence, which is the belief in one's ability to do something. But that belief has to be rational and well-grounded, because confidence lies uncomfortably between arrogance and timidity. For example, most people are confident that they can drive a car. But an arrogant driver who stomps on the accelerator before checking what's in front of him is more reckless than confident. A timid driver, meanwhile, might not even pull out of the garage because he's jittery about where he might end up.

Next is initiative, which is simply being able to begin, to engage in forward motion. In our car-driving analogy, it would be starting the engine. "The journey of a thousand miles begins with one step," as Chinese philosopher Lao-tzu so correctly put it, which means, in this example, turning the key.

Finally, there is optimism, which is knowing that once the car is moving down the road, you'll get to your destination. Maybe you don't know the exact way, but that's all right: You believe you'll figure it out as you go. Optimism is best tempered with realism, which acknowledges that there are going to be hiccups and challenges along the path. Being realistic up front allows for preparation and foresight: You check the spare because you might get a flat, and you put a can of gasoline in the trunk in case the fuel stations are closed. The trick is to keep realism from tipping into pessimism. Too much pessimism will make a person timid, which deflates confidence. Optimism without realism, on the other hand, risks arrogance.

———

YOU MIGHT BE WONDERING why all three of those—confidence, initiative, optimism—aren't individual attributes with their own chapters. After all, they each seem to be traits that would be hardwired into us to one degree or another, right?

Perhaps. But on their own, those traits are inert. They're only potent in combination with one another.

By itself, confidence is little more than a feeling, a faith in one's abilities. I'm confident that I can fly a plane. I grew up around flying, my father and brother are both pilots, and I've spent thousands of hours in a variety of aircraft. I know a lot about planes, and I'm sure I could fly one. I'm not arrogant in my confidence because I know that there are many things I would need to learn first. Nor am I timid because, really, I'd be pretty excited to give it a go. And yet after decades of this confidence, I've never flown a plane. Confidence alone does not produce results.

Unaccompanied initiative is no better. Put a child behind the wheel of a car and he'll certainly have the initiative to step on any pedal within reach. But that's frenetic energy, unguided, untrained, and quite possibly dangerous. Initiative without purpose is wasted.

Optimism alone accomplishes very little. I'm all for positive thinking, but if your idea of gardening is only to stare at freshly planted beds and think, "There are no weeds and I shall have a bounty," you'll be bitterly disappointed come harvest time. Optimism without action might put you in a pleasant mood—and there's nothing wrong with pleasant moods—but it won't get a job done.

But wrap those three together, let each play off of the others, and you've got self-efficacy. It's the belief that you can do something, the willingness to take the first step, and the optimism that you'll eventually reach your goal. Optimal performance requires self-efficacy, and a high degree of it.

———

SANDY TRAVIS SAT DOWN with me as I was sorting out the material for this book, going over the list of attributes, helping me refine my thoughts. I'd asked for her help because of our shared interests in performance and neuroscience and because she so clearly possessed many of the attributes on my list. There was fortitude, resilience, drive, selflessness, and on and on. But mostly, she almost vibrated with self-efficacy. And that was before I even knew her full story.

She describes herself as "an expert in pivoting," in sharply shifting her trajectory, often by choice, sometimes not. Growing up, she was her father's partner in adventure. Rock climbing, white-water rafting, hiking, camping, and exploring all helped foster her unique set of attributes, including self-efficacy. After all, it takes confidence to climb a rock face, as well as initiative to grab that first hold, and optimism that you won't fall.

She studied biology at Cornell and Yale, where, in 1973, she was halfway through a doctoral program when she contracted a bad case of mono. She had plenty of time to think and reflect during her extended bed rest, and one of the main things she thought was that she didn't want to get a PhD in biology, despite having earned a full ride (tuition, plus room and board) to a highly selective program. She chose to leave with a master's degree and went to the Congo as a Peace Corps volunteer. There were certainly downsides to that choice—she says that first year in Africa was "the only time in my life when I've crossed days off the calendar in half-day segments." But she was confident she'd made the right decision, optimistic it would work out, and she had taken the initiative to get on a plane. She ended up staying for three years—one year longer than the standard assignment.

Years later, she was living in Washington, D.C., and working as a consultant for an international firm. Burned-out on seemingly endless travel, and with no appealing career path, she made another abrupt pivot. Sandy put her possessions in storage except for two suitcases and flew to Seattle, where she knew few people and had no job waiting. Her friends told her she was nuts. But within a few months, she'd started her own consulting firm and was quickly building a list of clients. Again, she was confident and optimistic and took the initiative. Sandy always bet on herself.

Self-efficacy obviously is useful when it comes to making decisions. But it's also helpful in dealing with adversity, which Sandy has had plenty of as well. Years after moving to Seattle, she was married and living on a llama ranch in eastern Washington while still maintaining her business. Driving home one evening, another car ran a stop sign and crashed into her. She was rushed to the hospital with back and neck injuries. When her husband got there, she thought he seemed oddly grumpy. Sure, the ranch was an inconvenient two hours away, but his wife was badly hurt.

Two days later, her husband asked for a divorce.

For many people, maybe most people, that would be a crippling one-two blow, an accident followed by a divorce. And Sandy admits it was devastating. But within days she was buying a new car and looking for a place to live in Seattle. In the months that followed, in between physical therapy appointments, she designed an advanced negotiation program that her clients loved. In the end, that was the best year she had in business up to that point.

That's the power of self-efficacy. Not only does it allow us to stretch boundaries, explore our potential, and take risks, but it also enables us to successfully charge through unanticipated challenges, even when the outcome is highly uncertain. And few situations have a more uncertain outcome than being diagnosed with an aggressive cancer.

"Wham!" is how Sandy described it later. "The two-by-eight hit." For those not familiar with the term, a two-by-eight is a large piece of wood used in construction. Getting slammed by one is certainly not equivalent to a whisper or gentle tap on the shoulder.

She immediately drew upon her self-efficacy. She began her treatment with the same attitude with which she'd faced all the other challenges in her life—uncertain of the outcome but confident that she would figure it out along the way, step by step. She did, too. A year later she was cancer-free, and another adventure was in the books—literally this time, in *Passport to Freedom: Courage and Resilience on Your Cancer Journey,* which she published in 2017.

WE CAN SEE HOW self-efficacy manifested itself in Sandy. But how do we see or develop it?

Actually, Sandy is an excellent template, even if the specifics—the Congo, divorce, cancer—are extreme.

Hints of it can be seen in displays of the component parts. Instances of confidence, initiative, and optimism can all indicate self-efficacy. Most often it can be seen in the number of times we, or those we are assessing, deliberately pivot. It could be big pivots, like changing careers or moving to a different country, or it could be as simple as taking a new route to work or learning a different language. These are all examples of acting on and developing your own self-efficacy.

Why does this matter? It matters because if we take the time to deliberately make our self-efficacy stronger, then when we are hit with unexpected challenges, we have developed the qualities to get through them. Sandy was prepared for the pivots that life threw at her because she had deliberately made pivots before. Optimal performance is about doing the best that we can in whatever environment life throws at us. A big part of performing optimally is knowing that we can.

CHAPTER THIRTEEN

THE SELF-DISCIPLINED LOSER

Discipline: *The ability to remain focused and steadfast to achieve a result*

CONSIDER TWO MEN.

One was raised in a stable household with both parents and a couple of siblings but grew up to be a rebel. He smoked, he drank, he chased women. Even after he was married with children of his own, he had affairs. He considered himself a freedom fighter and organized and participated in many protests. He was jailed multiple times, and his government kept him under constant surveillance. He accrued a multitude of enemies and was eventually assassinated by one of his own countrymen.

The other man was a star student, loved by everyone in his class. He was plagued with tragedy, however, losing four of his five siblings and both of his parents before he turned twenty. As a young man, he found solace in his church, singing in the choir and even at one point considering the priesthood. He abstained from drinking and smoking, and he was a strict vegetarian. He also did not indulge his carnal desires, fearing them a distraction, and he remained single and unmarried until very late in life. He joined the military at a young age and fought for his country. He went into

politics and devoted himself to public service, eventually becoming one of his country's most famous leaders.

Which one of those men would you say was more disciplined?

BEFORE YOU ANSWER, LET'S define our terms.

Discipline is not the same as *self*-discipline. It's easy to
confuse the two, and there is some overlap. But the distinction is important. Self-discipline means resisting temptation,
overcoming your weaknesses, controlling your emotions.
The stakes can be low—declining that second piece of cake
or going for that morning run—or they can be higher—
quitting smoking for health reasons. In general, self-
discipline is a very good thing to have. The emphasis,
though, is on the *self,* on actions that are meant to improve
something about you.

Discipline is about accomplishing external goals. In terms
of optimal performance, to be disciplined means understanding the elements required to achieve an objective, and
then being steadfast in executing those elements. By these
terms, it is possible for people with very little self-discipline
to be extraordinarily disciplined, and vice versa. The fas-
tidious man who does a hundred push-ups each morning,
keeps a strict vegan diet, and never raises his voice no matter
how angry is *self-disciplined,* but he quits every endeavor at
the first hint of challenge because he is not *disciplined.* On
the other hand, people with very little self-discipline can be
very disciplined in pursuit of their goal; for example, James
Brown was a womanizer with a drug problem, but one of
the most brilliant musicians and disciplined performers of
his generation.

Self-discipline can be a component of discipline, in that
it can keep you focused on, and even help you achieve, ex-

ternal goals. But it's not required, and sometimes it's not even relevant.

THE OTHER IMPORTANT DISTINCTION is that self-discipline is a skill, whereas discipline is an attribute. That is, self-discipline can be taught, but a certain level of discipline, oriented toward external goals, is wired into each of us.

Very young children, for instance, are rarely self-disciplined. They throw tantrums, they blurt out whatever crosses their minds, they indulge each and every emotion immediately and fully. Yet infants as young as three months demonstrate goal-directed behavior—simply reaching to grab a bottle, for example. Discipline is the determined ability to remain focused until goals are accomplished. Think of it as the long-game version of perseverance.

We deployed overseas a lot when I was in the Navy. When we weren't deployed, we were often away at some remote facility training to deploy. To say that I wasn't home much would be an understatement. During one long stretch away, my older son was concerned that Dad wasn't home enough.

"Don't worry, Dad," he told me on the phone during one particularly long stretch away. "I'm taking care of Mom."

He was four years old. It was very sweet. He was also very determined to prove he was serious.

My wife woke up one morning, walked into the kitchen, and found all of the dishes clean (mostly) and stacked (very precariously) on the counter. Our son had woken up before the sun rose, tiptoed into the kitchen, found a sponge and the dish soap, and scrubbed every plate and cup as best he could. "I wanted to show that I can take care of you," he told my wife.

He has always been a disciplined kid. When he decides

upon a goal, he immediately figures out what he needs to do, and then does it. Not too long ago, he decided he wanted to be certified to scuba dive. He found the online classes, aced all the quizzes, and expertly handled himself at the pool and open-water sessions. He was twelve, and he didn't lean on Dad, the Navy SEAL, for much help at all. I didn't consciously teach him that—it's intrinsic.

So how do we develop discipline if we find ourselves low on the scale? The first step is to take a look at your track record. You might not be as low as you think, and you might be conflating self-discipline with discipline. Think first about those things that you have accomplished already. If you have been pretty good at accomplishing the goals that you've set, you are likely doing pretty well on the discipline scale. If your list seems largely unfinished, you might want to develop your discipline a little more. The good news is that simply being aware is half the battle. The rest is just deliberate focus.

BACK TO THOSE TWO men from the beginning, the philandering rebel and the buttoned-up soldier-turned-politician.

By now, it might have dawned on you that the first one, so undisciplined in his personal life, was the more disciplined of the two. He was Martin Luther King, Jr., one of the greatest leaders of a mass movement in history.

The other was Hitler.

Both were disciplined in that they had an objective, understood the elements involved in achieving that goal, and were steadfast in pursuing those elements. That Hitler's goal was a ghastly crime against humanity and King's was a righteous moral quest is beside the point: Both required a certain level of discipline.

But King possessed far more discipline.

Hitler surrounded himself with sycophants and rose to

power during a time of fear, suspicion, and economic tur-moil. He was immensely popular at the time, so his disci-pline was easy, as well as repeatedly reinforced and rewarded.

King, on the other hand, was constantly threatened, jailed, slandered, and surveilled. He had difficulty knowing whom to trust, and many people wanted him dead. His goal was opposed by a majority in his own country. His ap-proach, peaceful nonviolence inspired by Mahatma Gandhi, required even more discipline, as it was often met with vio-lence. His struggle was hard, and it was daily.

The discipline of optimal performance takes work, and usually a preponderance of the grit attributes as well.

CHAPTER FOURTEEN

A FISH IS THE LAST
TO DISCOVER WATER

Open-mindedness: *A willingness to consider and accept new ideas, opinions, or perspectives*

FOR MANY DECADES, HIGH jumpers at track-and-field meets got over the bar in the most obvious way: They took a running start and leapt as high as they could, leading with one leg, pulling the trailing one over, and landing on their feet, almost as if they were clearing an enormous hurdle.

Known as the Scissors technique, it was around the mid-1930s that American and Russian jumpers began refining that approach. Instead of keeping the torso mostly vertical, they started folding themselves, leading with one leg and their head, the chest parallel to the ground. They had to twist in midair to get the other leg over, which required a tricky bit of timing and coordination, but the new style allowed them to jump several inches higher. The Straddle, and a variation called the Western Roll, became the standard in high jumping for thirty years, because jumpers found it to be the most effective way to get over the bar.

Except for Dick Fosbury. He was a high school jumper in Oregon who found the Straddle so frustrating that he reverted to the Scissors. But the Scissors wasn't giving him enough height—at one meet, he couldn't even clear the qualifying five feet.

Fosbury was a teenager, and one marvelous thing about teenagers is that they question everything. Did he have to go over the bar in either the Straddle or the Scissors? No, those were traditions, not rules. The only rule in high jumping was that he had to take off on one foot. There were no other constraints.

That meant someone with an open mind—someone like Dick Fosbury—could figure out an entirely new approach.

"I knew that I had to change my body position," Fosbury told a reporter years later. "And that's what started first the revolution, and over the next two years, the evolution." The landing pits of sawdust and wood chips were being replaced with soft foam, which meant Fosbury didn't have to come down on his feet (there's no rule about landing, either). He began shifting his position in the air, lowering his shoulders and raising his hips. It was an odd and awkward technique, but he kept tweaking and adjusting.

By his senior year in high school, he was going over backward, headfirst, his body gently arcing, his legs coming over with a final kick, like the flip of a whale's tail.

Fosbury's new style was met with mockery. A photo of him in 1964 was captioned "World's Laziest High Jumper," and a local sportswriter announced that he "looked like nothing more than a fish flopping into a boat."

But he also set a high school record and took second at state. In 1968, he won a gold medal at the Olympics in Mexico City. And the standard high-jumping technique today, and for the last forty years, is the Fosbury Flop.

OPEN-MINDEDNESS IS THE ABILITY and the willingness to set aside our opinions, judgments, and preconceptions so that we can consider problems and environments from fresh, often unorthodox perspectives. It isn't simply being passively receptive to new ideas as they are presented but instead actively removing constraints on the imagination. This ability is highly advantageous to optimal performance, especially in uncertain environments. Rather than struggle to force uncertain circumstances into predefined and familiar parameters, the person with a high level of open-mindedness will strip away what *should* be in favor of what *could* be.

This is not easy. In some ways, it's contrary to human nature. There's an Ethiopian proverb that helps explain why: "A fish is the last to discover water." And why would it? A fish would have no reason to consider, let alone question, its environment. Water is an all-encompassing norm for a fish. People fall into the same trap. Most high jumpers were so conditioned to going over the bar forward that they didn't even consider that there might be a better approach. We are so accustomed to perceiving the world in certain ways that it's often difficult to consider alternatives.

Perception is at the core of the human experience. It's what creates each person's individual reality. All the tiny inputs—what we see and taste and hear and touch and feel—accrete into a staggeringly complex whole. Who and what we love or hate, what ignites our passions or triggers our fears, how we walk and talk, what we prioritize and what we ignore—in short, how we live our lives—are all the result of how we perceive the world around us.

And we each perceive it differently. The physical world is relatively standard for all of us. The sky is blue and roses have a certain smell and fire is hot and rain is wet. Everyone's brain recognizes those basic facts, more or less. But those tangible inputs are only a small part of perception. Whether rainy days make you happy or the smell of a rose makes you sad has to do with how your brain has interpreted and cataloged previous versions of those inputs. That's not as complicated as it sounds. Maybe you got married on a rainy day, or maybe there were big sprays of roses at your father's funeral. Those memories end up attached to those sensations, which then affects your perception. Now, take that same concept and repeat it several million times, in an endless variety of contexts. That's how reality becomes shaded and contoured for each of us.

We're all attached to our version of reality, even if we're not completely happy with it. We can't simply think our way into new perceptions. In part, that's because they exist as physical neural pathways in our brains. As we discussed in the mental acuity attributes (Chapters Eight through Eleven), every experience creates a neurological circuit that, like a well-traveled road, will be reinforced through repetition. Or, like a tunnel blasted through a mountain, they can be made permanent through intensity. Either way, those well-formed pathways are difficult for our brain to abandon. We perceive the world in a certain way because our brain tells us to.

TO SEE HOW THIS works, let's consider my perception of roller coasters, which is this: They're awful.

When I was ten years old, our family went to Disney World and we all rode Space Mountain. It was the first time any of us kids—me, my twin brother, our little brother, and our older sister—had been on a roller coaster, and we had no idea what to expect. Space Mountain would be a fairly tame coaster, except it's inside a dark building so you have no spatial awareness, no sense of where it'll lurch next. All I remember is a long, slow climb up a steep incline, a slight hesitation at the top, and then a plunge into a black abyss. Everything after that was utter disoriented fear.

When it was over and we stumbled into the Florida sunlight, I was dizzy with relief and motion sickness. So was my twin. Our little brother was a complete mess, scared and crying. My mother leaned down to comfort him, and he promptly threw up on her. My sister was fine, but my dad was pissed, as fathers tend to be when things go south on a vacation. "All right," he snapped at us, "that's it for roller coasters." Except it wasn't: for the rest of our time at Disney, the first, frightened question any of us kids asked before every ride was, "Is this another roller coaster?"

The intensity of that experience forged a neural pathway on our brains. To this day, neither my brothers nor I are roller coaster fans.

My wife's perception of roller coasters, on the other hand, is the complete opposite. She loves them. The taller, steeper, faster, and loopier, the better. And that's primarily because her brain got wired with a different neural circuit.

She grew up in western Pennsylvania, the youngest of three kids, and her family had been going to Cedar Point, an amusement park in Ohio famous for its roller coasters, for as long as she could remember. For years, she watched her siblings and her parents ride the Gemini—a wooden coaster 125 feet tall that reached sixty miles per hour— always whooping and hollering and having a grand time. When she was eight years old, she was finally tall enough to ride, too. Like me, her memory of that first ride is blurry, except for the end: Her brother and sister and parents joyously laughing, all of them congratulating her on being such a big girl. She was glowing with pride. So she rode it again. And again and again and again.

When my wife and I get on a roller coaster today, we physically experience the exact same ride. Same long climb, same precipitous drop, same sensation of speed. The sensory input is identical. But her perception of the ride is vastly different from mine because our brains have cataloged roller coasters differently. She loves it, and I do not.

And now the conspicuous question on the page: Why

am I riding roller coasters if I don't like them? Because I'm trying to develop my attribute of open-mindedness. Open-mindedness is about letting go of your ingrained interpretations and judgments about the world. Taking in new perspectives, even opinions about roller coasters, generates wisdom and can help build new neural pathways. It might require some mental gymnastics. To get on a coaster, for instance, I imagine I'm strapping into that fighter jet I always wanted to fly. I tell myself this is something I *want* to do. We can't erase those old pathways—indeed, that's why habits are so hard to break—but if the new ones are reinforced often enough, the brain eventually will prefer to use those.

I'm not there yet with roller coasters, though.

CURIOSITY IS CORRELATED WITH open-mindedness. The desire to learn and understand leads the mind to default, almost by definition, to the open position.

This makes obvious sense when you consider the opposite. A closed mind is a certain mind. It might not be *correct* in that certainty, but it is certain nonetheless. It also tends to be stubborn and judgmental, a rock-solid foundation for stereotypes. A closed mind is a terrible drag on performance in any uncertain, dynamic environment, where facts are unknown and details ever-shifting. To be sure of that which you do not understand is to court disaster.

Open-mindedness, then, can to some extent be a deliberate process. Decide and accept that there are possibilities you might not have considered. That doesn't mean miring your brain in a constant state of indecisive mush. The scientific method requires the rigorous testing of hypotheses, but there would be no hypotheses to test if scientists weren't first open to wondrous possibilities. Open-mindedness has taken us from cave dwellers to space explorers.

Yet open-mindedness can also be fostered and nurtured simply by bombarding the brain with information and ideas. Every new experience opens the mind to new possibilities; the most valuable part of discovery is that it reminds us that discovery is possible. So read more, watch more, listen more. Practice empathizing (Chapter Seventeen) with people with whom you disagree or are unfamiliar. Travel as much as possible—there's a truism that one can't have a thick passport and a narrow mind.

Stepping outside of your set boundaries can be intimidating. Familiarity is comforting. Our lazy brains want to use the well-worn neural pathways, the circuits we develop over time or through intense experiences that define reality for each of us. This is natural. But it can also be constraining. The first step to open-mindedness is accepting that our thoughts and perceptions might not be the only ones, or even the correct ones. Once you allow yourself to understand that the world—or any situation, place, or thing in it—might not be exactly as you believe it to be or want it to be, the possibilities are endless.

CHAPTER FIFTEEN

THE PRINCESS AND THE DRAGON

Cunning: *The ability to consider problems and circumstances from unusual and unorthodox perspectives in order to achieve a goal or objective*

LET'S TRY A PUZZLE. Get a pencil and some scrap paper and put three dots in a row somewhere near the middle. Put another row below that first one, and then a third beneath that. You should now have a nine-dot grid, three wide by three high, and in the shape of a square.

That's the easy part. The puzzle is this: Without lifting your pencil from the paper, connect all nine dots with no more than four straight lines. The lines have to be straight and there can't be more than four, and you can't pick up your pencil until you've connected all the dots.

Go ahead. We'll wait.

This is called, appropriately, the Nine Dot Puzzle, and it's pretty famous. Anyone who went through a management seminar in the 1970s or '80s is probably familiar with it. Consultants used it relentlessly to teach creativity, to encourage people to "think outside the box," so to speak.

If you're stuck, that's a hint.

The way the dots are arranged highlights a cognitive bias called "functional fixedness," which is the tendency to see objects as only able to work in a specific way. A three-by-three grid looks like a box, and thus the brain is biased to treat it as a box. Without even realizing it, most people put an imaginary border around the dots and try to keep all of their lines inside that pretend box.

That makes the puzzle impossible.

Extend the lines beyond that artificial boundary, though, and the solution is simple.

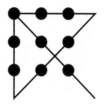

As an exercise in creativity, the Nine Dot Puzzle is ingenious. In one clever activity, it illustrates the invisible constraints people tend to put on their thinking and shows, literally, the advantage of thinking outside the box. And that's great, as far as it goes. Creativity on its own is the ability to develop new and original ideas, to imagine something that doesn't exist. Creativity is open-ended and free-flowing; the product is less important than the process.

But the puzzle *is* a product—it's a problem to be solved. And some people see the solution more quickly than others because they disregard that functional fixedness almost by instinct. Those are the people who have a higher level of cunning.

CUNNING **IS A PEJORATIVE** word. It implies sneakiness and deception, using trickery to an unfair advantage. But I'm using it in a broader sense, as a neutral term. It might include deception at any given time, but not always. Rather, I mean an ability to disregard the unspoken and often artificial rules when appropriate, to consider objects and circumstances from unorthodox perspectives.

Let's look at another famous puzzle to illustrate that point. The object of the Candle Problem is to mount a lighted candle to a wall in such a way that it doesn't drip wax on a table below. You have a limited, and curious, selection of supplies with which to work. There's the candle, of course, plus a book of matches and a box of thumbtacks.

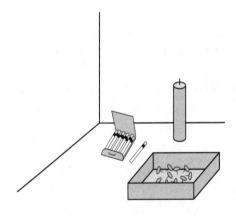

What do you do?

A Gestalt psychologist named Karl Duncker developed this puzzle in the 1930s, and most of his test subjects had a miserable go of it. Almost all of them tried to stick the candle to the wall with the thumbtacks, which of course didn't work. Using a gob of melted wax as an adhesive was another popular, and failed, idea.

Both approaches are a result of functional fixedness. Tacks are for attaching things, typically scraps of paper, to a flat surface. Wax is a bit more inventive, but using it as an adhesive isn't unusual.

The solution, though, is elegantly simple.

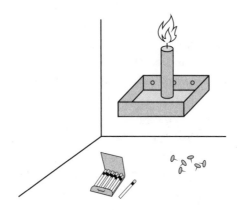

If Duncker tweaked the experiment and rearranged the supplies, most people solved it much more quickly. All he did was dump the tacks out of the box. His subjects then had a candle, matches, a pile of thumbtacks—and an empty cardboard box that could quite obviously be pinned to the wall as a makeshift shelf.

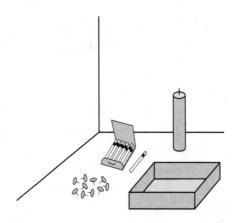

As with the nine dots, that is a creative solution. If we add a healthy dose of cunning, that creativity becomes a means to an end. Now we have the ability to creatively solve problems.

A problem, by its very nature, has two elements. One is that it requires a solution—a goal or objective. The second is that it has variables, the conditions and obstacles that describe the problem in the first place. Without both of those elements, you do not have a problem. If you have one but not the other, raw creativity will suffice. The artist who knows that she wants to create a sculpture of a bust but has no constraints on what materials or tools she can use does not have a problem to solve because there are no variables. Conversely, if the artist is given some clay, molding tools, and a grinder and told to create whatever sculpture she likes, she now has variables but no defined objective—and thus she has no problem.

But give that same artist some dry noodles, glue, and a pair of scissors and tell her to sculpt a bust of Beethoven—now she has a problem to solve. The objective (the bust) and the variables (noodles and glue) create constraints, whether real or imagined, and those constraints come with implicit biases. Cunning lets us neutralize those biases, to reconsider or ignore them altogether. Perhaps instead of seeing the scissors as a cutting tool, she stands them up on end to create a base, or maybe she carves the bust from a big glob of dried glue; I'm not a sculptor, but I'm sure a cunning one could figure this out. The point is that creativity metabolized with cunning leads us to creative problem-solving.

TOO MUCH CUNNING, I concede, can be detrimental. There's a reason the word has negative connotations. Mix it with too much narcissism, which we'll discuss in Chapter Sixteen, and it can be downright dangerous. Motive matters, too. Oskar Schindler's cunning, for example, saved twelve hundred Jews from the Nazi death camps. Bernie Madoff, on the other hand, used his cunning to swindle billions of dollars from thousands of investors.

But having just enough can be a key component of optimal performance. Sometimes we need to reconsider the rules, look beyond artificial boundaries, discard preconceived constraints. Cunning, after all, is how David was able to defeat Goliath. And cunning, in many ways, is at the very heart of the Navy SEALs.

SEALs are not, as a group, growling, overmuscled super soldiers. Sure, there are some big SEALS, but to look at them, they're a pretty unassuming bunch, mostly average-size and circumspect. That is by design—SEAL teams were never meant to be brute-force units. From the beginning, when Draper Kaufmann was selecting volunteers to swim unarmed and half-naked into enemy territory, the point was not to *outfight* the enemy but to *outwit* him. The job was to solve problems in ways that had not been considered before.

Modern SEALs are better equipped, better trained, and more physically fit than most of the military. But that ethos, that core idea, remains the same: SEALs are good at what they do because they're cunning.

Years ago, I was talking with some of my teammates about mixed martial arts, primarily about the dominance of Chuck Liddell and which opponents he could or could not beat. Some of the guys had been training in one form of MMA or another, mostly Brazilian jujitsu, so naturally the talk shifted to how they'd do against Liddell. To a man, they all conceded they'd be no match for him in the ring.

Then one quiet guy spoke up. "I'd fight him," he said, "if I could pick the time and place."

We all looked at him, astonished. He was a midsize, wiry dude whose athletic propensity leaned toward running and swimming. He spent some time in the gym lifting weights, but he had never had any interest in actual fight training.

"You're full of shit," one of the Brazilian jujitsu experts said.

"No, I'm not. I'm telling you, if you gave me the mission of beating this guy, I'd take it—as long as I could pick the time and place."

We were all curious now. Liddell is one of the greatest UFC fighters of all time, a heavyweight master of the sport. And our wiry SEAL was going to take him down? Even if the timeline was a couple of months, there is no way he could get better than the champ. Training would improve his technical skills, as well as his convergent and linear thinking; he'd figure out that if his opponent did X, he should counter with Y. But no matter how much practical knowledge he acquired, his experiential knowledge would be woefully inadequate. Maybe he'd get a slight home-court advantage by choosing where the fight would happen, but a ring is a ring—they would still be fighting where Liddell is most comfortable and most dominant.

"All right, tough guy," one of the MMA experts said. "Enlighten us."

The guy smiled. "All I would tell him is that I want the fight to be at two A.M., in open water, at a depth of fifty feet."

There was a collective groan before we all threw whatever was handy at him.

It's a playful example—we can safely assume Liddell would not have agreed to those terms—but it's also an example of a cunning mind. The pretend mission wasn't to beat Liddell in a sanctioned UFC fight governed by formal rules. It was to beat Liddell. The cunning person abandons the perceived constraints, like the ring and the referee, and instead focuses on his objective.

As long as we're playing with fantasy, imagine a special operator gets dropped into a medieval kingdom where a princess is imprisoned in a tower guarded by a dragon. All of the king's knights died trying to save her, incinerated by the dragon. That's because they couldn't shake off their functional fixedness. They saw the mission as "slay the dragon, save the princess." The special operator sees a different mission: "Save the princess. Who gives a damn about the dragon?" He'll use cunning to avoid the beast altogether.

CUNNING, WHEN USED FOR good, is incredibly advantageous for someone's overall drive. It allows us to actually "think outside the box" to find solutions and pathways to our goals. If you find yourself slightly deficient in cunning, you can develop it. When faced with a problem, take some time to deconstruct and understand all of the variables involved. Strip away the biases. Remember the Candle Problem? To the cunning person, the box wasn't just to hold thumbtacks—it was a shelf waiting to be pinned to the wall. Additionally, ask yourself hard questions about the rules and boundaries involved. Are they real or merely perceived to be? If they are real, can they be ignored? If so, what are the consequences?

Which is kind of what my younger son once did. He was about six years old and we were shooting hoops in the driveway. He wanted to keep score, a point per basket. I wasn't counting, or even trying to score, but he was getting frustrated that he wasn't sinking more than I was.

"Hang on, Dad," he said, then trotted into the house, coming back a moment later. "Mom needs to talk to you right now."

Right now seemed like something important. I jogged inside, but it took a couple of minutes to find my wife. For some reason, she was in the very back of the house, as far as possible from the basketball hoop. "What do you need?" I asked.

"Me? I don't need anything. I was told that you needed to see me and to meet you back here right away."

I could hear the ball bouncing as I walked back outside. My son was under the net, happily making layups. He smiled when he saw me. "Hey, Dad," he said, "I'm winning by thirty."

CHAPTER SIXTEEN

IT'S ALL ABOUT ME

Narcissism: *The desire to stand out, to be noticed, to be recognized*

WHEN I WAS LYING on a California beach in the dark, the cold Pacific surf crashing over me at the miserable height of Hell Week, I was not driven by selfless service to my country. I did not lean on my deep patriotism, and I was not inspired by a sense of sacrifice or duty. To be honest, none of those high-minded ideals were even the primary reason I wanted to be a Navy SEAL in the first place. All of those are a part of me, of course, but they aren't why I signed up for BUD/S training.

So why did I? For the same reason every SEAL does: to see if I could be a badass special operator. To prove that I was good enough, tough enough, strong enough. To be recognized as a member of an elite fraternity.

In a word, I was motivated by narcissism.

That's another one of those words that typically is considered pejorative. An excessive amount of narcissism, in fact, is a clinically recognized personality disorder. But in the layman's version of the term, narcissism is one of the elemental engines of human behavior, the innate attribute that urges us to strive, to succeed, to be noticed. In healthy doses, it is important for optimal performance.

THE ORIGINAL NARCISSUS WAS the son of a Greek god and a nymph, and it's fair to say he had a disordered personality. According to Greek mythology, Narcissus was so physically gorgeous that people fell in love just by looking at him. He was also kind of a jerk, rude and disdainful. He had contempt for his suitors, and his cruel, casual dismissal of a lovestruck nymph named Echo sent her wandering the forest forever, wasting away until all that remained of her was a distant, haunting sound. Nemesis, the goddess of retribution, was so angered by the way Echo was cast aside that she led Narcissus to a pool of water, in which he saw his own reflection. Except Narcissus at first didn't realize he was looking at himself—he just saw a person so beautiful that *he* fell in love. When he figured out the object of his love would never be real, though, he grew despondent and he killed himself.

Another version of that myth had Narcissus so enamored of the reflection that he refused to look away or disturb the water by dipping his hand in for a drink, and eventually he died of thirst. Either way, it should be obvious from that origin story why narcissism—why being like Narcissus—is generally not considered a good thing. The diagnostic criteria for narcissistic personality disorder are disturbing. Among other things, clinical narcissists have an exaggerated sense of entitlement, a diminished capacity for true intimacy, and a lack of empathy; they're self-aggrandizing, aggressively seeking to be the center of attention; and they're excessively motivated by gaining approval from other people. Those people are quite rare, though, comprising only about 1 percent of the population, give or take—narcissism only becomes a recognized, diagnosable disorder when all of those traits, plus a couple more, simmer together in a dysfunctional stew of malignant behavior.

But most people exhibit narcissistic *tendencies,* at least occasionally. Everyone wants to feel special at some point, wants to be significant, wants to be the center of someone else's attention, wants the approval of a friend, a boss, a lover, or a spouse. Those desires, and how urgently they are acted upon, are a measure of where one falls on the narcissism scale. They also are an inescapable part of being human, the result of biochemical reactions wired into our brains and bodies that are triggered and tweaked from birth.

From the first moment an infant is being held by his mother, when he is being played with and cuddled by his father, a basic physiological reward system is in play. The baby's brain is releasing the neurotransmitters dopamine and serotonin. Those are feel-good chemicals, the ones that tell our brain that something pleasurable is happening. The quick jolt of those chemicals makes us feel loved, admired, valued, and, most important, safe. (Indeed, a lack of serotonin is known to be linked with depression.)

All sorts of positive events trigger the release of serotonin and dopamine. The standing ovation you received after a talk, the big promotion the boss announced, the five hundred likes on your last Instagram post—the brain will react to all of those by calling for a burst of the happy neurotransmitters. The effect is immediate, yet it also is short-lived: Think of neurotransmitters as a fuel that burns bright, hot, and fast. Because our brains are wired to crave them, we naturally try to repeat the behavior or re-create the circumstances that cause them to be released. It's powerful stuff: The addict sniffing cocaine, to use a dark example, is in large part chasing shots of dopamine and serotonin.

But let's stay focused on the positive. When dopamine and serotonin are produced, they can in turn draw out a hormone called oxytocin. It's been called the "love hormone" or the "trust hormone," and it's stimulated by human interaction, especially sustained and intimate relationships. Physical contact, everything from long embraces to high fives and handshakes, causes the production of oxytocin. So does petting a dog or a cat. But touch isn't required. Paul Zak, a neuroeconomist and author of *Trust Factor: The Science of Creating High-Performance Companies,* has spent years studying the role oxytocin plays in human behavior. His research shows that eye-to-eye contact, sharing a meal with others, and telling someone that you love them all increase oxytocin. Even acts of generosity toward others—surprising someone with a gift, helping a buddy move his piano, bringing a meal to a sick friend—stimulate the production of oxytocin.

Compared to serotonin and dopamine, however, oxytocin is longer lasting. If neurotransmitters are the accelerants that start a fire, hormones are the logs that keep it burning long into the night. They're slower to produce but also slower to dissipate. While all those Instagram likes will feel good for an hour, the pleasant feelings from a long conversation with a close friend might linger for a day or two.

Another benefit of these neurotransmitters and hormones is that they're a two-way street: When you do something kind for another person, you both get the benefit. By doing something nice, you produce oxytocin; by having something nice done for them—because they feel special—the other person produces serotonin; you then feel appreciated, which releases your own shot of serotonin. Or think about an actor receiving a standing ovation. He's getting soaked in serotonin, but the people in the audience applauding are generating their own dose of feel-good chemicals.

This is by evolutionary design. Those chemicals are nature's way of getting us to take care of one another and to join together into cohesive social groups, which we needed to survive. But within those groups there needed to be individuals who stood out as the biggest, strongest, fastest—the alphas who could protect the others. Being the protector was a rough job. He or she, depending on the species, was the first to meet threats, the one who had to fight for the group's safety. Because that was an inherently risky role, one that often led to injury or death, nature needed a biological way to ensure that someone would both be the alpha and be supported in that role.

Enter serotonin and oxytocin. The protector was rewarded with the adoration of the tribe, the first choice of food and mates, deference from the others. By showing that deference, by simply supporting the alpha, the others in the group were rewarded with smaller, yet still effective, doses of serotonin—which encouraged them to continue supporting the alpha.

THE BOTTOM LINE IS that we are designed to crave significance, admiration, and adoration. This continual quest is the foundation of narcissism. At reasonable levels, it can be perfectly healthy and serve as a powerful enhancement of performance. Narcissism is what drives us to take risks, to get noticed, which in turn can help us discover potential we didn't know we had.

People who fall too high on the narcissism scale, however, can be dangerous. In a simple sense, those more narcissistic types favor the quick hits of serotonin and dopamine over the longer-lasting oxytocin. They need those constant reinforcements because their self-esteem is either very fragile or very low; despite presenting as arrogant, they generally feel unsafe and insecure. They're extremely sensitive to perceived injuries from criticism or defeat, and they very easily feel humiliated or degraded. To prevent that, highly narcissistic people try to put themselves at the center of small, tight, sycophantic tribes. They are rarely loyal—loyalty requires trust and a sense of safety—so their tribes are inherently unstable: Healthy members tend not to stay long and new ones are let in only when they show the requisite deference. Those who do leave usually suffer a disproportionate amount of wrath from the person to whom they once deferred—because defectors are considered enemies.

So beware the highly narcissistic people in your sphere. Their energy and effort will, more often than not, be to prop up their fragile egos rather than to achieve shared objectives or serve a common purpose. They are by definition not team players. Yet if they sense you are distancing yourself—if you are not obviously on *their* team—they'll likely lash out, diminishing you in an effort to inflate themselves. Worst of all, narcissism doesn't show up clearly in a mirror: The more narcissistic a person is, the less likely it is that they'll recognize that behavior.

WHERE IS THE BALANCE? How do we effectively metabolize our own narcissism without tipping the scales?

The first step is to be honest about it. You have narcissistic tendencies. I do, too. We all do, and that's okay.

The second is to understand the biological chemistry at work so that you can separate the quick, powerful jolts of serotonin and dopamine from the more enduring and foundational oxytocin—separate the candy from the vegetables, so to speak. Serotonin and dopamine are seductive, always luring you back for more, so pay attention to where you're getting your fixes. Social media, for instance, is wildly addictive. Are you wasting time checking the comments on your Instagram posts? Eyeballing likes and retweets? Stop. Put aside your virtual friends for the real ones, the people, or even pets, who adore you and help build your oxytocin levels. Once those oxytocin-based bonds are established, research shows that just *thinking* about them will fire up those feel-good neurotransmitters, too. The cycle is self-reinforcing.

Finally, remember that narcissism is invisible. We have a hard time seeing even the healthy amounts in ourselves. Those close relationships, vital for our mental health, can also serve as a warning system, or a grounding wire when our circuits might be running a bit too hot.

My wife is one of my grounding wires. We've been married for over twenty years, and she's always been my biggest proponent, which includes being an honest critic. About halfway through my SEAL career, sometime around 2007, I came home from a particularly successful deployment. The apex of SEAL popularity was still a few years away, but we were getting a fair amount of attention even then, in large part because special forces were doing a disproportionate amount of the nation's war-fighting. My wife, meanwhile, was raising a two-year-old and a newborn and running a household by herself—she was growing a little weary of hearing how her mostly absent spouse was totally awesome.

I was catching up on chores and projects one afternoon shortly after I got home when she called me from the back of the house, where she was juggling both kids. She needed me to get a box of cotton swabs from the bathroom. I wasn't happy about having my project interrupted, but I grudgingly marched to the bathroom and looked in the closet.

No swabs. "They're not here," I yelled.

"Yes, they are," she hollered back. "They're right there on the middle shelf."

I looked again. "I can't see them."

"They're right on the middle shelf!"

"I'm telling you, *they're not here.*"

I could hear her stomping toward the bathroom. We were both agitated, but I at least would have the satisfaction of being proven right.

She reached around me and grabbed the box of cotton swabs. "They're right here," she barked. She turned, started to walk away, and called loudly back at me. "It's no wonder you guys haven't found bin Laden."

Ouch.

My narcissistic tendencies helped make me a SEAL. My wife helps keep that narcissism in check. It's those close and trusted relationships that help us see and keep track of things we might miss in ourselves. Nurturing those we love and trust not only helps our overall lives but also serves to tell us the hard truths and keep us grounded.

DRIVE ROLL-UP

Thousands of years ago, a group of people lived together at the edge of a forest. Remember that story from a few chapters back? With the stream running dry, food becoming scarce, and a hard winter bearing down, a handful of those people took the first brave steps into the forest.

They walked off looking for safe shelter and abundant food and water. They were driven, in other words, to satisfy intrinsic needs, and possibly extrinsic ones, too. The path was long and uncertain and treacherous, but those few travelers had higher levels of the drive attributes than those who stayed behind.

They had enough self-efficacy to believe they could accomplish the journey and the discipline to keep going. They were open-minded, willing to believe there was a better place beyond the distant ridgeline. Instead of hunkering down for the scarce winter, they had the cunning to consider the novel, almost radical, approach of wandering into the unknown. Probably at least one of them was narcissistic enough to want to lead a party of explorers, too.

Drive is the behavior of staying focused on and pursuing a goal, and those five attributes all contribute to the behavior.

We introduced those prehistoric travelers in the context of courage, which is one of the grit attributes. That's because they would have needed both drive *and* grit to survive an arduous journey. Drive is concerned with longer-term objectives, aspirations that require time and diligence to achieve. Drive is what kept them walking day after day, week after week. Grit is about the short term. Grit got them through the worst moments of those days and weeks—fighting off bears, crossing wild rivers, scaling steep, rugged slopes.

Drive needs grit to be effective—it's difficult to push toward a goal if you can't get past the inevitable obstacles. Moreover, no single drive attribute is very effective in isolation; drive as a behavior typically requires functional levels of at least two of the underlying attributes.

Someone who has a high level of only discipline, for example, will likely have meticulously thought out plans that are never acted upon. Cunning by itself tends to present as maliciousness, and narcissism shows up as preening arrogance. A person who's very open-minded but extremely low on the other attributes is . . . well, probably just very nice.

Developing several or even all five, though, will increase your drive immensely. Combine drive with grit while exercising your mental acuity attributes, and that's a powerful formula for optimal performance, anywhere and anytime.

THE LEADERSHIP ATTRIBUTES

Leadership is not a position. It's a behavior. And you don't get to decide if you're doing it well.

Let me explain. I spent my entire career in the Navy as an officer, retiring as a commander. That meant that I was always in charge of somebody or something. But that's all it meant: My rank made me a boss, not a leader. And I'm sure that's how at least some of the guys under my command saw me, as the person who just happened to be in charge, for good or ill. I also know that some of those men saw me as a leader, but only because they told me so.

Leaders are identified and defined by those whom they lead. You can't declare yourself to be a leader. That's like announcing that you're funny—you might think so, but if you can't make anyone laugh, then you're not funny. Whether you're actually a leader, not just the person in charge, is entirely up to other people.

That said, leaders also aren't a few rare people at the very top of the social hierarchy. Leadership is everywhere. Sure, there are CEOs and commanding officers, people with clear authority over others. They might be leaders. They might just be in charge. But parents can be leaders. So can coaches and teachers, or the front man in the local bar band. There's the friend who always has wise advice, and that person in the office everyone turns to when the mercurial boss is on a tirade. You don't need a title to be a leader. You just need to behave like one.

In the work that I've done with the Chapman & Co. Leadership Institute, we've asked thousands of people around the world the same question: What do great leaders do? We've asked that question on the East Coast, the West Coast, and in the Midwest; in Europe, Africa, and Asia; among Boomers, Gen Xers, and Millennials. The answers are always the same.

Great leaders, we're told again and again, are trustworthy. They listen and they care. They're selfless, authentic, and accountable.

Some of those answers describe skills—listening, for one, is a greatly underappreciated skill—but most of them are attributes. There are five that are key to leadership: empathy, selflessness, authenticity, decisiveness, and accountability.

Certain skills, like time management, delegation, and listening, will enhance those leadership attributes. But they are not critical. In fact, mastery of any particular skill is not required. Most of us have people in our lives whom we go to for advice or help—people who by definition we consider leaders—regardless of their particular expertise. As a lawyer for fifty years, for example, my dad doesn't know much about plumbing. But that didn't stop me from giving him a call when I was having issues with the pipes in my first house.

Not every situation requires leadership for optimal performance, of course. There are many niches, even entire professions, that are self-directed. A world-class comic, for instance, does not need to lead or be led to that position. Having too much empathy might even be a detriment to top-notch comedy.

But most of us at some point will be identified as leaders. Maybe not as the boss or the commanding officer, but as a parent, a friend, a confidant. And most of us will need to be led, at least occasionally. These are the attributes that will help you identify the optimal leaders and improve your own leadership potential.

CHAPTER SEVENTEEN

NO ONE CARES HOW *YOU* FEEL

Empathy: *The ability, whether deliberate or not, to join the emotional state of another person; to feel what someone else feels*

BARRY-WEHMILLER IS ONE OF those big, indispensable companies that you've probably never heard of. It supplies manufacturing technology and services to other companies, which means, basically, that it makes the machines and provides the systems that other companies need to make their products and services. Let's say you make an energy drink and need a machine to put caps and labels on plastic bottles. Barry-Wehmiller can make that machine for you. A machine that cuts, shapes, and prints pizza boxes? Or one that spins toilet paper into rolls? It can make those, too. About 75 percent of the products we use every day have been touched, in one way or another, by a Barry-Wehmiller machine.

BW was formed more than a hundred years ago in St. Louis to supply equipment and machinery to the city's many breweries. In the 1980s the company began expanding, acquiring other companies that supplied machines or technological services to other industries. By the early 2000s, BW had bought up almost a hundred other manufacturing firms.

In the process of buying all those other companies, BW's CEO, Bob Chapman, spent a fair amount of time on manufacturing floors. A company is only as good as its people, and Chapman had both the curiosity and the fiduciary duty to check in on the workforce BW was bringing into the fold.

You know what he learned? A lot of people didn't like coming to work.

That's not wildly surprising. Making things—the actual physical labor of creating a product on a factory floor—requires long hours of hard and often monotonous work. Shift work is guided by rigid rules, and typically there are many layers of bureaucracy between the people on the floor and the suits upstairs. And because manufacturing generally operates on an ethos of producing more with fewer resources, including people, workers can understandably feel like expendable cogs in a faceless system instead of people with thoughts and feelings and something valuable to contribute.

As a long-run proposition, unhappy workers aren't in anyone's best interests. So Chapman decided that the company's primary focus needed to shift from profits to people— to creating a workplace to which people wanted to come, where they felt appreciated and fulfilled and safe. But how? Chapman could read a million suggestion-box notes and analyze a library of performance spreadsheets, but he knew that that wasn't going to be enough. That would just give him a long list of grievances. To fix the reasons shift workers were dissatisfied, Chapman and his team needed to fully *understand* those reasons, not simply list them. They needed to know what it *felt* like to be a shift worker.

They needed to have empathy.

———

FOR CHAPMAN, SYMPATHY WAS not enough. To sympathize with someone is to be aware of their woes, and that is largely a passive experience: An unfortunate event happens to someone else, and you reflexively acknowledge that they are embarrassed or sad or frustrated. You might feel pity toward that person or sorrow on his or her behalf, but those are *your* emotions directed at someone else.

Empathy is different. It's an active experience that requires emotional projection. Instead of merely *knowing* how someone feels, you're *feeling* how that person feels. Empathy is the ability to fully and genuinely imagine another person's emotional state, even without those emotions being explicitly communicated. It means, basically, putting yourself in someone else's shoes.

Sometimes that's easy. You instinctively empathize with someone who's suffering through a situation you've been in. Anyone who's struggled to quit smoking, for instance, understands how hard it is for another person to give up cigarettes. More difficult, though, is feeling real empathy for people completely unlike you involved in unfamiliar experiences—like the way a swing-shift machinist experiences work compared to the way an executive does. In a situation like that, genuine empathy requires a deliberate shift in perspective and, as you might imagine, a fair amount of open-mindedness (Chapter Fourteen).

There's one key rule about empathy: It can't be faked. False empathy stands out like a lighthouse in the fog. Think of bad acting in a straight-to-video movie, where the emotions are stilted, awkward, and obviously phony. That's what people see when you pretend to be empathetic—and insincerity is the polar opposite of empathy.

Fortunately, you don't need to fake it. Humans, and many other animals, are wired for empathy. One of the things Andrew Huberman studies in his lab is what is called "emotional contagion," or the contagious nature of emotion. In tests, merely watching someone in a heightened emotional state caused physiological changes in the observer that aligned with the person experiencing the actual emotion. If subjects observed someone experiencing fear, for example, they would begin to experience the increased heart rate, rapid respiration, and dilated pupils that typically come with being afraid. The results were similar for other emotional states—sadness, excitement, joy—as well. Being attuned to others' emotions is part of being alive.

THERE IS A PHYSIOLOGICAL basis for this idea of emotional contagion. In the mid-nineties, neuroscientist Giacomo Rizzolatti and his team of Italian researchers found neurons in the brains of macaque monkeys that fired when the monkeys grabbed an object—*and when they watched another monkey grab the same object*. Rizzolatti called them "mirror neurons" and suggested that the discovery could help explain how humans can "read" others' emotions and empathize with them.

Mirror neurons haven't been pinpointed with the same precision in humans. Rather, it's possible people have a more general "mirror system," which Huberman notes has been essential to our evolution. "Animals, including humans, that are reliant on groups for survival," he says, "needed to have mechanisms that helped them pay attention to the feelings of others."

Partly, those mechanisms helped form closer bonds among members of the group. But empathy also plays a role in survival. If one of our primitive cave-dwelling ancestors watched someone fall terribly ill after eating berries from a certain bush, those mirrored feelings helped everyone remember to avoid those berries later. In the same way, if you see someone howl in pain when they touch a certain object, you'll know to keep your distance. You don't need to feel the pain yourself—your most primitive form of empathy does that vicariously.

That kind of utilitarian mirroring is common among most animals. But humans have something extra, and it's the reason why some people seem to be more empathetic than others. "We have a really powerful forebrain," Huberman says, "which ultimately becomes that gateway to how much emotion we choose to experience."

The limbic brain—the ancient brain—is the central processor for interpreting emotions, both our own and others'. We see someone weeping, and the limbic brain recognizes that as sadness. But our forebrain, the more evolved part, is responsible for reasoning, for rational thought, for our ability to make nonemotional decisions. And it also can control what gets sent through from the limbic brain. "There's a circuit in the forebrain," Huberman says, "one of the decision-making circuits of the neocortex, that relegates our own experience to the background so that we can allow the external perception to override."

That means empathy, as a neurological matter, follows a specific sequence. It begins with an emotion from an external source—a crying child, a frustrated co-worker—that gets processed through the limbic brain. Then our forebrain allows (or does not allow) that external emotion to temporarily set aside our own emotions. It allows us, in other words, to *feel* that external emotion. The extent to which those external emotions come through, both how readily and how intensely, is a measure of where we fall on the empathy scale.

If empathy comes easily to you, you probably have a more dominant limbic brain. Most people, in fact, begin life highly empathetic because the limbic brain is one of the earliest parts to fully develop. Anyone who's been in a nursery of newborns understands this: When one starts crying, the rest start joining in even though they're in no apparent distress. They're simply mirroring another's emotions, unrestrained by the forebrain. Or consider pets. They don't have developed forebrains, which makes them empathy machines. Your dog will always stay quietly with you when you're sad, growl at a threat when you're scared, wag his tail and slobber when you're happy. Animals feed on our emotions.

The forebrain, on the other hand, takes a couple of decades to fully develop. That's why teenagers are such an emotional roller coaster. Their limbic brains are running full tilt, but their forebrains, the part that regulates emotion and behavior, are still baking. A fully formed adult, on the other hand, who is driven more by the forebrain and is therefore more rational than emotional, is probably slower to feel emotion.

The fact that the forebrain is involved, that decision-making circuits can fire or not, suggest that empathy is, at least in part, a choice. Your empathetic response can be controlled in either direction. People who need to engage in a little more empathy can choose to try to internalize more of the emotions of others. It's not a magic bullet; simply deciding to be more empathetic will not make it so, and remember, fake empathy is worse than no empathy. But with practice, it will get easier. Conversely, those who get too easily mired in others' emotions can learn to dial it back. It will feel unnatural at first, deliberately separating from someone else's distress, but in time it will be liberating.

Anyone in a leadership position needs to find an empathy balance, the Goldilocks spot of not too much and not too little. It's often been said that leaders need a switch that allows them to turn empathy on or off, depending on the situation. I'd modify that and make it a dimmer switch, one that can slide up and down, refining the depth and intimacy of empathy as needed. Human interaction is never black and white, so our emotional response shouldn't be, either.

A lack of empathy in any leader obviously is a huge detriment. But too much empathy can be just as damaging. It's hard to be productive if you're functioning at the whim of other people's emotions. Because empathy is typically focused on the feelings of an individual or small group, employing too much of it can make others, with different feelings, feel dismissed. The boss who is always hyper-concerned about the feelings of one person or group will likely find herself alienating others. Finally, too much empathy can negatively affect logical, nonemotional decision-making—a critical skill when leading big, diverse groups. A leader often has to make big-picture decisions unfettered by the emotions of others.

Empathy is an invaluable tool, so long as it is properly calibrated.

THE FIRST STEP TO creating those genuine empathetic bonds, as Bob Chapman knew, is to listen. That's harder than it might seem. People tend to *hear* more than listen. Usually our brains are trying to sort out a response or figuring out how whatever is being said relates to us.

But empathy requires *really* listening. Chapman and his team had to focus, cleanly and clearly, on the person who was speaking, had to clear out all of those stray thoughts about how to respond, and had to eliminate any sense of defensiveness. It also meant shutting up and staying quiet, so that whoever they were talking with felt fully free to speak his or her honest mind.

When they listened, they stopped merely hearing and started empathizing. They no longer heard a shift worker complaining about a long walk across a parking lot in the cold—now they felt the resentment of a man who came to work at six in the morning during a Wisconsin snowstorm, parked two hundred yards from the door, and had to walk past row after row of spaces reserved for executives who rolled in at nine. They felt the embarrassment of having to ask a supervisor to use the bathroom or pay phone while the back-office staff free-ranged around the plant. They understood the frustration of workers wasting time having to sign out tools one at a time from a locked cage instead of being trusted to do their jobs properly and efficiently.

Once those emotions were internalized—once Chapman and his team empathized—the solutions were obvious and swift. Rearrange some parking spots, allow workers ready access to tools, let people use the bathroom and phone when they needed. Treat people like professionals, and they will be professional. Morale began to soar, efficiency blossomed, retention increased, and, as time went by and the new systems took hold, profits increased.

Barry-Wehmiller's drastic shift spurred the creation of an internal training course focused on what Chapman calls "Truly Human Leadership." The first course? A three-day workshop teaching people how to listen empathetically. Word began to get around the manufacturing world that BW had figured out a better way of leading people. Smaller manufacturing plants, looking to be acquired, sought out BW because they wanted to be a part of a unique and powerful business philosophy.

It hasn't stopped there. In 2015, Chapman released his book, *Everybody Matters,* and supported the creation of the Barry-Wehmiller Leadership Institute (since renamed the Chapman & Co. Leadership Institute) to export those lessons to other companies and leaders.

Those lessons are powerful because they are so simple and, once you see them, obvious. I met Chapman shortly before I retired from the Navy and was so impressed with the philosophy, and its success, that I later joined the institute as its director of outreach and senior facilitator. In all of my experience with leadership in the military, empathy was not specifically emphasized. Yet it is fundamental. Leaders don't lead organizations—they lead the people who make up those organizations. To do that effectively requires empathy.

CHAPTER EIGHTEEN

IF IT DOESN'T HURT,
YOU'RE DOING IT WRONG

Selflessness: *Placing the needs and well-being of others above one's own despite a real or perceived risk*

THE MOST IMPORTANT ISSUE in the elections of 1854 was whether slavery would be allowed in the territories of Nebraska and Kansas.

For more than thirty years, the Missouri Compromise had prohibited slavery in any new territories north of the thirty-sixth parallel, roughly what is now the top of the Texas panhandle. But the Kansas-Nebraska Act repealed that compromise: Congress in the spring of 1854 decided that the matter of human bondage on the frontier should be settled by a vote of the people living there. Six months later, in the fall, candidates were defined largely by whether they were for or against the act legalizing the potential expansion of slavery.

In Illinois, Abraham Lincoln was of course against it. He ran for the U.S. Senate that year as an "anti-Nebraskan," as opponents of the act were known, against the pro-Nebraskan incumbent, James Shields.

State legislators elected senators back then, and the anti-Nebraskans held a slim majority in Illinois. On the first ballot, Shields got forty-one votes, Lincoln received forty-four, and another anti-Nebraskan named Lyman Trumbull had five (nine other votes went to other candidates). Since no one had the requisite fifty votes to win, another ballot was called. Then another, and another. After nine ballots, still no one had a majority.

Lincoln really wanted to be a U.S. senator. But he knew Trumbull's few die-hard supporters would never support him, and it was more important that whoever won be against the Kansas-Nebraska Act.

Before the tenth ballot, Lincoln announced, "I'm for Trumbull." He told his supporters to throw in their lot with Trumbull, too. "You will lose both Trumbull and myself," he said when some of them protested, "and I think the cause in this case is to be preferred to men."

Lyman Trumbull was elected U.S. senator.

While personally devastated, in letters he wrote later, Lincoln explained that his "larger number of friends had to surrender to Trumbull's small number" because the stakes were worth sacrificing his own success. "I could not . . . let the whole political result go to ruin," he wrote, "on a point merely personal to myself."

SELFISHNESS IS EASY. THAT'S not necessarily a bad thing. In the animal kingdom, of which we surely are a part, being selfish can at times be a matter of survival. When nuts are scarce, after all, the squirrel that hoards the most is going to make it through the winter. At a primal level, selfishness is a reaction to fear—fear of losing vital resources, of being denied that to which we think we're entitled, of dying—and, as we now know, neurologically, fear is a powerful motivator.

Selfishness, rightly or wrongly, has also been one of the organizing principles of human civilization. In fact, it's practically encouraged by the way people too often keep score. Gazillionaire publisher Malcolm Forbes, for instance, had a plaque in his kitchen that read, "He who dies with the most toys, wins." But leadership is about people, not accumulating toys. And because selfishness means deliberately prioritizing one's own interests over those of others, it is inherently antithetical to leadership.

To be selfless, the polar opposite of being selfish, means placing someone else's well-being above your own, and then acting accordingly. Depending on the situation, that can be difficult because selflessness involves either a personal cost or some level of risk; simply being kind is not the same as being selfless.

For example, a healthy, wealthy, and well-fed businessman buys himself a sandwich for lunch. As he's walking back to his office, he passes a homeless man on the corner, dirty and disheveled and holding a sign that says, "Will work for food." The businessman stops, decides he's not really that hungry, and gives the man his sandwich. Is that selfless? No. Altruistic, perhaps, or generous. If the businessman is trying to cut down on his calories, it might just be utilitarian— doing the most good for the highest number of people. But it's not selfless because there is no risk involved, and no real cost beyond a couple of bucks for the sandwich.

Let's take that story one step further. The homeless man is grateful for the sandwich because he hasn't eaten in two days. But he knows there's a man on the next block who hasn't had a scrap of food in *three* days. Rather than eat his free lunch, he delivers the sandwich to the other guy. That *is* selfless because there's a cost involved—namely, the man's belly stays empty.

The key is that the selfless person—the giver, so to speak—prioritizes the needs of another—the receiver— over his or her own. That dynamic is so reflexive in some relationships that it's not even a conscious decision. Parents, for example, will instinctively sacrifice their material wealth and physical comfort for their children. In extreme situations, even complete strangers can willingly put themselves at grave risk for others. When Kansas City Chiefs running back Joe Delaney saw three children struggling in a small lake in 1983, he immediately went in after them, despite the fact that he couldn't swim. Two of the children drowned, but Delaney saved one before he unfortunately drowned, too.

Those are all classic examples of selflessness, born of parental love or dramatic circumstances. But let's focus on the more routine episodes, the ones that require neither heroes nor deep personal relationships. There is still a risk or cost involved, but it does not need to be substantial. It could be as seemingly benign as letting a co-worker take credit for a project you completed together because he needs points with the boss. Or giving blood—it takes time and makes you briefly woozy for the benefit of strangers. The cost is minor, but it's still a cost.

"A LEADER IS BEST when people barely know he exists," the ancient Chinese philosopher Lao-tzu wrote. "When his work is done, his aim fulfilled, they will say: We did it ourselves."

Robert K. Greenleaf said much the same thing in his 1970 essay, "The Servant as Leader," in which he inverted the classic hierarchical pyramid. Rather than exercising power from the top, sending orders cascading downward, Greenleaf argued that a leader functions more successfully by attending to the needs of the team. By helping others to be successful—by serving them—the leader sets an example that others will readily follow. Subordinates who feel more valued will see more value in others and believe they are all invested in a worthwhile endeavor. Leadership means inspiring others.

Great leaders want those who follow them to gain

enough competence and experience that, eventually, they don't need to be led. Often, that means conceding your own obsolescence. I always told my junior officers that they had to accept the irony of working themselves out of a job. Consider that for a moment: That kind of relationship, a superior consciously knowing that he is gradually surrendering control, requires a deep level of trust. A leader who trusts his subordinates will, in turn, be trusted.

Acts of selflessness will rapidly build that trust. Again, the cost involved does not have to be extreme. A friend of mine likes to say that "time is the currency of leadership." Spend it. Give your time to advise, to mentor, even just to listen. Find ways to allow others to excel, to shine in such a way that illuminates them and not you. Those are all measures of selflessness. Look for those opportunities and practice being selfless; it's a close cousin to kindness and altruism, and those are both behaviors to be encouraged.

CHAPTER NINETEEN

YOU CAN'T HIDE YOU

Authenticity: *The degree to which a person's actions are consistent with his beliefs, values, and desires, despite external pressures*

THREE YEARS AFTER I left the Navy, my friend Brian McCabe invited me to speak to a few hundred people at Pegasystems, a global software developer. Brian is the company's vice president of solutions consulting for the Americas, and he wanted me to talk about high-performing teams at the kickoff for a big sales push.

I'd first met Brian fifteen years earlier, at my sister's wedding. He used to work in a cubicle next to her, and she would tell him stories about me and my twin brother, the Harrier pilot. She couldn't tell him very much—a lot of our work was classified, so she didn't know very much—but she'd offer snapshots. "He's out somewhere doing practice landings in the Harrier," she'd say about my brother. Or, "Rich is skydiving out west." Little things like that. Brian hung on every word. He was fascinated by the military and had even considered enlisting in the Marines at one point.

My sister told me about Brian, too, so I knew what to expect when I finally met him at her wedding in 2004. He asked a million questions, which wasn't unusual. After a decade as a SEAL, I'd gotten used to superfans, mostly young guys who wanted to be SEALs or old guys who wished they had been. But there was something different about Brian. I liked him right away but couldn't exactly say why. Maybe it was the way he asked questions—curious without fawning—or maybe I just liked him because it was obvious he cared about my family.

I brought a gift for Brian when I met him that first time, a SEAL challenge coin. Challenge coins function mostly as souvenirs these days—the one I gave him had the SEAL insignia on one side and the name and symbol of my specific command on the other—but they have a noble history. There are a few different origin stories but the most common is that the first ones were struck by American pilots who volunteered to fly for Allied squadrons before the United States officially engaged in World War I. One of the young pilots kept his medallion in a leather pouch he wore on a cord around his neck. When he was later shot down, the Germans put him in a prison camp but, for some strange reason, let him keep his pouch. He still had it when he escaped during a night of heavy bombing, snuck across no-man's-land, and came upon a French outpost. The French were going to execute him as a spy—remember, Americans weren't officially fighting the war—until one of the soldiers recognized the medallion. They sent him back to his squadron with a bottle of wine.

Those Americans agreed then to always carry their medallions. At any time, even years later, one of those pilots could challenge another to prove he still carried his coin. If he produced it, the challenger had to buy him a drink; if he didn't, the next round was on him.

Most military units have a challenge coin now, but the tradition didn't hold. In fact, they're often called command coins because the challenge part faded away. They're mostly given as gifts or mounted in plaques as mementos. Some people have whole collections they display in cases.

But Brian was so touched that he promised he'd honor the history and carry that SEAL coin with him always, just like those original pilots. Frankly, I'd heard that before but never took it seriously. People mean well, but it's just not realistic to keep an odd souvenir in your pocket day after day, year after year.

We kept in touch after the wedding. Brian rose through the ranks at Pegasystems, and he asked me once or twice if I'd come talk to his team about leadership. I couldn't do that when I was in the Navy, but I was happy to do so after I retired.

When I saw him in person, he asked if I remembered giving him that coin. Yes, of course I did. He pulled it out of his pocket. It was worn, the colors fading, the hard edges gone smooth. That doesn't happen in a display case.

"I still carry it," Brian told me, "every day."

That's when it clicked. That's when I figured out what I saw in him fifteen years earlier. There's no bluff in Brian, no pretense, no artifice. He did what he said he would do, and he is who he presents himself to be. He's authentic.

AMONG ALL OF THE leadership attributes, authenticity is the most important for building trust.

Authenticity, by definition, can't be faked. It can't be copied: There's no template, no checklist of external behaviors or attitudes that are the model of authenticity. Being firm and taciturn doesn't make one any more or less of a leader than being easygoing and funny. What matters more is whether that person is *authentically* firm or *authentically* easygoing.

The simplest measure of authenticity is consistency: consistency of action, consistency of thought, consistency of values. Consistency builds trust, and a lack of consistency instills doubt. Think of it this way: If stepping on the brake pedal didn't consistently stop your car—if sometimes it made the engine race or turned on the wipers instead—you wouldn't trust the brakes, right? The same idea applies to humans. If you don't believe you're seeing authentic versions of people, if you suspect they're play-acting or pretending, presenting insincere façades that shift with their audience or their own whims, it's impossible to build an honest foundation of trust.

To make it even simpler: Authentic people are genuine. They aren't markedly different in private than they are in public.

There are, of course, caveats. Manners, social norms, and basic decency are all fine reasons to temper your authenticity. Rude is rude, even when it's authentic, and the world would be a better place if everyone tried to be a little kinder. But being authentic does not require being pleasant. Authentic people are not necessarily nice or enjoyable to be around or even self-aware enough to realize that no one likes them. That doesn't really matter, though, because you can adjust to unpleasantness as long as you know it's genuine.

For example, many years ago one of my new commanding officers immediately struck me as cold and grumpy. New COs are installed every two years in the military, so in a career you see the gamut of personalities and leadership styles. But this one really stood out. The first time I met him was at the change of command ceremony, but in an instant he was on me about some equipment our unit had that wasn't being used. It was gear that had been shelved long before I got there because, I'd been told, it was ineffective, cumbersome, and too much of a hassle to maintain. And that's what I repeated to the new CO.

"How do *you* know it doesn't work?" he growled at me. "When was the last time you used it? How many hours have you used it?" He grew more agitated, and I was more uncomfortable with each question and every unsatisfactory answer.

This was at the ceremony where the point is to welcome the new boss. I walked away rattled, certain the next two years were going to be rough.

But over the next few weeks, from my own interactions and from talking with buddies, I figured out that the CO was *always* like that. In his office, in the chow hall, out doing physical training, with junior officers, senior officers, enlisted sailors—it didn't matter. He was always curt, always demanding, always grumpy. In other words, I could depend on him, I could *trust him,* to always be the cranky salt he authentically was. That allowed me to adjust my strategy, to tweak the way I performed under his command.

That CO, despite his personality, was an excellent leader. Years later, I was assigned to work for him on an overseas deployment, and he greeted me as cheerily as he did the first time: a quick, cold handshake and a stack of work that needed to get done yesterday. "I run a tight ship," he told me. "You're gonna feel the full pain of staff duty." It was weirdly comforting.

My experience isn't unusual. You've probably been there or can imagine something similar. Let's pretend you've got a choice of three managers, all of whom typically are cold and unpleasant, offering little praise, saying nothing that isn't directly related to work. One of them, though, is remarkably pleasant to his superior or to anyone he thinks can help him. Another is cranky one day, bubbly the next, and in a completely unhinged rage on the third. And the third, like my old CO, is consistently, genuinely grumpy.

You, and every rational person, would pick number three, the authentic one.

———

BRIAN'S FATHER WAS THE main orthodontist in the small New England town where he grew up. "He ran his practice out of our house—it was designed to have a commercial office space attached to it—so if you had braces in Hingham, chances are you came to my house to see Dr. McCabe," Brian told me. With all of those townsfolk and kids from school coming to Brian's house, it was hard for him to be anonymous. And if everyone knew who he was, there was no point in Brian pretending to be someone he wasn't. He learned from an early age that it was easier to always be his authentic self.

Decades later, Brian's natural authenticity is part of what makes him an effective leader. "One of the key things about being an authentic leader is transparency," he said. "The higher you go up in an organization, the more exposed you are, the more people see you. Everyone knows who you are. And they see you from angles that you don't even see. You cannot hide who you are because everybody sees you."

This is key. Leaders are watched more than they are heard. Every parent knows children model the behaviors they see. Albert Bandura demonstrated the effect of behavioral modeling with the famous Bobo doll experiment in 1961. Bandura had groups of children between the ages of three and five watch an adult interact with an assortment of toys, including an inflatable clown called Bobo. For one group, the adult ignored Bobo; for the other, he spent most of his time being physically and verbally aggressive with Bobo. The results won't surprise you. When given the same toys, the first group played quietly and rarely interacted with the inflatable clown. The second spent most of their time hitting and kicking Bobo.

Humans never fully shed that tendency to model behaviors. So by being authentic, you encourage those around you to be authentic, too. Especially for those in leadership positions, being honest about who you are—even if it means being vulnerable—helps others to be honest about who they are, too.

Here's part of how Brian does that. He's a drummer, and has been since he was a kid, and during corporate events he'll get onstage with a band in front of hundreds of employees and put on a show. He's led the crowds in full-blown karaoke, even though Brian is not, in fact, a singer. He's dressed up as a shagadelic Austin Powers, complete with awful teeth and a big gold Male medallion, occasionally shouting "Oh, behave" to the audience.

It's all in good fun, and it's obvious Brian is having a great time. But there's a purpose behind it, too. "Authentic leaders model the behavior they want to see more of," Brian says. "Opportunities to play music, sing, or ham it up in front of my team show the team that it's okay to let it out there. And that's one of the reasons why a team is so successful."

Once you start to question your level of authenticity, it should be plain to see. You know if you're faking it, if you're pretending to be someone you're not, if you compromise your values to please or placate someone else. Chances are that if you are markedly different at work than you are at home, then in one of those places you are lying. Of course you will modify some behaviors in public to respect social norms, to be polite and decent, even to accommodate the sensitivities of others. Just because you're an authentic carnivore, for instance, doesn't mean you should bring a steak to a vegan dinner party. You might also genuinely want to conform to your social group, just as you might be a genuine contrarian. (The latter might make you tiresome and annoying, but not necessarily inauthentic.) The irony is that while only you can define your authentic self, others can often spot your inauthentic self.

CHAPTER TWENTY

MANY A FALSE STEP IS MADE BY STANDING STILL

Decisiveness: *The ability to make decisions quickly and effectively*

AT 3:15 ON THE morning of June 22, 1941, more than three million German soldiers, supported by divisions of Finns, Hungarians, and Romanians, invaded Russia. It was, and still is, the largest military invasion in history, and it was not unexpected. Hitler had already blitzkrieged through Europe, and he'd massed men and matériel along Russia's border. Soviet and British intelligence warned of an invasion, and a German deserter even told the Soviets exactly when it would happen.

If any country could stop Hitler's armies and Panzer divisions, it was the Soviet Union. The country had twice as many tanks and aircraft as the Germans, an enormous population, and robust industrial production that could rearm and resupply almost six million notoriously tough troops. And yet the initial attack was a debacle for the Soviets. The Axis powers stormed over the border and, within weeks, were hundreds of miles inside Russian territory.

How could such an apparently superior military force get so badly overrun? One factor, historians concluded, was Joseph Stalin's poor leadership. Before the invasion, he refused to believe it would happen. When it did, he was unable to issue firm commands because he wasn't decisive. "Stalin left the Commissariat of Defense that night of June 22 and returned to his dacha at Kuntsevo," Edwin P. Hoyt wrote in his book, *199 Days: The Battle for Stalingrad.* "No orders were given, no word came from the dacha. Stalin was completely paralyzed with shock and incapable of action. For a week he hid in his country retreat and abandoned all his responsibilities. . . ."

Without direction from Stalin, there was chaos at the front. In the first hours of the invasion, commanders (who were generally inexperienced because of Stalin's earlier purges of the military, but that's another story) were paralyzed by Stalin's uncertainty. Should they try to slow the Axis armies? Should they counterattack? Should they shoot back at all?

"So fearful were the generals of Stalin," Hoyt wrote, ". . . they would do nothing to provoke their leader. . . . If they shot, they might be shot."

Because of a lack of decisiveness, that first catastrophic week almost doomed the Soviet war effort. The Axis invasion continued for six months, and the fighting came within two hundred miles of Moscow. Some eight hundred thousand Soviet soldiers were killed, and millions more were captured or wounded before the crippling cold of the Russian winter finally ground the campaign to a halt.

DECISIVENESS IS THE ABILITY to make clear, well-informed, and timely decisions. The last criterion, timeliness, is what separates the person with a high level of decisiveness from someone who merely makes solid decisions. In any dynamic environment, taking too long to make even a good decision is ineffective because the environment changes so quickly.

Let's break this down, starting with decision-making.

The ability to make decisions is a crucial component of leadership. Effective leaders need to identify and obtain critical information, gauge when enough detail has been collected in light of the potential outcomes, then decide and act. This suggests several things.

First, those with well-developed mental acuity attributes will have an advantage in making decisions. After all, the decision-making process is simply the internal mental acuity process made external. It obviously requires situational awareness, which in this context also often includes the perspectives of others to be more fully informed. That might be intuitive, basically reading the rest of the team—are they wary or optimistic, enthusiastic or reluctant—or it can be more active and collaborative, perhaps a discussion about current and historical data and possible outcomes. Once the information has been taken in by the decision-maker, the next step involves compartmentalization: assessing relevance and prioritizing. This, too, can involve external perspectives and input, rather than just the signals bouncing through our inferior temporal cortex, hippocampus, and forebrain. Once the decision is made, a dose of courage and some self-efficacy (to bolster the courage) will translate it into action. Finally, learnability is useful in properly evaluating and absorbing the results of the decision.

Second, effective decisions are final decisions. The Latin roots of the word literally mean "to cut off"—that is, to eliminate all other possibilities. A decision that isn't clear and firm isn't a decision at all—it's permission to consider a list of options. That said, *final* is not synonymous with *permanent*. Every action has a reaction. Circumstances change. Some well-made decisions are nonetheless wrong decisions. This is where another attribute, adaptability, comes into play. When the results of a decision become apparent, sometimes the best course of action will be to adapt, to decide to do something else.

While those other attributes are helpful in making decisions, they are not required. In fact, great decision-makers can even be a bit low on those attributes if they're willing and able to lean on others for support. Sharing knowledge and building consensus can be excellent strategies in a protracted, complex decision-making process. In fact, great leaders often will deliberately involve others in order to foster inclusion and trust and to reduce or eliminate bias.

Finally, decision-making is a skill. It can be learned. Evaluating data, balancing competing interests, predicting probable outcomes—those things can be taught and practiced. Certain attributes, as we've discussed, will make those skills easier to perform, but they are still skills. Decisiveness, on the other hand, is an attribute.

THE DISTINCTION BETWEEN DECISIVENESS and decision-making is speed. To be decisive means having the ability to move through the decision-making process quickly, efficiently, and, especially for a leader, sometimes independently.

Making quick, sure decisions is easy when you have all of the information, you understand the environment, and the stakes are low. Should you make a ham sandwich for lunch, or go with the sushi that's been sitting on the counter for two days and is starting to stink? Most people can be decisive in that situation. The stakes can even be higher, so long as the relevant information and circumstances are well understood: If a man with a known heart condition is having debilitating chest pains, you would quickly and firmly decide to call an ambulance.

Decisiveness, then, is most valuable and most easily assessed when things are uncertain and fluid and the stakes are high. Imagine you're running late for a meeting you have to be at, a meeting on which your job depends. The roads are jammed, but the GPS says you'll make it with five minutes to spare. But you know these roads—traffic is likely to get worse before it gets better, which could turn into a thirty-minute delay. There's a back route you could take if you turn left right now, but that's guaranteed to make you fifteen minutes late. What do you do?

Maybe there is no one correct decision, but you have to make one, and do so swiftly. Speed matters. Important decisions can't always wait until every option has been dissected and analyzed. As Winston Churchill famously said, "If you're going through hell, keep going." That's exactly right: In times of stress, uncertainty, or complexity, movement is the key to optimal performance, and movement requires that decisions be made.

Decisiveness is also critical in establishing credibility as a leader. A speedy and well-thought-out decision, backed by logic, gut instinct, and a willingness to take personal responsibility for the outcome (we'll discuss accountability in the next chapter), inspires confidence in those we're leading. Additionally, being decisive illuminates other attributes—courage, discipline, awareness—that reinforce that confidence. Conversely, appearing *indecisive* creates doubt. Imagine the distress, if not panic, at the Russian front when there was no clear directive on how to respond to the Axis invasion. Vacillating, waffling, or flip-flopping suggests incompetence, a lack of confidence, or both. And you can't inspire confidence if you don't demonstrate it. Indecisiveness is rarely, if ever, seen as a positive trait.

Can you go too far? Of course. Being effectively decisive implies that one is making competent decisions, that one is absorbing and processing the appropriate amount of information instead of just immediately barking random commands. Go back to that lunch choice. The fact that you like sushi more than ham isn't enough information for a proper decision—you need to consider that the sushi has been spoiling for two days. Choosing without considering that information isn't decisive. It's reckless.

"IN ANY MOMENT OF decision," Theodore Roosevelt said, "the best thing you can do is the right thing, the next best thing is the wrong thing, and the worst thing you can do is nothing."

Roosevelt, like Churchill, is correct. Paralysis is never a good thing. But there is a caveat: When Roosevelt said *nothing,* he really meant *not make a decision.* There are situations where deciding to do nothing is actually the best thing you can do.

For example, there's a military tactic called reconnaissance by fire. Basically, soldiers fire at where they think the enemy might be in order to provoke a reaction, thus confirming that the enemy is, in fact, there. But special operators, for example, work in small units where silence and stealth are critical and big firefights are usually best avoided. So they're trained to suppress the urge to immediately return fire. In other words, when they're getting shot at, they might make a deliberate decision not to shoot back, which is not the same as doing nothing.

A special-ops unit holds its fire as a tactic to help accomplish an objective. The soldiers firing upon them are also trying to accomplish an objective, namely, to figure out where the enemy is. "Ready, fire, aim" normally is pejorative slang for moving too fast, for doing something consequential without properly preparing—putting a product on the market too quickly, writing a stern memo in the heat of emotion, or punishing your kid without figuring out the facts. Reconnaissance by fire, though, is the literal expression of that maxim: Soldiers are firing, and revealing their own position, so that they can find an enemy at which to aim.

Both of those decisions—to fire on an unseen enemy and not to shoot back—carry risks, but they are calculated risks. They are risks in service of a broader mission. One side is trying to gather information, and the other is trying not to reveal information. The point is, knowing your purpose is tremendously valuable in being decisive. Small decisions that might seem dangerous or counterintuitive, that might even lead to negative results, can nonetheless help clarify circumstances and inform the next decision. Understanding your mission, your values, your objective, can make some decisions remarkably straightforward and easy in the ability to be decisive.

But beware too many decisions. Unlike most of the attributes, overusing decisiveness can be detrimental. Psychologists call it "decision fatigue," and it settles in after a long string of deciding too many things. Many highly successful and decisive people, in fact, actively reduce the number of decisions they have to make, especially the little ones. Former president Barack Obama and Mark Zuckerberg, for example, limit their wardrobes to one or two outfits. You can do this as well, even if it's as simple as making some of tomorrow's small decisions tonight.

CHAPTER TWENTY-ONE

DON'T BE A MEDIATOR

Accountability: *Taking responsibility for, and ownership of, your decisions, actions, and the consequences thereof*

NAVY SEAL TEAMS, LIKE any military outfit, have both officers and enlisted men, and the best officers—like the best leaders in any organization—typically have a distinct set of attributes. When I was in charge of selection and training, we designed a separate weeklong program specifically to screen officer candidates. There was a myriad of activities, both physical and cognitive, to help us get a better glimpse of the attributes in each man. One of the most important things we were looking for was accountability.

For years, we'd used a mission-planning exercise in officer screening. A candidate would be given the basics of a mission—the type of target, location, available assets—from which he would design a plan that he would brief to a panel. The original purpose was to measure things like knowledge of an environment, the ability to employ assets, and competence in presenting a coherent briefing. Those, as you understand by now, are skills. To explore attributes, though, I added a twist.

When I outlined the mission parameters, I began including two stipulations. One was that the candidate had to include soldiers from the host nation; for instance, Afghans in Afghanistan or Iraqis in Iraq. The other was that the mission had to be executed as a callout, which is exactly what it sounds like: Forces surround a target and use a megaphone to call out the occupants. There are strategic advantages to both of those tactics, especially if a broader objective is to win hearts and minds in a particular theater. Using local soldiers allows them to share ownership of the mission; and a callout is much safer for civilians than kicking in doors and blowing holes in walls. On the other hand, there are also distinct disadvantages to each. No one likes embarking on a high-stakes mission with unfamiliar comrades, and loudly announcing your presence eliminates the element of surprise.

Once I'd delivered those instructions, the officer candidate was sent off to develop a plan with some of my instructor staff, who were acting as members of the officer's team. This was more realistic than having the candidate pencil up a plan on his own because real-world mission planning always involves the whole team: Reconnaissance guys will map routes, assault teams will plan their portions of the mission, and so forth. I gave each candidate thirty minutes and told him I'd be in my office if he had any questions.

Here was the important part of the twist: I instructed my men playing the role of team members to vehemently protest both stipulations.

After the comic relief of listening to my guys in the next room screaming obscenity-laced complaints, I typically would see the candidates standing in my doorway, sheepishly asking to talk. They would articulate concerns about both constraints. In every case, I would hear them out, then concede on one but hold firm on the other. That is, I might let them off the hook on the callout but insist they use local forces, or vice versa. Then I would send them back to continue planning with a team I knew wouldn't be satisfied.

This exercise highlighted several attributes, including social intelligence, adaptability, and conscientiousness. But it was particularly effective at revealing accountability or a lack of it. How? By the way each candidate framed his concerns to me and explained my response to the men. In most cases, the candidate would explain to me why *he* was troubled by the stipulations, and then to the men why *he* was holding firm on one or the other.

But one candidate was different. He came into my office after the tirade of protests looking a little more rattled than the others. "Hey, sir," he said. "The guys are really protesting these stipulations." He went on to give me a few decent reasons, all of which I'd heard before, and, as usual, I relented on one but held firm on the other. When he returned to his team, I could hear him through the wall. "Guys, the boss has decided," he said. "He'll concede on using local forces, but he's putting his foot down on the callout." The candidate suffered some more scripted grumbling and then went back to planning the mission.

To his credit, his plan wasn't bad, actually. But there are many times in a combat environment when an officer might be tasked with something that he or his men don't fully agree with. That officer still has to implement that order, and doing that effectively means taking ownership of the whole process, especially if it's contentious. That candidate showed me he wasn't willing to shoulder that kind of responsibility. Implicit in his reasoning to me was, "It's the guys who are saying this, not me," and his rationale to his team was, "It's the boss telling us this, not me."

That's what a lack of accountability looks like, and it's dangerous in any leader. It creates an us-versus-them situation, puts distance between the different levels of a team, and unconsciously (or, in the worst case, consciously) labels higher-level decision-makers as the enemy. Next, and maybe more important, it suggests to those being led that the person in charge might not be willing to be accountable for the big stuff that will inevitably come down the road. Trying to remain neutral, and therefore clean, is incompatible with leadership.

Leadership attributes are not required in all roles. Freelance writers, stand-up comics, or truck drivers don't necessarily need to lead anyone. They might, however, have people in their lives who look to them as leaders: Every parent, for instance, is in a position of leadership, no matter what they might do to earn a living. Even without that responsibility, though, having a few of these attributes can be handy. Accountability, specifically, helps optimize performance in other areas.

IN COMPLEX ENVIRONMENTS, TAKING action is paramount. Even if that action is making a decision to do nothing, it's important to understand what you're doing and why. Just as important is recognizing that any consequences of that action are your responsibility—you have to fully own those decisions.

Being accountable and owning our decisions and actions serves several purposes. One, it requires that we understand *why* we're doing whatever action we've chosen, which in turn helps us to be fully committed to it. The officer candidate who effectively processed the profanity-laced complaints of the team members—as opposed to merely hearing them as baseless whining—could understand the logical, legitimate concerns and explain them to me. He could also cogently explain to the men the logical and strategic reasons why I was putting my foot down and allow everyone to come up with a better plan. Purpose provides clarity. It's nearly impossible to truly own an action if you aren't clear why you're taking it. If you fully own your decisions, you will be better able to explain the reasons behind them.

Two, being accountable allows us to look objectively and critically at the results of a decision, which helps us assess the results more accurately and make the next decision more effectively. If the mission plan ends up not working as well as possible, the accountable officer and men will studiously figure out what could have been done better rather than dismissing any flaws as "the boss made us do it that way." Better decisions will be made next time, and everyone will improve—a far better outcome than repeating a cycle of grudgingly doing what the powers that be demand.

Finally, taking responsibility for a decision and its results immediately engages the learnability attribute (Chapter Eleven). Remember, we human beings are wired to make sense of our environment. While much of that happens automatically and unconsciously, part of that process is very deliberate. At the risk of oversimplifying, this takes place in the form of questions we ask ourselves and which our brains reflexively try to answer.

Try this experiment to see what I mean. Get a blank sheet of paper and set a timer for two minutes. At the top of the paper, write an open-ended question; let's use "What are some ways I can double my income?" Now start the timer and start scribbling answers. Don't worry about how practical they are—just jot down as many as you can.

Time's up. Now you should have a list in front of you, maybe two or three ideas, maybe a dozen. Some of them might be fanciful, like winning the lottery. Some—get a second job, work a lot of overtime—are probably practical. Maybe a few are inane, because robbing a bank and selling a kidney are both terrible ideas. But that's okay! The specific answers don't really matter. The point is, you lodged a question in your frontal lobe and immediately began to come up with answers.

We do this to ourselves all the time, only we don't always pay attention to the quality of the questions. Without even realizing it, all sorts of distracting queries start to pollute our thinking.

Why does stuff like this always happen to me?

Why am I so bad at this?

Why are they always out to get me?

Once asked, our brains can't help but start trying to answer those questions. Many times, the answers will be no more than random, anxiety-driven guesses, a flailing attempt to make sense of forces and factors we can't control. When we have a high degree of accountability, however, we shift from unconsciously foundering on the unpredictable external to consciously considering the internal.

What are ways that I can get better results?

How can I improve?

Who are those people who can help me?

We can't control a complex environment, but we can control how we decide to act and react. Accountability prepares us to ask critically useful questions about performance, as opposed to less useful ones about what unseen or unpredictable forces are to blame. Leaders who are accountable—in their actions, reactions, and thinking—inspire confidence and develop trust among those they lead.

ACCOUNTABILITY CAN BEST BE seen and measured in environments that make being accountable both difficult and consequential.

Let's go back to those officer candidates. That exercise was useful because it put them in a pressure cooker. They were being told by a senior officer, whom they wanted to impress, to do things in a way that might be risky and that really ticked off the team members, whom they also wanted to impress. Moreover, saddling them with two stipulations was intentionally problematic: In that particular scenario, adhering to both would most likely put the immediate mission and men at risk, while ignoring both would damage the broader strategic objectives. Candidates were trapped between their superiors and their subordinates.

Most of the candidates would deliver my orders to the team members, then hear out their complaints. The style with which those complaints were delivered—with shouting and obscenities—was meant to throw the candidate off-balance, but the substance was legitimate. Accountable candidates listened closely, separated the serious concerns from the grumblings, then delivered a cogent explanation to me. Those candidates did not tell me the men were unhappy—they told me why the mission was unworkable under my stringent conditions.

Every officer, like every employee or teammate, will at times be asked to do something with which he does not fully agree. There also will be times when a directive from above is flawed or just plain wrong. Leadership means knowing the difference, speaking up, and standing firm on what's right. Speaking truth to power is never easy, but it's critical in high-performing teams—especially as a leader. In this case, one of those two constraints—the callout or the local forces—had to go. Did any of the candidates fully agree with keeping even one of those conditions? Probably not. But they could understand my reasoning and recognize why my rules were necessary even if not ideal, then embrace my order and present it to the team in a way that inspired confidence. They were, as I put it before, fully owning that decision.

But there was that one candidate who told me *the guys* were complaining, and who told his men that *the boss* was holding firm. He didn't explain what *he* thought because he wasn't accountable.

As a senior officer, I saw in that candidate someone who'd too easily placate the whims of those under his command. Also, it was clear that he hadn't processed the concerns of his men. Instead of analyzing their input, weighing competing factors, and then expressing his own considered perspective, he was merely passing the decision-making from his guys to me, and then from me to the guys. He was being a mediator, not a leader.

As with most attributes, no single test should be the sole judge of someone's accountability. Even those of us who are pretty high on accountability can think of times when we were less accountable than we wanted to be. This is where environment and intensity matter. Different situations allow us to see accountability in a variety of shades. Accountability might manifest differently in combat drills than it does in the office, out partying in town, or when no one is looking at all. Accordingly, we didn't definitively peg that officer candidate as having low accountability until we'd put him through a few other accountability-heavy situations that week. We saw similar results in each, which gave us confidence in our assessment—after all, we needed to be accountable for the reasons we weren't selecting him.

LEADERSHIP ROLL-UP

One thing that I learned during my military career is that when it comes to being in charge, there are generally two kinds of people: drivers and leaders.

Drivers see their organization or team as a mechanical system, and they consider the people they're in charge of to be parts—buttons to push, levers to pull, pedals to press. Because they believe their vision is the most important one or the only valid one, they exert control through heavy-handed direction and overt manipulation, sometimes with rewards but more often with punishments. If one of those parts doesn't perform as demanded, it's replaced without a second thought. There is no empathy because parts are expendable; no one mourns the worn-out brakes on their car.

Drivers might get results for a while, maybe even a long while if they churn through enough parts. But like any overworked and poorly maintained mechanical system, the gears eventually begin to grind. Depersonalized workers become demoralized subordinates. No one follows a driver—they're being pushed instead.

Leaders are different.

All types of leaders—parents and siblings; commanding officers and CEOs; presidents and priests; athletes and office managers—have one thing in common: They inspire.

People follow leaders willingly, eagerly, because leaders motivate and influence. They might instruct but they do not dictate, encourage but not manipulate. People perform at their best for leaders not because they were ordered to but because they want to.

Leaders are able to inspire because they have high levels of most of the leadership attributes: empathy, selflessness, authenticity, decisiveness, and accountability. You already know that, you have *always* known that, even if the concept was never broken into those specific components. Just think of the people you consider leaders in your own life—you can see those attributes clearly.

You don't need to have exceptional levels of all five. You don't need to be perfect. Anyone who's been in charge understands that's an impossible standard. (That's precisely why accountability and empathy are key: Effective leaders understand the effect of their mistakes on others, and take responsibility.) At times, leadership might even require briefly behaving like a driver.

And that will be okay. When leaders inspire and influence, they also build trust, nurture confidence, and earn respect. Remember, other people decide whether you're a leader and whether they will follow because leadership is a behavior. Develop it and become one.

THE TEAMABILITY ATTRIBUTES

A high-performing team is defined less by how often it wins than by how well it loses.

Winning and losing are how we typically keep score. But that's not always the most effective measure of performance. When the rules are clear, the obstacles are known, and the competition is predictable, winning can be fairly easy, especially for those with an abundance of practiced skills.

But what about those times when the rules aren't clear, obstacles keep cropping up, and the setbacks and disappointments outweigh the achievements? When circumstances are uncertain and situations are unstable?

That's when the teams that merely win a lot get separated from those that are truly high-performing.

Let's be clear about what a team is: any group of two or more people who work together toward a common goal or objective. The New Orleans Saints are a team, obviously, but a marriage is a team, too. So is the accounting department, the teachers in a school, the staff at a hospital, the local bar band, three friends on a long road trip. How a team—the members and the collective whole—absorbs hardship, challenge, and outright defeat matters. The degree to which teammates trust one another, how well they relate to one another, how comfortably they lean on one another matters. Teams that do those things well are able to perform their best in any situation and environment.

Those teams are more than high performers—they are *optimal* performers.

Sometimes exercising skills at a peak level is difficult. Sometimes the best possible performance is messy, gritty, and uncomfortable. Optimal performers, people and teams, have the confidence and ability to keep moving forward anyway.

TEAMABILITY IS ABOUT HOW well people work and play together, how deeply they connect, and how effectively they collaborate. Much like with being a leader, you don't get to decide whether you're a good teammate. Others will instinctively make that assessment for you, and they will do so based upon how well you perform and interact with them. How relatively important each of those criteria is will vary from team to team and person to person. Sometimes the grumpy guy is worth keeping around because of his specific talent, and sometimes the person who struggles with learning specific tasks is nonetheless a calming influence on everyone else.

The most important factor, though, the one underlying the others but often unspoken and unexamined, is trust.

Trust is not an attribute. It's a belief. In the context of teams, it's a belief that the other members will do their jobs, that they will support one another, and that they will maintain the cohesion of the group. In fact, when teams fail—that is, when they are unable to remain together as a team—it is almost always because of a lack of trust on some level.

We can't force other people to trust us. We can only behave in a manner that allows others to make the decision to trust us. The next four attributes—integrity, conscientiousness, humility, and humor—inform behaviors that encourage trust.

Those are each useful in other settings, too. But people who have high levels of all or most of them likely are successful members of teams. Those with lower levels probably find teamwork fractious, ineffective, and disappointing—and their teammates would almost certainly agree.

As with all of the attributes, these are not set in stone. The levels of all four can be increased with enough practice and determination. But remember: Just like with leadership, you don't get to decide if you're a good teammate or if other people trust you. That's up to your teammates. If you're functioning well in a high-performing team, especially during rough patches, you can be confident that you're doing the right things.

CHAPTER TWENTY-TWO

THE SUBJECTIVITY
OF RIGHT AND WRONG

Integrity: *The ability to act in accordance with relevant moral values and social and cultural norms*

IMAGINE YOU'RE TAKING THE final exam in a college course. Sixteenth-century European history is interesting, but the class was harder than you expected. Still, you haven't missed a lecture, you've done all the reading, and you've been studying every night for the final. If you can concentrate during the exam, you should be fine.

But you're distracted by the guy next to you. His name is James, but you don't know him well. He's been absent a lot, and he spent most of his time texting when he did show up. He even dozed off once or twice. And now he's fidgeting. He's turning up the corner of his exam every few minutes, stealing glances at a slip of paper he's trying to keep hidden. Jim is obviously cheating. He finishes when you've still got seven questions left.

The exam is over, and you see James out in the hallway, texting. You turn to a friend, about to unload about Jim, when you hear your name. It's the professor. She wants to talk to you.

You follow her to a quiet corner of the room. She tells you she thinks the student sitting next to you was cheating, and she wants to know if you noticed anything unusual. Cheating is a serious offense, she says, and the consequences are severe, a failing grade at the very least, maybe even expulsion. If you have anything to say, come by her office later. She'll make sure you remain anonymous.

What do you do?

Some of you—we'll call you Group 1—will go to her office. Of course you'll say something! James is lazy and dishonest! It's wrong to cheat, and it's unfair to the students who actually put in the effort.

Or perhaps you're in Group 2. Sure, cheating is bad, but, c'mon, it's sixteenth-century European history. There's probably not much use for the information beyond the final exam and, besides, who wants to be a rat?

And the rest of you, Group 3, just don't want to get involved either way.

Which group has integrity here?

Now, before you go patting yourself on the back, Group 1 people, let's game this out one more step. You leave the classroom and catch up with your friend. He asks what the professor wanted. You nod toward Jim and tell your friend the professor thought he might have cheated.

"Oh, man, that poor bastard," your friend says. Turns out he knows James better than you do. He lives in a poor neighborhood the next town over with his mom, who raised him by herself. James is the first in the family to go to college, but only because his mom saved for years and he got a couple of small academic scholarships. But four months ago, his mom was diagnosed with stage IV breast cancer. They don't have insurance and they can't afford help, so James has been taking care of her. When he's not home, he texts her, checking in, trying to keep his mom's spirits up. He hasn't gotten a lot of sleep, and he's just squeaking by in his classes. But he's got a job lined up as soon as he graduates, a good one with good benefits. Neither his job nor his major have anything to do with sixteenth-century European history. He took it as an elective for the same reason you did—he thought it would be interesting. But if he fails, he won't graduate and he won't get the job.

Now what's the right thing to do?

THERE IS NO OBJECTIVE guide to behaving with integrity. We often fool ourselves into believing that there is, that there is always a right thing and a wrong thing and that the choice between them is binary. But deep down we all know better. Right and wrong are almost never black and white because the world is shaded in grays. Context is everything.

Certainly there are guideposts. Laws, both criminal and civil, lay out a detailed list of what things people are not supposed to do. But there is also an entire legal profession, lawyers and judges and arbitrators, to argue about and interpret and properly apply those laws. Religions dictate moral codes, but there are caveats and exceptions within those, too. Thou shalt not kill, except for all the times it's acceptable to kill. Philosophers have pondered secular ethics for millennia. Is it always wrong to hurt another person? What if hurting one person helps a hundred people?

All those different codes and dogmas and rules, meanwhile, are in conflict with one another. Immoral things have been perfectly legal, moral acts have been illegal, and the definitions of both shift with time and perspective. Surely we can now all agree that slavery was immoral. But what about the death penalty? Abortion? Leaving jugs of water in the desert for migrants illegally crossing the border who might otherwise die of thirst? One person's atrocity is another's triumph: ISIS fighters are as certain of their righteousness as the Spanish Inquisitors were of theirs. Even zealots can act with integrity.

Humans evolved as social creatures. As we've already discussed, the need to belong to a group was a matter of survival, and that instinct is still powerful. We are all shaped and conditioned by the groups to which we belong—family, friends, co-workers, congregants, fellow citizens, and so on—and we tend to behave in ways that will maintain our status within those groups. To take an extreme example, a gangster who behaves with integrity *within his group* is less concerned with being a law-abiding citizen than he is with keeping his mouth shut about crimes committed by his fellow gangsters.

The truth is, there is no one set of absolutely correct instructions for doing the right thing. As a society, we've ballparked some guidelines, and most of us agree on the big generalities. Lying, stealing, murdering—there's not an enormous amount of disagreement that such things are bad. But even within what seem like consensus rules, there are gray areas. If you don't tell the professor that James was cheating, is that lying by omission? Is the right thing to tell the truth, get James expelled, cost him his job and his mother her health care?

WHILE BEHAVING WITH INTEGRITY is relative, the attribute is not. Each of us knows what right and wrong feel like. Each of us can grope through those gray areas and find the decent, proper, and correct thing to do. Those who are high on the integrity scale will do so consistently, regardless of the personal consequences. If admitting a mistake gets you fired, if standing up for a friend gets you punched in the head, if paying for the damage to the neighbors' fence cleans out your savings, so be it. Having integrity, and acting upon it, means having a clear conscience regardless of the detriment to you.

Doing the right thing, again, depends on how you define the right thing. And that takes us back to your personal values. Let's revisit James. As you read those first couple of paragraphs, you immediately began applying your values. Some of you would never cheat, ever, under any circumstances, and would report anyone who did. Others mentally shrugged: *Meh, it's a history test, sometimes you gotta play a little loose with the rules.* And many of you would never cheat but couldn't care less if someone else does.

None of you are necessarily wrong. You just have different values. Perhaps you value the sanctity of the test as a measure of academic achievement. Or maybe you value the knowledge gained through the course but think tests are an imperfect, and thus meaningless, metric of that knowledge.

Yet when you learned more about James's circumstances, your values were still being applied and, quite possibly, your perspective shifted. Most of us place a higher value on empathy and compassion than a random, one-off test. The meaning of *do the right thing* changed with the context.

SO HOW DOES INDIVIDUAL integrity apply to teams? In two ways, one building on the other.

First, integrity is a foundational element of trust, both in ourselves and with others. As individuals, if we can't trust ourselves to do what we believe is the right thing, we lose confidence in ourselves. And if you don't trust you, why should anyone else?

Second, integrity among individuals naturally leads to integrity within the group. Trust is imperative to any team that hopes to function at an optimal level. When members of a group trust one another, unity and cohesion are easier to maintain. Each member of the team can expect the others to do the right thing for themselves *and* the larger group.

Again, what that "right thing" is will vary from group to group. Indeed, it will be defined by the members, their mission, and the circumstances. One sports team, for instance, might value fair play as its highest priority. An athlete who cheats, then, would violate the team's ethos and be a drag on performance. Another team might value winning above all else—which means a player who's a stickler for the rules might never gain that team's trust.

Integrity can't be assessed in a team environment until the values and culture of the team have been identified. And that has to be done honestly and candidly. Whatever that ethos is, it can't be forced upon the group. In other words, integrity within a group can't be defined by what a few leaders or executives *want* it to be. Ideally, those leaders have exemplified and rewarded behavior that aligns with their definition, and in that way have assembled a team that mirrors it. But the group always sorts out its own standards.

Then it requires time to assess. Integrity is an attribute that only matters if it's consistent across myriad environments. If someone or some team does the right thing in times of stress, in times of uncertainty, under the glare of a spotlight, and when no one is looking, that's integrity.

CHAPTER TWENTY-THREE

THERE'S ALWAYS SOMETHING TO DO

Conscientiousness: *The ability and inner drive to work hard, to be diligent, and to be reliable*

I MET CHRIS WITHROW IN the late summer of 1996, when we both began BUD/S class 210. He was one of the youngest guys in the class, a kid at only twenty, and he was little, a skinny blond who might have weighed 120 pounds soaking wet.

But that's why he stood out, or why I remember him.

The first phase of BUD/S involves a lot of time in IBSs, or inflatable boats that are a slightly smaller version of the rubber Zodiacs you're used to seeing in the movies (the S in IBS stands for *small*). Every day, the boats had to be pulled out of the water and washed. The floorboards had to come out, the paddles had to be put away, and the whole thing had to be inspected for rips and punctures and, if necessary, patched. Those boats are heavier than you probably imagine, too—it takes at least four guys to carry them, and part of the torture of Hell Week is lugging them around on your head for hours at a time.

We called it PMS-ing—planned maintenance system— and it was grunt work. No glamour, no badass overtones. But Chris was always first in line. And in the morning when the boats had to go back in the water, he was first there, too. He always had his own gear ready for inspection, which gave him time to help other guys get their gear ready.

When we moved to the second phase, Chris was constantly volunteering to do something, maybe maintenance on the dive gear, maybe hauling out the trash.

"That's one of the qualities they're looking for in BUD/S," Chris says. "They're always looking for guys who'll go the extra mile, guys who are willing to help out."

True. But most of us have to decide to go that extra mile. We need to put in the effort to convince ourselves to put in the effort. With Chris, it seemed to just happen, as natural as breathing. If something needed to be done, Chris was willing to do it. And if nothing needed to be done, he would find something.

He was diligent, reliable, and one of the hardest workers in the class. In a word, he was conscientious.

ONE OF THE MOST common models psychologists use to explain personalities is called the five-factor model or, using an acronym built from the five factors, OCEAN: openness, conscientiousness, extroversion, agreeableness, and neuroticism. As a personality component, conscientiousness is an amalgam of traits and behaviors. Persistence, thoroughness, and predictability are key parts of a conscientious personality, as are resourcefulness, energy, and planning.

As mentioned before, however, personality traits are different from attributes. Personalities are built from patterns of behavior that emerge over an extended period of time. It's the outward expression of all the things that make you *you*— your skills, habits, emotions, perspectives, and, yes, attributes, all blended together. A multitude of factors influence your personality, from genetics to upbringing to environment.

Attributes, as you understand by now, are more elemental. They can be tweaked and developed, but they're wired into our personal circuitry. Conscientiousness as an attribute, then, has a narrower focus than it does in the OCEAN model. Chris is a good example because at the level of an attribute, conscientiousness involves three things he consistently displayed—the ability and innate desire to be diligent, to be reliable, and to work hard.

To hear Chris tell it, he wasn't always conscientious. His father died when he was young. As the only child of a single mother living in a rough neighborhood, Chris remembers feeling like he grew up in survival mode. He was a quiet kid who kept to himself, didn't reach out to others for help, and didn't offer any to others, either.

His uncle, his dad's twin brother, was the closest he had to a father figure. As an ATV enthusiast, he used to take Chris and his own kids, Chris's cousins, out to the sand dunes for long days of riding.

Chris was the youngest among the cousins, and for a while that got him a pass on the labor required to get the ATVs ready. "I was always kind of oblivious," he says. "Everyone was working hard, getting everything ready, and I was just bebopping around, not even conscious that I was being a slug."

Until one trip when he was approximately ten years old. "One of my cousins pulled me aside and just lit my ass up," he says. "He was yelling at me. 'You need to help! You notice how hard we're working here? You're doing nothing! You should always be looking for something to do!'"

At that moment, something clicked for Chris. Embarrassed and upset with himself, he immediately found a task that needed to be done, and when he finished that one, he found another. Getting yelled at was a shock to his system that seemed to jolt him into being a conscientious person.

But was it really that moment? Did he become conscientious right then?

No. Some attributes can lie dormant, or seem to, if there's no particular need to use them. Chris had simply never been in circumstances that teased out an obvious show of his conscientiousness. "Looking back, I'd always been someone who didn't want to let other people down," he says—which is a pretty good description of a latently conscientious child. When his cousin chewed him out, it was easy for him to step up his game, put himself to work, and then look for more. His cousin had simply summoned an attribute that Chris had all along.

And it stayed with him. When he played hockey in high school for a coach with "an old-school Russian mentality"— tough, raw, brutal—he trained harder, practiced harder, played harder. When he left the SEALs after eight years and became a law enforcement officer, his diligence, reliability, and hard work led to one promotion after another. As the commander of a SWAT team, his conscientiousness established the tone for the team. As we discussed in the leadership attributes, leaders need to model and reward the behavior they want to see more of. *If the boss is always looking for something to do,* the theory goes, *maybe I should be, too.*

"It's all in line with what my uncle and cousin told me," he says. "Always be looking for something to do. Give the extra effort all the time. Be someone people can count on."

CONSCIENTIOUSNESS MATTERS IN THE context of a team because it fosters trust. This isn't an esoteric concept, no trick of brain chemistry. It's common sense, and you understand it intuitively. Think of the people in your own life, personal or professional, whom you trust. Odds are most of them are dependable, reliable, and hardworking in one way or another. Maybe they don't follow through on everything, and maybe they're a little flaky now and again. But in the areas in which you trust them, they display a respectable level of conscientiousness. Otherwise, you wouldn't trust them.

That same concept applies to teams. Trust is paramount. Each member can operate more efficiently and more confidently if all the other members can be counted on to do so, too.

Being conscientious, however, might look slightly different depending on the type of team. On some, staying focused on a particular task, regardless of how others are performing, is paramount. On a football team, for example, an offensive lineman isn't expected to pick up the slack in the quarterback's passing game—his job is to block, and if he is a conscientious lineman, that's what he'll stick to. Other types of teams, though, are more fluid. Even among groups with a rigid hierarchy and distinct levels of responsibility, being conscientious might mean blurring the roles. When my troop chief, Hank, and I were stuck in the planning room working on a mission brief, guys would filter in to see if they could help. And once the mission was set and briefed, Hank and I would see what we could do to help the guys get ready. There was always something to be done, and always guys looking for help. (Except for the snipers. They don't like people touching their guns.)

As with perseverance and resilience, it's difficult to argue that someone can be *too* conscientious or that a team can have too many conscientious members. But it's important to remember the three components of conscientiousness, and that they all are necessary. A hard worker isn't much use if he's not diligent once he gets started or isn't reliable enough to show up. A reliably lazy person doesn't bring much to the table, either. But someone who shows up and works hard until the task is complete will be an asset to any team.

CHAPTER TWENTY-FOUR

PLAY BLACK, NOT RED

Humility: *The ability to be self-aware and transparent about one's strengths and weaknesses*

THERE'S A DECEPTIVELY SIMPLE game we play in one of the leadership workshops at the Chapman & Co. Institute. It's called Red/Black, and it involves two teams, each of which is given two laminated cards. On one card the word *black* is printed in black ink, and on the other is the word *red* in red ink.

The rules are minimal. First, teams can't talk to one another; that is, they can only communicate with their own teammates. Second, for each round the teams simultaneously lay one card on the table. We do a countdown to add a little excitement: "Three, two, one . . . reveal!"

Scoring is as follows:

- If both teams play their black card, they both get a point.

- If both teams play their red card, they both lose a point.

- But if one team reveals red and the other shows black, the red team gets a point and the black team loses one.

The objective is to accumulate the maximum number of points. We play for several rounds—although we know how many we'll play, and thus how many points are possible, we don't tell the players—and see where the score ends up. The exercise is designed to highlight a few different ideas and discussion points, such as creating competition where none exists (the objective is to accumulate points, not beat the other team) and the power of communication (not being able to communicate a strategy between teams usually results in them feeling like they are against each other). But the most interesting part is what happens in the very first round. Each team immediately faces a choice:

Do we go on offense and play red? Or do we take a risk, play black, and hope the other side does, too?

Let's game this out. If you play red and the other team plays black, you'll get a point. But the other team is only going to fall for that once. Next thing you know, both teams are throwing red and losing points in a mutually destructive aggression pact. But if you play black and the other team plays red, you'll lose a point. But you're no dummy—you'll only fall for that once, too.

But here's the thing: Both teams are debating that same decision. Each team could start with black, but that only works if the other team does, too. So that choice is risky. It requires laying down arms, the red card, and extending an olive branch, the black one. It means being vulnerable and extending some trust in their opponents' motives.

What do you do?

I can tell you from experience that leading with red is a losing strategy. In fact, the only time we've seen a team collect the maximum points is when both teams consistently play black. And that almost always begins with that first round. If both teams lead with black cards, the odds rise exponentially that they'll continue playing black. That initial act of trust compounds upon itself and is reinforced with each round.

Building trust with others is a generative act. That is, the trust you are willing to place in others generates the trust they will place in you. And deciding to trust often follows from a position of vulnerability.

Think of every trust-building exercise you've ever been a part of or even heard about. Falling backward into the arms of co-workers, or answering creepily silly questions, or doing anything blindfolded (blindfolds, if you're new to this, are very popular among the trust-building set) all require being vulnerable in one way or another. You could actually fall on your head. What's one thing people don't know about you? Probably something you don't want people to know. The blindfolds mean, you know, you can't see.

But those exercises are popular because they work. Vulnerability leads to trust, and trust builds upon itself.

Yet there is an underlying component that sets that process in motion. In order to allow oneself to be vulnerable, it helps to have a healthy level of humility.

HUMILITY OFTEN IS STIGMATIZED, especially in high-performance arenas. It can be seen as weakness or a lack of confidence, "a modest or low view of one's own importance," as one dictionary puts it.

As an attribute, though, humility means being transparent about your weaknesses. That's not the same as false modesty or the occasional humble brag but rather an honest assessment of one's abilities. That also means being vulnerable—admitting weakness by definition requires vulnerability—but it's critical in the context of teamability.

One of the strengths of any high-performing team lies in understanding its weaknesses. Being open about your own allows others to understand where they can help.

Humans are designed to recognize hierarchy in groups, an outgrowth of the animalistic instinct to recognize the alpha. As we discussed in the chapter on narcissism, we are biologically rewarded for being an alpha or even supporting an alpha. Among people, however, alpha is not always a static position—it can shift depending on the situation and circumstances. In our cave-dwelling days, this wasn't difficult to figure out: If a bear is attacking, Dad steps up; if the baby is crying because it's hungry, Mom becomes the alpha.

Among modern humans, with all of our specialized skills and competencies, it gets even fuzzier. Our brains don't like fuzzy, though, so mostly we default to whoever has been designated *the leader* in a particular hierarchy. The ship is taking on water? Look to the captain. Department falling short of its quarterly goals? Talk to the department head. Military mission went sideways? Take it up with the senior officer.

Ideally, the people in leadership positions would always be the most qualified to handle such problems because—again, ideally—the hierarchical systems have placed the most experienced and knowledgeable people at the top. But we don't live in an ideal world. Too often, we conflate the alpha with the person in charge, and that's not always the case. The best person to step up for any given problem could come from anywhere on a team. But to do so, they must first feel like they can.

Dan Coyle, in his book *The Culture Code,* describes the vulnerability loop, which is the ability of members of a group to rapidly and comfortably signal their weakness to other members. This is an admission of vulnerability, of course, in that it shows that they don't have all the answers. But that display also encourages trust and cooperation, giving every other member tacit permission to speak up and act as needed. Coyle, who highlights several experiments that have tested that theory, explains that deliberate vulnerability increases human cooperation—even among strangers. That cooperation is the key to teamwork, especially in demanding, high-stakes environments.

The great leaders understand the vulnerability loop, even if unconsciously. And they take it one step further by not overemphasizing their own experience, knowledge, and strengths. That, too, is a component of humility, and it has a similar effect to admitting weakness. A boss who brags about his strengths can be intimidating, often to the detriment of the team. Yet by remaining humble, while still confident, in those abilities, that same boss quietly encourages others to offer ideas that might be better in some ways. A chief who boasted incessantly about his ability to kill bears with a club, for instance, might have dissuaded the kid with the new-fangled spear from speaking up.

A few years ago, at a workshop about high-performing teams, I met a prominent heart surgeon who routinely performed eight- to ten-hour surgeries. That's the epitome of a high-stakes environment that requires an optimally performing team.

"One of the primary rules in my operating room," he told the group, "is that we only use first names."

There is a well-defined hierarchy in an OR, with the lead surgeon at the apex. But in the midst of an operation, where a mistake can jeopardize a patient's life, it's critical that every member of the team feels free to speak up if they see something going wrong. Using first names, the surgeon explained, helped break down the psychological barriers built into the hierarchy. It's a small tweak with enormous implications. After all, it's much easier to say, "Hey, Doug, I think this might be wrong," as opposed to, "Excuse me, Doctor, are you sure you're doing that right?"

That sort of thing is not uncommon among high-performing teams. As a troop commander, for example, none of my men called me "sir" or called Hank "chief." Frankly, it would have felt weird if they had. They called us Rich and Hank. This is standard practice among SEALs and was designed that way by Draper Kaufmann in the beginning. Since the inception of the Naval Combat Demolition Units, officers and enlisted men have gone through the exact same training, side by side. This is different from most other services, where enlisted men and officers have separate training. SEALs even extend that practice to their warfare pin. In most of the rest of the Navy, the enlisted pin is silver and the officers' is gold. Every SEAL wears a gold pin, an eagle with its head bowed and clutching a U.S. Navy anchor, a trident, and a flintlock pistol. Although not an official canon, many SEALs regard the eagle's bowed head, typically held high in other military insignia, as exemplifying the humility of a true warrior, honoring all those who have come before him.

THERE IS A SWEET spot on the humility scale, and it is quite wide. But there is danger at either extreme end, either too much or too little.

A lack of humility often resembles arrogance. While that's almost always a by-product of fear or insecurity, arrogance on any team is detrimental. It breeds resentment, stifles communication, and, as a result, is brutal in terms of results. Just think back to Julie's imploding dream team from the opening chapters.

Too much humility, though, risks teetering into meekness, which in turn can lead to inaction. Deference in support of empowering others is necessary for optimal performance, but there are times when you need to step up and be the alpha. You will be the expert in the room, the one who's been empowered by the deference of others, at which point you will need to take charge and perform with confidence. Great leaders understand this balance. They will defer until they've squeezed every ounce of potential out of their team, but they will not hesitate to assume control when required.

Moreover, an overabundance of humility can also mask an underlying lack of confidence. A lack of confidence, real or perceived, inevitably will begin to erode trust—which in turn will undermine any team.

Your own level of humility is difficult to self-assess. "Humility is a strange thing," Sir Edward Hulse, a nineteenth-century British politician, once said. "The minute you think you've got it, you've lost it." In other words, it's a paradox to boast about your own humility. It is, however, comparatively easy to ascertain in others—those who are transparent about their weaknesses and quietly certain of their strengths demonstrate a healthy level of humility. It also can be sussed out in the context of a group. In any team environment where there is little or no cross talk, sharing of ideas, or honest debriefs, that most likely speaks to a low level of team humility, which is determined by a similar deficit among its members.

So how do you encourage a healthy level of humility in others and yourself? Start with generosity. Being generous on a team—with your time, your effort, your compliments, respect—establishes a tone of giving instead of taking. Sincere, expressed appreciation for what each member brings to the table sends a powerful message with a resonant echo: *I need you because I can't do what you do.* That's what humility sounds like.

Next, when it comes to those things that you have mastered, those tasks and problems for which you are the alpha, remember the old adage: Mastery is a journey, not a destination. We've all known a blowhard who believes he's already arrived, that his expertise is final and eternal. No one likes that guy. No one trusts him. Accept, instead, that you are still on your journey.

Let me give you an example. We used to interview candidates to join our cadre of training instructors in the Navy. These were panel interviews, the candidate sitting at a table with three or four instructors who all asked questions. I went last, and I asked only one: How would you teach someone to ride a bicycle?

Seems simple, right? Except now you're thinking about it, and you don't have an easy answer. The reason is, you've already mastered riding a bike. You don't have to think about it while you're doing it. But now try to break it down into discrete, usable components so that you can explain your mastery to someone else. Really try to figure it out.

That feeling you have right now is humility.

CHAPTER TWENTY-FIVE

HONOR THE CLASS CLOWN

Humor: *The ability to find the funny—and laugh even when times are tough*

WHEN MY YOUNGER SON was five, he had a goldfish named Swimmy.

We also have a cat. His name is Leo. He killed Swimmy.

This was not completely unexpected. Leo is a cat, after all, and he'd already killed our older son's goldfish a few months earlier. We'd taken precautions, fortifying the tank with some heavy books stacked on top, and that seemed to work well until one day when it didn't. While the four of us were out, Leo managed to nudge the books off the tank, grab Swimmy with a paw, and toss him into the middle of the room, where Leo apparently batted him around and chewed him a bit.

Fortunately, our older son saw the carnage first. My wife diverted the younger one into the living room while I cleaned up the mess and flushed Swimmy down the toilet. Then we told our younger son.

He burst into tears. My wife and I held him, tried to comfort him. The death of a pet is wildly traumatic for a five-year-old. He caught his breath long enough to tell us he wanted to see Swimmy one more time to say goodbye and then bury him in the yard.

I shot my wife a look of mild panic. She didn't flinch. "Oh, honey," she said in her most soothing voice, "Daddy already flushed Swimmy down the toilet."

"What?" He resumed sobbing. "Why would you do *that*?"

She rolled with it. She told our son about Fish Heaven, a wonderful place where all goldfish end up, and how, because it's made of water, the fastest way for Swimmy to get there was through the plumbing.

He kept crying, deep, heartbreaking sobs. It was awful. Parents can feel the pain of their children acutely. His suffering grief for Swimmy became our grief for him.

But then he abruptly stopped and looked at us with a dead-serious expression.

"Wait," he said. "Does our *poop* go to heaven?"

He was quiet for a moment. Then he laughed at the absurdity of his own thought, and we started laughing with him.

HUMOR IS A POWERFUL attribute. The ability to laugh, to find the sliver of funny amid the tragic and the trying, can be calming, comforting, empowering, and encouraging. We've all heard the joke that broke the tension, the one-liner that smoothed an edge of fear, the wisecrack that distracted us from that nagging pain. Exactly *what* we find humorous is a matter of taste, but we've all been some version of that five-year-old, devastated by the loss of a pet, who was briefly relieved by our own silly thoughts.

"Laughter is the best medicine" is a well-worn cliché because there is an enormous amount of truth to it. When we laugh, our bodies release an assortment of feel-good chemicals that have both neurological and physiological effects. "We don't laugh because we're happy," the psychologist and philosopher William James said more than a hundred years ago. "We're happy because we laugh."

The chemical rewards begin with the neurotransmitter dopamine. As a reminder, it doesn't create a pleasurable sensation but rather tells the brain that a certain activity is pleasurable—in this case, laughter. Immediately, and in even the most dire of circumstances, a jolt of dopamine brightens the mood by creating a mental echo of joy and amusement.

Laughter also triggers the release of oxytocin, the appropriately nicknamed "love hormone" stimulated by human interaction that we covered in Chapter Sixteen. If you've ever wondered why laughter seems to be contagious, oxytocin is part of the reason why. The other reason is those mirror neurons that we talked about in Chapter Seventeen on empathy. Much like a physical hug or even an affectionate gaze, hearing or seeing someone else laugh or smile both stimulates our mirror neurons and causes the release of oxytocin, which helps to build bonds between people.

And then there are endorphins, another neurotransmitter. In the early 1970s, researchers discovered that opiates, like heroin and morphine, interact with specialized receptors in the brain that hinder or block pain signals. But why would human brains have opiate receptors in the first place? The most plausible theory is that the body must produce its own opiate-like substance.

That substance is endorphins, the body's own wonder drug. You know that euphoric rush that comes after a hard workout or in the middle of a long run? Those are endorphins flooding your system, minimizing pain and discomfort, maximizing pleasure and well-being. From an evolutionary perspective, endorphins are critical. If people needed to trek for days or run for miles to hunt down dinner, or if they needed to sprint away from becoming dinner, endorphins encouraged them to keep moving. The body also releases endorphins during pleasurable activities, like eating, drinking, and sex—all the fundamental requirements for surviving and procreating.

That combination—dopamine, oxytocin, and endorphins—is extraordinarily potent. And they're all released when we laugh. The process is involuntary, too; you'll be flooded with those chemicals whether you want to be or not. William James didn't understand all the neurochemistry, but he figured out the cause and effect: Laughing makes us feel good.

ONE NIGHT DURING HELL Week when we were lying in the freezing surf, the instructors taunted us from the edge of the beach. "We got warm blankets," one of them yelled. "Warm blankets for anyone who rings that bell. Anyone who wants to quit, we got hot coffee and doughnuts, too. Just get up and ring the bell."

It was meant to tempt us, but it was almost cruel. The water was bone cold, and the spray stung like wind-driven sleet. Every second seemed like a minute, every minute an hour. Hell Week is a miserable experience, and the surf zone was one of the most immiserating components. I tried to block out the instructor's voice; even thinking about a warm blanket was torture.

The guy next to me piped up. "You got any chocolate glazed ones?" he hollered over the rush of the surf. "Because I ain't quitting unless you got chocolate glazed!"

I burst out laughing. I knew right then that guy—the guy who could make a joke during a singularly awful experience—wasn't going to quit, and I knew that I wouldn't, either. But I looked at the man to my left. He was grim-faced, shivering, unable to laugh because he was lost in the pain of the moment. I remember thinking, *He's not gonna make it.*

Five minutes later, he rang the bell.

I heard there weren't any chocolate glazed doughnuts.

As an attribute, humor is not necessarily synonymous with being funny. If you can make other people laugh, terrific. You're probably fairly high on the humor scale. But more important is whether you can laugh, because that can have a direct effect on your performance and that of your team—especially in difficult circumstances.

Let's break down what happened in the surf that night. On the surface, it's fairly simple: A little quip eased the tension of a wretched experience and, in doing so, encouraged me to stay in the water and momentarily forget my pain. But that wasn't a completely conscious thought. When that joke set off my laugh, it automatically unleashed all of those feel-good chemicals.

We discussed dopamine in Chapter Four in the context of courage, which is the ability to step into fear. Fear is unavoidable in life; at some point, and probably at many points, each of us will face a challenge that scares us, an objective that intimidates us, circumstances that stir a withering dread. Courage allows us to move through that fear because a courageous act is one of the things that prompts the release of dopamine. It does not require that we conquer fear—simply confronting it is enough. That shot of dopamine is the brain saying *Yes! Keep going!*

It doesn't matter how that dopamine is produced. When I laughed, I got a dose of it that encouraged me to keep going. That makes laughter a kind of courage hack, as it replicates the neurochemical rewards of courage. (Just toughing out the night—which was its own kind of courage—generated some dopamine, too, but you can never have too much when you're getting drenched by icy ocean waves.) That applies to endorphins, as well: A good dose of them will ease pain and soothe anxiety no matter whether they're produced by a workout or a laugh.

My laugh also caused the production of oxytocin, the hormone that reinforces family and social bonds by rewarding certain kinds of contact. That warm feeling you get when you hug someone you care about, for instance, is oxytocin at work. It doesn't have to be physical contact for the love hormone to be released. A gaze into a lover's eyes or a long conversation with a friend will have the same effect. So will laughter. This phenomenon is obvious when we think about it. A shared laugh is a primal bonding experience, one that we've all experienced. Even strangers feel more connected to one another when they laugh together. Why do you suppose a sense of humor is among the top qualities people say they want in a partner? It's because humor generates a biochemical attraction and signals that a partner will help when times get rough.

This is why humor is so important in teams. An effective team is a cohesive team, and laughter strengthens bonds between members. It also helps the entire group to work through difficult problems; remember, think of laughter as a courage hack. In fact, I've yet to come across a high-performing team in any field—business teams, medical teams, SEAL teams, sports teams, marriages, families—that didn't rely on humor. There might be a primary *class clown,* or everyone might chip in with wry asides and goofy jokes. But the point is, they know how to laugh, and that enhances their performance.

CHAPTER TWENTY-SIX

DYNAMIC SUBORDINATION

NOT LONG AFTER I started working with business organizations, I found myself standing next to a whiteboard, stumped. The executives in the room wanted me to draw an organizational chart of a high-performing team, like, say, a SEAL team.

I had options. The most obvious was the classic pyramid with the leader at the top and widening layers of subordinates below. Originally designed by a Scottish American engineer named David McCallum in 1854, it was adopted by most businesses and other teams as a succinct visual representation of who reports to whom and how information and decisions flow down from the top. The military, with its hierarchical chain of command, is basically a giant pyramid.

But that didn't seem to fit a SEAL team. Special operators in a combat zone aren't quite as rigid with military formalities.

I briefly considered the flat model, which was sort of a mild rebellion against McCallum's pyramid. The pyramid was clear and authoritative, but it could also be cumbersome. Information and decisions had to move through each wicket, so if the guys at the bottom had a brilliant idea, it had to work its way up, level by level, to the peak, where a decision would be made and then passed down, level by level. "Flat" organizations, by contrast, reduced or even eliminated layers of middle management and decentralized decision-making. That definitely sped up the flow of information, but it was unmanageable for large organizations. Plus, it was often difficult to figure out who was in charge.

Then there was Robert K. Greenleaf's "servant-leader" model, which turned the pyramid upside down (and which we discussed in Chapter Eighteen). But Greenleaf was on a more philosophical mission to change the way executives view their relationship with employees, not necessarily improve organizational function.

Standing in front of those executives, a blank whiteboard next to me and a marker in my hand, I realized that none of those models adequately described my experience with SEAL teams. The flat model wasn't right because "decentralized" in practice often means "compartmentalized," and nothing on a high-performance team is walled off: Every action by any member affects the group. And the upside-down pyramid, while very noble, placed a tremendous load on the leader at the bottom. Yet in any optimally performing team, that load is distributed for maximum efficiency.

I stood there for a few moments, pondering my options. Finally, and mostly in frustration, I drew what looked like an amoeba. A blob.

"There," I said, tapping the whiteboard with my marker. "That's what it looks like."

My audience nodded thoughtfully.

"Now," I asked, "where would the leader sit in there?"

"In the center," someone said. "At the front edge," another one guessed. "At the back edge," said a third.

I smiled. "Correct," I said. "All of you are correct."

———

IN A HIGH-PERFORMANCE TEAM, leadership shifts to wherever, and whomever, the leader needs to be at any given moment. Those teams understand that information, challenges, and obstacles can come from any angle at any time. And they're effective because the teammate closest to the problem is able to step up and lead, while the rest of the group defers to that temporary leader.

I call this, my amoeba-shaped organizational plan, *dynamic subordination.* I figured it out in close-quarter combat training, where teams practice clearing rooms and buildings. As I explained in Chapter One, CQC is fluid and dynamic, and success depends on each member of the team adapting to an ever-changing environment. There needs to be a constant awareness of the most dangerous and immediate threat, and the man in the best position to know that, and direct a response, isn't based on rank or seniority.

Let's say a four-man team is securing a building with multiple rooms. The lead man enters and sweeps right, which means the second man sweeps left, and so on. The room is clear. But now the third man in is closest to the door to the next room. He has become the leader, and the rest of the team followers. The cycle repeats multiple times until the entire building is secure.

But what if, in that first room, there was a threat to the left? Then that second man, in that immediate moment, is leading the response. It doesn't matter if the first man is technically the boss—what matters is neutralizing the threat as quickly and efficiently as possible.

Dynamic subordination isn't limited to combat units, of course. Any high-performing team or organization can operate that way. In fact, it happens more often than you might think, especially where safety is paramount. The captain of a commercial airliner has absolute authority on his aircraft.

But if a mechanic calls him back to the gate because he wants to double-check a maintenance issue, any pilot worth his wings will automatically defer to the mechanic's expertise. When the flight attendants begin deplaning all those annoyed passengers, the captain doesn't take the lead on that, either—he gets out of the way and lets professionals do their jobs. That process—rapid, smooth, and efficient—is dynamic subordination.

There are two necessary elements. One is trust among all members of the team, which should be obvious. Everyone must believe that everyone else is competent, consistent, and working in the interests of the group. Allowing a renegade narcissist to assume the leadership role, even briefly, can shatter a team.

The other is a diversity of attributes specific to the mission or environment. That's not the same as the human-resource definition of diversity, but it is in alignment with it. People of different genders, races, ethnicities, and sexual orientations all bring different perspectives and experiences to the table, and those differences can influence which attributes develop more fully. As a general rule, the more diversity of attributes there is on a team, the better equipped it will be to deal with uncertainty and challenge.

There is no single list of best attributes for any given team. The attributes required for a SEAL team are different from those for a sales team, an accounting firm, or a human-resources department. Even teams that appear to be operating in the same general arena might need different attributes. A company of dramatic actors, for instance, would certainly insist on empathy being near the top, while a sketch comedy troupe might push it farther down the list. I'm guessing it's easier to find the funny in a funeral if you don't have a surfeit of empathy.

———

THE FIRST STEP IN developing an optimal team that can effectively utilize dynamic subordination is deciding which attributes would be most useful.

Start by asking that fundamental question: What attributes does this team need to accomplish its objectives? Then start throwing down answers. There are twenty-five attributes in this book, but they are not an exhaustive catalog. There are others out there—creativity and sociability, for instance—and you'll probably come up with more on your own. Don't be shy in this initial stage; if you think it's a useful attribute for your team, write it down.

Let's take a look at Julie's team, from the beginning of the book. Had she asked this question prior to assembling her team, she might have come up with a list that looked something like this:

ADAPTABILITY	MASTER CODER	CUNNING
LEGAL EXPERT	LEARNABILITY	ACCOUNTABILITY
DISCIPLINE	HUMILITY	MARKETING EXPERT
OPEN-MINDEDNESS	GRAPHICS MASTER	HUMOR

These twelve might not be the entire list that she came up with, but they are a healthy start.

Once you have your list, you'll need to pare away the skills. It's extremely easy to confuse skills with attributes. "Good listener," for example, is not an attribute but rather a skill that can be taught, and more easily to someone with a high level of empathy. Likewise, "great presenter" is a skill rooted in situational awareness and self-efficacy, and "critical thinking" can be taught to anyone with reasonable levels of the mental acuity attributes. Remember, if you can teach it or be taught it, it's a skill, not an attribute. The reason you sort this out *after* you make your first list is that it allows you to clarify what skills your team needs, which in turn will help pinpoint the most useful attributes. In Julie's case, things like master coder, legal expert, marketing expert, and graphics master could be culled. Again, they are not discarded but simply moved to another list as a guide to some of the skills that will also be important.

Now carefully consider your team members. It's unlikely that any one of them will have high levels of all the attributes on your list. But all of them should have some, and collectively they should fill the spectrum. And are there critical attributes that everyone needs? Are there some that can be covered by only one or two people? Because Julie's client already is known to be mercurial, all of her team members ideally should have higher levels of adaptability and accountability. Generous amounts of attributes such as cunning and humor, on the other hand, could be reserved to only one or two people. Those are both assets to any team, but in manageable amounts; the last thing Julie needs is six colleagues turning their cunning on one another or laughing too hard to get any work done.

This exercise also works well for a team that you might already be a part of. Understanding your current team will allow you to identify strengths, weaknesses, and any gaps that need to be filled.

ASSESSING ATTRIBUTES IN OTHERS is perhaps the trickiest part. The process outlined in Chapter Twenty-eight will help you get started. The key, though, is to shift your own focus from skills to attributes. That's what we did in our SEAL selection course. We had an excellent training program in which skills could be clearly identified and measured. But attributes could be, too—once we realized that we had to look for them. In CQC, for example, an operator was employing skills such as precision shooting, target acquisition, and breaching entryways. But the most successful ones were also displaying, and developing, attributes like awareness, compartmentalization, decisiveness, and adaptability. In dive training, the practiced skills were underwater navigation and pacing yourself to swim at exactly one knot while the attributes teased out included patience, self-efficacy, and humility (nothing humbles someone like the ocean).

This concept, this shift in focus, can be applied to almost any training regimen. Enhance it by tossing in some surprise uncertainty from time to time. I call this "training for the periphery," where you can use existing skill-training environments to develop attributes as well, and it's done all the time in special operations.

Remember, the environment matters. You're not going to see Larry's decisiveness and adaptability when he's sitting at a desk plugging sales numbers into a spreadsheet, though you might get a good peek at his level of conscientiousness. To help highlight certain attributes, you might need to create new environments for your team. That's what makes a well-constructed offsite so valuable: If you put a group of people into a situation none of them have experienced before, they might reveal attributes you've never seen before.

But even those situations need to be carefully calibrated and analyzed. Friendly competition can be a fine team-building exercise—except for all of the non-competitive people on your team. Whatever attributes you were hoping to draw out of those folks will be skewed by what a pain in the ass they find the whole thing to be. An outing to one of those "escape rooms" might be more effective, but beware of the loud guy in the group who starts barking orders. That might *appear* to be leadership. But if you're watching for attributes, you might see too much narcissism and self-efficacy manifesting as arrogance and too little open-mindedness and humility.

Be creative in developing scenarios, but keep the context relative to the attributes you're looking for. Take an accounting department to the beach for some predawn surf torture, and several attributes, or a lack thereof, will be apparent—though those likely won't be relevant to efficient accounting.

Finally, be certain to separate skills from attributes, just as you did with your list when you started this process. A sales team looking for a new associate, for example, might have an applicant present a sales pitch to a group. She has a day to prepare, and she nails it. Fantastic: She has spectacular preparation and presentation *skills*. But add an unexpected challenge. Change the product she's pitching at the last minute. Switch the task from making a pitch to fielding a complaint. Then you'll see her resilience, adaptability, and cunning.

Make no mistake: Those presentation skills are vitally important. Skills are the way most people measure the world, how they assess competence, how they determine which person belongs on which team and in what role. There's nothing inherently wrong with that. It's just not enough. A team built on skills will be great when everything goes as planned. Which is never. And that's when attributes matter the most.

CHAPTER TWENTY-SEVEN

THE OTHERS

EVERYONE HAS ALL OF the attributes. If any of the twenty-two I've described seem so unfamiliar that you can't imagine they're wired into you, trust me: They are. Remember, attributes aren't exotic quirks bestowed only upon elite performers. They are a basic part of being human. They are elemental.

Now, you might have a very low level of one or more of the attributes, maybe even a level approaching zero. That's okay. You, me, all the other humans—we all have a different mix. We're all low on some, high on others, and middling on the rest.

Let's go back to that idea of each attribute being represented by a sliding dimmer switch. When the dimmer is all the way down, it means there is very little of that attribute present; when the switch is higher, that attribute is more developed. Next, imagine all of those switches lined up in a row, side by side, and you plot a line across the position of the dimmers. Almost everyone will have an undulating, irregular wave, and almost no one's will be exactly the same as anyone else's.

In general, the more developed an attribute, the higher that dimmer, the better. There are a couple of notable exceptions—narcissism and cunning should be tempered—but it's hard to argue that someone can be *too* resilient or have *too much* learnability or be *too* courageous. And as you already know, you *can* develop attributes; we'll discuss the process further in the next chapter.

Before we move on, though, there are three more attributes I want to discuss. They're such obvious ones that you already might be wondering why each hasn't gotten its own chapter. Patience seems like a pretty key attribute, right? So does competitiveness. Give me a chance on fear of rejection.

These three *are* important. But they're also outliers. None of them fits the dimmer-switch model because each of them has an opposite that can't be ignored. Most of the attributes can be measured on a straight line that begins at zero. If you have low accountability—or empathy or discipline, whatever—the dimmer switch will be at the bottom. Your level of accountability can't go lower than that; negative accountability isn't a thing.

But what if you have zero patience? What if you have *less than zero* patience?

Then you are *impatient*.

Patience or impatience can be present at varying levels of intensity. That is, you can be mildly impatient or, as the saying goes, you can have the patience of a saint. That makes it what I call a bidirectional attribute, and it's better represented by a seesaw. Patience is sitting on one end, impatience on the other. If you're neither notably impatient nor patient, that seesaw will be pretty well balanced. If you're more patient than the average bear, then the seesaw tips to that side.

The same idea works for competitiveness/non-competitiveness and fear of rejection/insouciance to what others think. Those, too, are balancing on a seesaw.

There's one more thing that sets these three apart, and it's the most important. From my research and experience, I've learned that optimal performers can work with any of them. It doesn't matter which side of the seesaw you're on. Neither side is necessarily better than the other. This is different from the first twenty-two attributes, where being near zero on any of them doesn't promote optimal performance. But while patience is invaluable in some circumstances, so is impatience. Non-competitive people are sometimes the most successful. Fear of rejection can help form cohesive groups while insouciance can encourage iconoclasm. These three—or these three pairings, if it helps to think of them that way—are so situational that truly optimal performers can turn either to his or her advantage.

PATIENCE/IMPATIENCE

One day when my younger son was three, I was home alone with him while my wife was out and our older son was at kindergarten. I had a few things to get done around the house, so I put my son in his room with a stack of his toys. He was happily playing when I moved to another room. Within a few seconds, though, I heard his bedroom door close, followed by the unwelcome *click* of the knob locking.

I hurried back to his room, knocked, and gently called his name, trying to coax him to open the door. No response. I tried again, then a third time. Nothing. I wasn't hearing anything—no laughing, no crying, no answer at all. I wasn't worried, exactly, but I could feel a sense of urgency building in my veins.

But I have an abundance of patience, and I could feel that kick in, too. That allowed me to start processing the available information. That required situational awareness, of which I have a relatively high amount. I had not heard any loud noises, such as my son falling or furniture crashing down on him. I knew the room was pretty toddler-proof, no sharp edges or small objects a three-year-old might put in his mouth. I tapped my empathy: Panicking and yelling would likely cause my son to panic and yell, too, so that was out.

A tool! I remembered I had one that could pop the lock from the outside. I just had to find it.

I jogged outside. My son's room was on a ground-floor corner with windows on two sides. The shades were drawn on the first one but halfway up on the second. I could see him on the floor, still playing, not a care in the world, and, apparently, completely tuned out to any of my knocking. But I knew I had time.

It took me about ten minutes to find the tool, partly because I went back outside to look through the window a couple of times while I was searching. But I got the door open and all was fine. When my wife got home, I told her the story and we both practiced with the tool to make sure we knew how to use it.

A few months later, I came home from work one night and my wife sheepishly told me she had something she needed to show me. She led me to our son's room where I immediately noticed there was a hole in the door about the size of a grapefruit. Our son had locked himself in his room—and his mother is an *impatient* person. She did try the lock tool, but it wasn't working quickly enough for her. The sledgehammer, though, was easily accessible, so she whacked a hole through the door, reached through, and unlocked it.

Not the most elegant solution, but effective. Then she led me to the bathroom. Another hole. Apparently, the boy had locked himself in there, too. I had to laugh. Busted doors can be fixed, after all. "You could be a breacher on one of the SEAL teams," I told her.

My patience and my wife's impatience have always balanced beautifully. When a situation requires patience—like, say, quietly figuring out how to extricate a perfectly safe child from a locked room—she usually steps back and lets me take the lead. But when impatience is required—like when a child could be in tremendous peril if he's not freed from a locked bathroom *right now*—my wife will take charge. There are plenty of times when my patience can begin to look like procrastination, and that's when she really steps up.

The point is, both patience and impatience have pros and cons depending on the context. If two people can balance each other, all the better.

Leaning heavily toward the patience side will likely help emphasize other attributes, such as perseverance, learnability, and discipline. Patience helps in overall skill development and even managing the stress response. But there are also cases where impatience becomes a powerful attribute as well. Impatience can help speed up some critical attributes such as decisiveness, adaptability, and task switching. Wherever you fall on the scale, patient or impatient, the key is to recognize where that can be advantageous or disadvantageous—but remember that neither is bad.

FEAR OF REJECTION/INSOUCIANCE

There is no single mix of attributes that defines a SEAL. Like members of any other group, SEALs each bring their own unique blend. But there are some common threads. Ask pretty much any SEAL how he got through Hell Week, and he'll likely give you a variation of this answer: "There was no way I wanted to be the one who got up and rang that bell. I would have rather frozen in the surf zone than be that guy."

That's a fear of rejection talking, and SEALs tend to have

a bit more of it than most people. This is different from narcissism. Narcissism puts your opinion of yourself at the center, while fear of rejection is concerned with the opinions, or perceived opinions, of others.

Most people have some level of that fear, and it's perfectly healthy. (A pathologically high amount can tip a person into a debilitating psychological disorder called rejection sensitive dysphoria, but that's rare.) We're born with a biological need to belong to a group because it's a requirement for survival. As we discussed in Chapter Sixteen, this is why a hormone like oxytocin exists in the first place—to push us into social bonds. In earlier times, the group was necessary to fend off predatory animals and other clans. Resources were shared—hunters needed gatherers and vice versa. To be cast out of the group wasn't only humiliating but also potentially deadly.

We've evolved to be social creatures, to instinctively want to belong to a group and, with that, a fear of being rejected. The groups and the fears shift with time and circumstances. Children and adolescents generally have a higher level of that fear. Their confidence and sense of self are still developing, and they're busy figuring out how to navigate the world. Peer pressure works because it plays on that fear of rejection, and it's especially effective on adolescents because kids typically want to fit in, or at least not be left out.

The level of fear usually decreases as we get older and become surer of ourselves. But it rarely fades completely. When you behave a little differently in public than you do in private or with your closest confidants, for instance, that's your fear of rejection showing. At that level, a fear of rejection helps to maintain a polite society and perpetuate norms. Does anyone really enjoy wearing a tie to work? Probably not—but many people fear not fitting in enough to knot one around their necks anyway.

So how does this relate to optimal performance? Curiously, a fear of rejection can push us to overcome *other* fears. With an elevated level, you'll follow the group out of your comfort zone and achieve things you were afraid to try. If your friends are training for a triathlon, maybe you will, too, if only to fit in. Maybe you'll visit some exotic destination or try a strange new food or stick with a job for longer than you imagined possible.

This is one of the ways SEALs do what they do. Of course, there's more to it, but the fear of rejection, of standing out in a negative way, is part of the reason why guys who hate heights keep jumping out of airplanes, why guys who hate being underwater keep diving, and why we all went into the most dangerous parts of a war zone without hesitating. Guys pushed through their own fears and trepidations for fear of not serving the group.

That fear of rejection is sometimes at work even among those who don't make it through SEAL training. In some cases, classes will go on for days or even weeks without anyone quitting. Then, usually during Hell Week, one person decides to quit and ring the bell. Many times, as soon as that happens, there is a deluge of quitters, as if suddenly they now have permission. Because now they are not alone in quitting—they are part of another, different group.

For all of that, though, you don't need to fear rejection to perform optimally, or even function day-to-day. The opposite of that fear, not caring what people think, can be just as healthy and empowering. Most of us know someone who doesn't care what other people think. They do what they want, and if people like it, cool; if not, that's cool, too. You might even consider yourself one of these people. If you are, great. Just keep in mind that while *saying* you don't run with the crowd or conform to what others expect is very empowering, actually *meaning* it is quite difficult.

But for those who truly aren't constrained by the thoughts of others, who sincerely enjoy separating themselves from the herd, they open themselves to endless possibilities. They can explore unfettered and wander paths—intellectual, creative, even physical—that others overlook or reject. Some of the most famous and influential iconoclasts possessed this quality. Steve Jobs, Richard Feynman, and Vincent van Gogh are all examples of people who would likely not have broken the ground that they did had they cared what the group thought. The group isn't always correct, which we know only because a few rare people have broken cleanly from it. And if nothing else, not worrying about one's status in the group reduces stress, which in turn allows one's other attributes and talents to function more effectively.

Wherever you sit on the fear-of-rejection seesaw, there is potential.

COMPETITIVENESS/NON-COMPETITIVENESS

This is probably the most counterintuitive of all the attributes. Everyone in the performance-coaching business—researchers, writers, motivational speakers—agrees, and maybe even preaches, that a competitive drive is one of the keys to overall success. I completely agree.

But I disagree with the implied corollary—that being non-competitive is a detriment to optimal performance.

The value of competitiveness as an attribute is self-evident. Competitive people want to win. They want to be the best. The competitive athlete wants to win games. The competitive salesman wants to have the most sales. For those people, competition is motivation, one of the things that drives them to be successful.

But what if you're not competitive? Does that mean you don't want to be successful? Of course not. More likely, it just means you probably define success differently.

I have never been competitive, even when I played sports.

I enjoyed the intricacies of lacrosse—the precision ball handling, executing plays, and working as a team—but I never really cared much about winning or losing. Often, I would look at my teammates, who mostly seemed to love the competition and were very emotionally moved, in either direction, when we won or lost. I wondered why I didn't feel the same way, but usually mimicked their behavior the best I could so I would fit in (there's that fear of rejection). I kept trying to fake it when I applied for SEAL training because, frankly, I assumed my lack of competitiveness would be a liability.

To my surprise, it wasn't. BUD/S neither favors nor rejects the competitive attribute. The program doesn't care if you were an all-state quarterback or a Rhodes scholar or the homecoming king. SEAL training is designed to strip you to your core and then find out if you have what it takes to keep going. There's no "winning" BUD/S: You either make it or you don't. No one finishes first or ninth or last in the class. Everyone who completes the training has proven himself capable of being a SEAL, and everyone who rings the bell has not. It's binary.

There are, however, two awards given at the end of BUD/S. One is the Honor Man, which does favor the competitive spirit—it's a combination of running, swimming, and obstacle course scores, plus votes from the instructors. The other award, Fire in the Gut, is equally prestigious but takes none of those objective scores into account. Instead, the students and instructors vote for the man who shows the most grit and drive through the hardships of BUD/S. Often, it's one of the guys with the lowest scores. There's no competition for the Fire in the Gut award. It can't be won. It's earned.

That both awards are given out emphasizes the fact that SEAL teams, like all optimally performing teams, benefit from having both types of people. Competitive and non-competitive people approach problems differently and see the world through a slightly different lens.

Simon Sinek, in his book *The Infinite Game,* sketched the basic dichotomy. Working with a concept developed by James P. Carse, he explained that finite games have rules and boundaries and clear delineations between winners and losers. The easy analogy is sports. Every game or match has a fixed end point, marked by time or innings or sets or distance; identifiable players; clear rules; and an objective goal, such as scoring the most points or finishing faster. In the business world, there's the fiscal year and profit margins and gross revenues—clear markers for who wins and who loses.

Infinite games, on the other hand, are fuzzier. Players come and go, the rules are malleable, and the game never ends—the game exists to perpetuate itself. An infinite game can't be won in the traditional sense. It can only be navigated or managed with shifting degrees of success over extended periods of time. Think about the long-term business cycle or the continuing experiment in self-governance or even raising a family. Any of those can go well or spiral into disaster, but that's not the same as winning or losing.

Competitive people thrive on finite games. They tend to look at a situation or problem, identify the players, rules, and criteria for winning, and then attack it from that perspective. Non-competitive people can be more adept at infinite games. They might look at that same problem and search for solutions outside the immediate rules and boundaries, recognize that the players can, and probably will, change, and thus define success as something other than a clear and immediate victory. They will often watch what the competitive pack is doing and then purposefully avoid it and instead search for an alternative path. That's an invaluable perspective for any team or business looking to disrupt current markets and trends.

Neither approach is better or worse than the other.

They're just different. But there is tremendous power in combining competitive and non-competitive people on a team. Every infinite game has within it a series of finite games. An election is a finite game, but politics is infinite; the fiscal year is a finite game, but business is infinite; a date is a finite game, but marriage is an infinite game.

As Simon likes to remind us, life really is an infinite game, not a competition but a journey.

Both polarities of all three of these attributes have pros and cons. You would do well to figure out where you stand and figure out where those on your team sit as well. Doing so will allow you to capitalize on the pros and cancel out the cons.

CHAPTER TWENTY-EIGHT

DECODING YOUR PALETTE

By NOW YOU UNDERSTAND that attributes are not cryptic. They are not mystical, hidden clues to our personalities, nor are they buried deep in the subconscious. Dormant attributes might need a traumatic moment to tease them out, but our fixed and known attributes are visible every waking minute.

We just need to pay closer attention and know what we are looking at.

When you're walking down the street, driving a car, or sitting in a meeting, are you aware of your surroundings? Do you notice the details, the out-of-place stranger, the car trying to merge, the moods in the room? If so, you probably have a good amount of situational awareness. Or maybe you like to throw on your headphones and get lost in your thoughts. Maybe it's easy to sneak up and surprise you—you're likely on the lower end of the scale.

See? Once we're aware of the attributes, we can't help but begin to notice them in ourselves.

Still, assessing where we fall on each attribute scale is a

deliberate task. Simply noticing isn't enough. We've got to put in some work to better understand what's driving our behavior. Here's how to start:

FIRST, USE THE ASSESSMENT tool found at theattributes .com. The assessment tool is designed to give you a snapshot of where you stand compared to other people. Answer each question honestly and authentically, as who you are, not who you want to be—you can't move forward unless you know where you're starting. Keep in mind, though, that the assessment tool offers only a guide, a kind of head start— a questionnaire can't possibly reveal attributes as well as real-time events can.

Once you have completed your assessment, it's time to refine the results. This will be inherently subjective because the process relies on your memory. Recall how you behaved during times of stress or uncertainty, when your attributes overpowered your skills. Those situations don't have to be extreme. Think about the last time a flight got canceled. Were you fairly adaptable and patient? What about the last time you heard someone express political views completely opposite your own? Were you open-minded and empathetic? Or maybe you remember an especially stressful project at work. Did you persevere? Were you disciplined and conscientious?

If you're honest with yourself, you can develop a comprehensive sketch of your attributes relative to one another.

Also, it helps to ask friends and family members for their perspectives. While the first three categories—grit, mental acuity, and drive—are largely introspective, other people have seen you in stressful and uncertain environments and can probably give you an idea of where your tendencies lie. And the last two categories, leadership and teamability, require input from those who interact with you. Remember, you can't appoint yourself a leader or declare yourself a good teammate.

UNDERSTANDING YOUR CORE VALUES will give you insight into your attributes, too. Our behavior is informed by our attributes, but our core values also factor in.

Consider this scenario: You're the coach of a youth sports team. The kids, all ten- and eleven-year-olds, have had a spectacular season, undefeated straight through the playoffs. Now they've been invited to the national championship, a weeklong tournament at Disney World. The kids will miss a week of school, but that's not the problem: Teams are limited to twelve players, and you've got fifteen—so three can't go. It's not a financial issue, so you can't bake-sale your way out of it. All of the kids are able to go, and none of them are volunteering to stay home. The parents have left the decision up to you.

What do you do? Take a moment to think about it.

An answer likely popped into your head almost immediately. A few other possibilities probably followed, but focus on that first, almost reflexive response—because it's a clue as to what you value.

At the Chapman & Co. Leadership Institute, we've presented that dilemma to thousands of audiences. The list of potential solutions is always similar.

- Draw twelve names from a hat, lottery style.

- Take the best players, based on objective statistics if you have them.

- Pick the most dedicated players, the ones who always show up to practice and work hard.

- Reward academics by selecting the kids with the best grades.

- Refuse the invitation in solidarity with the entire team; if they can't all go, no one goes.

None of those answers—and yours as well, whether it's on the list or not—is right or wrong. Each of them is simply a window into what you value most. If that happens to be fairness, you likely thought about a lottery. Maybe you value competitiveness more and went with the top performers; or hard work and decided to take the most dedicated. If academics are paramount, that's what you chose; and if unity matters more than anything else, you canceled the whole thing.

This exercise illustrates how our core values influence our behavior. Most of us know our values, of course, and can list them if anyone asks. But rarely are we forced to place our values in competition with one another, to rank them in order of importance. You probably value competition, fairness, *and* academics. Fine. But which one do you value more? Probably the one you chose first.

Understanding your values can help you assess your attributes. For some, the relationship is obvious. If you value competitiveness, you have a high degree of the competitiveness attribute. The same is true with attributes like integrity, courage, and authenticity—if you value those things, you're high on the corresponding attribute scale. Others need a little more thought. If creativity is a core value, that suggests you have an abundance of open-mindedness or cunning. If you value recognition more than fitting in, your narcissism clearly outweighs your fear of rejection.

So how do you determine your core values? One quick and simple way is to look at the values in Appendix Two.

Pick a few that resonate the most with you, but no more than seven; we're digging for *core* values here. Be clear in how you define those terms, too, because you might not agree with the dictionary. A word like *freedom* can be liberating or terrifying depending on one's perspective.

Once you have your list, ask yourself some hard, clarifying questions. For example:

Have I abandoned this value when I was stressed or challenged?

Let's say integrity is on your list. But there was that time when you blew a deadline at work and instead of admitting it, you called in sick to buy yourself an extra day. Integrity, it turns out, is not one of your core values. It might be *a* value, but it's not part of your solid, immutable foundation.

Here are two more questions:

Would I sacrifice this value for money, say a million dollars?

Can this value explain some of the key decisions I've made in my life?

Ask these three questions about each of the values you listed. Be brutally honest—no one's looking over your shoulder. If the answer is "no" to the first two and "yes" to the third, you've got yourself a core value. If not, you might want to reconsider.

Now that your list is narrowed down, put those values in order of importance. If you could choose to satisfy only one, which would it be? Your answer goes at the top of your list. Repeat the question for the remaining values, and you'll have your values ranked.

Those core values are going to be, and have been, fairly consistent throughout your life. But the order in which you prioritize them can shift. A young man, for instance, might value adventure and recognition above love and belonging, but thirty years later, married with three children, the order switches. He still values adventure, just not as much as belonging.

SO YOU'VE GOT A good sense of where you fall on most, if not all, of the attributes. Now what?

First, don't judge yourself. Be neither critical nor prideful—aim for *understanding*. Attributes are like a unique palette of paints, custom designed for each individual. Some of us have more cadmium red or cobalt blue, and some have less ocher. But what we create with those paints—a masterpiece or subway graffiti—is up to us. Understanding what you have to work with, that maybe you could use a little more yellow, is the first step.

You'll rank high on some of the attributes and won't need to focus as much on those. Know that those are constantly running in the background, guiding your behavior. You can hone them just by being deliberately aware of them. As you go about your day, take note of when your empathy or adaptability comes into play, the moments, even little ones, when you lean on them. Recognize when they are strengths and when they are weaknesses. As I've mentioned, I love riding the subway in New York City because it allows me to indulge my situational awareness—I notice everything around me, and in that situation there are a million things to notice. But sometimes I just need to relax, and my hypervigilant situational awareness isn't helpful.

What about the ones where you're low? What about the tiny dot of yellow on your palette?

You can get more yellow! You can increase any of the attributes with enough time and effort.

Neural plasticity, which we discussed in Chapter Eleven, refers to the brain's ability to change with learning. Every thought, feeling, and movement is the result of a series of electrical signals traveling through circuits of nerve fiber. When we have a thought for the first time, or experience a feeling or move in a certain way, our brains create a new neural pathway. When those thoughts and such are repeated, a substance called myelin wraps around the nerves, making that pathway slicker and faster—imagine a rustic footpath that eventually becomes a six-lane superhighway.

Let's break down that neural evolution in the context of learning a complicated skill, like driving a car with a manual transmission. There are four phases in learning any new task:

- Unconscious Incompetence: *I don't know how bad I am at this.* When my dad first took me out to the big parking lot across the street from our house to teach me how to drive a stick shift, I thought, *This is going to be easy.* It was not, and I immediately moved to the next phase.

- Conscious Incompetence: *I now know how bad I am at this.* I'm in the driver's seat, and the car is jerking and stalling. Dad made it look so easy! With practice, I graduated to the next phase.

- Conscious Competence: *I'm getting better, but I have to think about everything I do.* If I concentrate on depressing the clutch, shifting gears, and then pressing the accelerator and easing up on the clutch at the same time, I can keep the car moving. I'd be a menace in traffic, but Dad can take me out on the back roads to practice. This is typically the longest phase, when the myelin is really wrapping around those nerves.

- Unconscious Competence: *I can do this without thinking about it.* This is the entry point into mastery. It's when Dad feels comfortable enough to take me onto busy city streets. I can manipulate the pedals and the shifter without thinking about either and fully focus on the road. Those neural pathways are now highways, sheathed in layers of myelin.

Those neural pathways are very durable. As I've mentioned, I drive a stick almost every day and never give it a second thought—unless I'm in Scotland.

Learning a skill is different from developing an attribute. For one, developing an attribute must be a deliberate, conscious choice. It can't be imposed upon you. Many people learn to type, for instance, as a side effect of using a computer. Not so with attributes. If you want more self-efficacy, you have to put your mind to it. Also, developing an attribute takes much longer. You're not only building new neural circuits but also bypassing well-established ones that your brain likes to use.

Still, the process is basically the same as in learning a skill: Practice, practice, practice. For any attribute you want to develop, try following these five steps, which you can remember with the acronym START.

SLOW down. In any situation, but especially stressful and uncertain ones, the key is to use your logical forebrain. That means remaining, or getting, calm. Highly charged emotional states set off a feedback loop between your brain and your body—feelings are processed through your limbic brain, which tells your body to rev up the sympathetic nervous system, which encourages the limbic brain to maintain control. Breathe, slowly and deeply. Focus on soothing thoughts. Allow the sympathetic response to notch down enough for your frontal lobe to engage.

THINK. That's why you engaged that forebrain. Where are you and where do you want to be? Are you rigid but want to be adaptable? Closed-minded when you want to be open-minded? Think through the attribute you want to develop and the behaviors that would follow.

ACT deliberately. You're calm, and you've thought out what you want to do and why. Do it. It probably will be difficult—you're bypassing a convenient and speedy neural highway—but it will get easier over time.

RECOGNIZE results. How did that work out? Was it difficult? Easy? What were the results? Consciously noting and analyzing those things will make the behavior stickier in your brain, easier to recall, and thus easier to repeat—or adjust if it didn't go well.

TRY a new environment. The problem with training for uncertainty is that, after a few runs, the training environment is no longer uncertain. So mix it up. Did your deliberate resilience when your flight got canceled work well? Great. Now try it after you get chewed out by the boss or have a tense argument with your spouse. In order to truly develop any attribute, you have to make it a habit. You might never get to unconscious competence, but conscious competence is definitely within reach.

For all that, remember that the combination of attributes already in you is perfectly fine. You aren't required to have more self-efficacy or courage or learnability. The important part is to be aware of which of your attributes are strong and which are weak. That will allow you to better understand what drives your behavior, which in turn will help you optimize your performance.

CHAPTER TWENTY-NINE

GO PERFORM OPTIMALLY

IN 2014, FOUR YEARS after I'd first started thinking about attributes, I happened to be in San Diego for a few days. I had business with the Naval Special Warfare Command, but there was also an officer on one of the SEAL teams I wanted to check in with.

A couple of years earlier, he'd been one of the candidates handpicked for the selection and training course. On paper, like all of them, he was perfect. In practice, like half of them, he didn't make it.

We met for a beer at one of the bars in Coronado. I wasn't sure what to expect. People have all kinds of reactions to profound professional disappointments. Most make their peace with it, but some are bitter even long after the fact.

This guy, to my great relief, was actually happy. He'd rebounded quite well after being dismissed from our program. He'd been promoted to task unit commander for one of the SEAL teams (each team is made up of several task units) and was getting ready to deploy again. He liked where he was and what he was doing.

I was happy for him. But I was curious, too. I asked him what he thought of his weeks in our program.

To my sincere surprise, he smiled. "Hands down," he said, "the best professional development experience of my career."

I was stunned.

He told me that when he realized he wasn't going to make it through the program, he thought about getting out of the Navy. Being selected for our program had been his only focus, what he imagined would be the pinnacle of his career. If he was going to fail, he wasn't sure there was much point continuing in special operations.

But then we dismissed him. My instructors and I sat down at the same table where we'd had to dismiss so many other good men. By the time he came to the program, though, we were deep into the attributes.

"When you guys gave me that first list, the one about all the things I didn't have enough of, that was tough," he said. "But that second list, man, that made all the difference."

The second list was of the attributes he had high levels of. We tried to do that with every candidate; it was in everyone's best interest for guys to leave as allies with a solid understanding of their strengths and weaknesses.

"Not because it was like, 'Oh, at least I can task switch' or something," he said. "It was more that I could see where I'd be a good fit."

I was smiling now, too. That's exactly what we hoped would happen.

Teasing out attributes, helping that man identify which he was short on and which he had a preponderance of, reframed how he saw himself and his future. He understood that he had a lot to offer the spec-ops community, even though it wasn't through a role in our unit. When he took over his task unit, he understood how his strong attributes—accountability, empathy, authenticity—would help him perform as a leader.

With his senior enlisted chief, he tweaked the training for the men in his unit. As with our program, the change wasn't in what was taught but rather how we, the instructors, looked at the results. Skills *do* matter, and those standards never wavered; it doesn't matter what extraordinary attributes a team brings to CQC if they can't clear a building. But his training wasn't a selection course—at the task-unit level, every man has to be ready to deploy, and by adding attributes to the equation, he was able to more quickly spot and address deficiencies. Sometimes that meant shifting a man to a different role, and sometimes it was helping a guy concentrate on developing what he needed more of. Solutions to issues came faster, and he was able to see his team with more depth and clarity.

But it was more than that. Sitting in that Coronado bar, he told me that he began to see how he could also be a better husband and father. Instead of getting frustrated when his wife got so focused on a project that she lost track of everything else, he relied on his abundance of task switching to step up and help. He targeted his humor more precisely, especially with his teenager, which smoothed out a lot of bumpy days. He was fascinated by the interplay between the natural narcissism of youth and the empathy now illuminated in his kids.

As he spoke, I recognized the true power of understanding attributes. Up until then, I'd been hyper-focused on applying them to spec-ops selection and training. But suddenly I realized that they affected *everything*. Here was a badass special operator who came away from a crushing disappointment empowered. By understanding his hidden drivers, he was able to perform better at work and at home, anywhere and everywhere.

That is what I hope for you.

———

I'M INSPIRED BY HUMAN potential. We are a species that in only ten thousand years evolved from cave dwellers to space explorers. Humans have the unique and brilliant gift of being able to imagine something and bring it into existence.

We are able to do this because of our grit, our mental acuity, our drive and leadership and teamwork.

Understanding your attributes is one of the keys to unlocking your potential.

You now know yours.

Maybe you've got more discipline and humility than you thought. Or perhaps you're a little short on situational awareness or adaptability. That's okay! You can always work on developing an attribute. But the important part is to understand what you already have.

Talk to your friends and your family about their attributes and help them discover their own palettes. They will gain the gift of their own self-awareness but then you can also see how each of yours complements the others. My wife and I have done that—which is exactly why we are a high-performing team. Knowing these elemental details will allow your relationships to soar.

That means all of your relationships. If you're part of any kind of team—in business or sports, medicine or education, professional or personal—you will mesh better as a group once you start understanding one another's attributes.

Also, figure out what attributes your specific group is looking for, then see how you all stand. Are you looking to bring on some new members? Now you will know the gaps you need to fill—and exactly what to select for in potential candidates. Don't rely solely on a flowery résumé that highlights accomplishments and skills—instead start inquiring about attributes. Does this person have the patience, integrity, or open-mindedness that we need right now?

This all will likely be a dynamic process as you maximize the attributes you are high on, develop the ones you'd like more of, and, possibly, uncover dormant ones that you never knew you had. You might discover attributes that aren't among the twenty-five in this book. That's great, too! Remember, this is not an exhaustive catalog but a solid foundation. Write down those new ones, explore them, deconstruct them, figure out what they mean for you or your team.

I CAN TRACE THE beginning of my attribute journey to a point in time, but I've always been curious about human behavior.

Why can some people do extraordinary things while others flail and founder?

What is it that allows apparent underdogs to perform and prevail?

How do Davids beat Goliaths?

Finding those answers became even more important to me as I navigated my own journey. The Navy, the SEAL teams, war, marriage, parenthood, even transitioning out of a military career for civilian life—each of those came with its own uncertainty and challenge. Maybe some chapters in my story are more extreme. But the fact is, every one of us—and every team, business, and organization—has their own hero's journey. Everyone hears their own call to adventure, has an urge to cross into the unknown, faces challenge and temptation, then endures revelation and transformation.

That's life.

My hope is that you can now use this tool for your journey.

Know your attributes. Use them to understand yourself, your relationships, your business, your teams. Use them to become better.

Use them to perform optimally.

ACKNOWLEDGMENTS

Naively, I thought that writing a book would be a fairly simple endeavor. It is decidedly not. It takes time. Hours upon hours of work, many of which are spent simply staring at a blank screen wondering what to say, doing tons of research, and typing and then deleting a lot. There are weeks upon weeks of tweaking, editing, and reviewing. And months upon months of prepping strategy, marketing, and getting it out to the world. The truth is that this type of hard work, to be done correctly, takes a team: family, friends, and experts in the business. I've been so honored, humbled, and grateful to have people in my life who have constantly believed in me, even when I've had trouble believing in myself. This book would not exist without them.

TEAM

Sean Flynn. I could not have done this without you, my friend. You've not only helped me put together a book that I'm proud of, but also taught me an enormous amount about writing, storytelling, and the power of language. You've been a mentor, guide, and sounding board on not only the book but many things. Thank you for all of your hard work, caring, and effort. I look forward to our continued friendship and many future projects.

Celeste Fine. I (and Kristen) could not have dreamed of a better agent to have our backs and lead me through this process. This book would quite literally not exist if it wasn't for your astounding ability to draw out powerful concepts and ideas. You are truly the best. Also, to John, Anna, and the entire small but extremely powerful team at Park & Fine—thank you for supporting and believing in me. It's deeply comforting to have all of you in my corner.

Ben Greenberg. I'd been told stories about editors that range from horrific to heroic. Thanks for being at the right end of that spectrum. But heroism is not the correct term because it's usually conditional, sporadic, and often dramatic. You've instead been a guardian—constant, consistent, and grounded. Constant in your support and guidance, consistent in your word to allow me to steer the narrative, and grounded in your feedback. My "editor story" has now been forged—thanks for making it a great one.

Andy Ward. Since you and I first met on the phone many years ago, I've never come across anyone who has anything bad to say about you. Instead, people use words like "honest," "brilliant," "trustworthy," and "caring." They say things such as, "He's awesome," "he's my favorite guy in the business," and "just one of the greats." Frankly, I was starting to get suspicious—until I actually met you and I realized it was all true. You are the definition of a class act, my friend. Thanks for being who you are and believing in me. I'm honored to now be another Andy Ward superfan.

To my other awesome team members. *Lisa Shannon* at Big Sky Bold and *Derek Mann*—thanks to both of you for helping me take an idea of an assessment tool and turn it into reality. *Nick Platt* at Navigo and *Rob Mohr* at Hit Hard Media—you guys are awesome teammates. Thanks for bringing everything you have to the table. Kaeli Subberwal, Luke Epplin, Tom Perry, Robin Desser, Gina Centrello, Greg Mollica, Ayelet Gruenspecht, Debbie Aroff, Maria Braeckel, and the entire Random House team—thanks for constantly making me feel like this book was your number one focus, even though there are so many other great books you are working on. You are all true professionals.

FRIENDS

HB. Every one of us SEALs hopes to go to combat, to finally put to use all of our training, to test ourselves in the real world—to prove ourselves beyond the cold surf and heavy logs of BUD/S. Actually getting that chance is something for which I will always be grateful. But being able to do that with you is a fortune that I will never be able to appropriately explain. You have always been the ultimate SEAL leader. That I have been able to lean on you, trust your guidance, and know that you'll always have my back is more than any man (let alone SEAL officer) could ever dream of. Thank you for leading Two Troop with me, thanks for showing me what resilience and perseverance look like every day, thanks for helping me with this book, and most important, thanks for being such a great friend, teammate, and brother.

Andrew Huberman. Your friendship, encouragement, and deep care and concern for my family and me is something that I've cherished since the day we met. It's amazing to think that all this came from some ideas we threw around over sushi one afternoon in Palo Alto. Thanks for being a great friend, a brilliant adviser, and a trusted business partner. I'm excited for the future, brother.

Dan Coyle. I tell the story all the time: "I read this book and it was so good that I decided I had to meet the author." That book was *The Talent Code,* and you were my first "author mentor." I still have the notes that I penned during our first sit-down in my living room to talk about writing. More important, you are a true friend, to my family and me. Thanks for all the advice, guidance, phone calls, introductions, and for just being you in general. I am proud to make you proud.

Simon Sinek. It is a certainty that I would not be where I am today were it not for your help, care, and friendship as I made the transition to civilian life from military life. You have been and continue to be a great friend, guide, and teammate. But I've also always enjoyed our conversations and your unique and inspirational view of the world. I look forward to continuing to bring ideas, old and new, into the world together. There is very little we disagree on, but when we do, the conversations are even more enlightening. However, *The Empire Strikes Back* is still the best movie of the Star Wars canon—not *Rogue One* (though I'll admit it's a close second). To the Simon Team—*Sara, Lissa, Christina, Jeff, Shed, Heath, Matt, Lee, Jessica, Justin, Laila, Lori, Sharin, Tim, David H., Siobhan,* and *Mikayla;* fellow Optimists *Kim, Kristen,* and *Jen;* and old friends and alumni *Darrin, David M., Peter,* and *Monique*—thanks for all of your hard work in supporting me and all of us while spreading the message of inspiration and hope. You are all rock stars.

Steven Kotler. You are a true friend and mentor. Thanks for all the phone calls, time spent over beers, and emails back and forth. I have learned from you since our first conversation. Your deep fascination with explaining the unknown and intangible through science and fact will continue to change the world for the better—and has had a massive effect on me. Your optimism is infectious, and exactly what the world needs. I look forward to continuing to tag along and peeking over the fence at what you are up to.

Bob Chapman, Matt Whiat, Sarah Hannah, Brian Wellinghoff, Susan Conrad, and the entire Chapman & Co. Team (*Aaron, Courtney, Ania, Jill, Maria, Tim, Jessie, Grace, Jami, Andrew, Mike & Astrid, Jane, Ian, Michaela,* and *Lungile*). Thank you. Also, fellow facilitators *Torian, John, Mark,* and *Paul*—I can't effectively describe what it meant to leave the Navy after twenty-plus years and be able to drop right into a team like you all. Your support, belief, encouragement (and, sure, the paycheck also) were all absolutely essential to my journey. You consistently helped me jump outside my comfort zone, gave me a beautiful and powerful message to transmit, and had my, and my family's, back the whole time. You all mean the world to us, and will always.

Josh Waitzkin. To steal a quote from you and turn it back on you, "You have a beautiful mind." You really do, and my mind grows and expands from every conversation we have. Our "whenever I was in the city" lunch linkups, which have now become periodic Zoom calls, are always enlightening. You are amazingly grounded, empathetic, and caring. Although I left the service short on confidence to succeed in the civilian world, you made sure to emphasize a key idea to me every time we talked: "You have everything that you need. Go out on your own and forge a new path." This book is a result of you constantly reminding me to believe that. Thank you, brother. Big hugs (another one of my favorite Josh sayings).

Sandy Travis, Brian McCabe, and *Chris Withrow.* Thanks for being both wonderful friends and perfect contributors to this book. It is richer and more powerful because of your stories and experiences. You are extraordinary people and I am grateful to have you in my life. *Jamie Wheal,* thank you for your friendship and guidance through the years—as well as pulling me along with you to gigs and events that I would have never experienced otherwise. You and your family are awesome. *Jonathan Fader,* I appreciate our friendship and always appreciated your encouragement, always urging me to "go do my own thing." I always listened. *Brian Hackett,* I've loved staying connected all these years, from the creation of the Mind Gym until now. Our periodic conversations were great on their own, but your commitment to getting my message in front of people has kept me on my toes and forced me to stay ahead of complacency. Thank you, my friend. I look forward to our future of continuing to share ideas.

FAMILY

Rusty. "Just down the street" for almost twenty years. You'll never know the full impact you've had on our family, though we'll always keep trying to tell you. You opened your heart and your home to us since the day we met, and the four of us (six with pets) couldn't imagine a neighborhood or a life without you being a part. You are family, and we look forward to always staying that way.

Mom. I got my own doses of open-mindedness, perseverance, authenticity, and many more attributes from you. You are strong and tough; you don't whine and complain but simply get things done; you are also faithful and loyal—I try to model all of those things. Thank you for always telling me to go do what I want, even though it was often dangerous. And thank you for all the prayers while I did just that. I love you, Mom.

Dad. Adaptability, situational awareness, and decisiveness are a few of the many attributes that I got from you. You also showed me the power of my own patience and gave all of us experiences that expanded our minds. Thank you.

More important, thanks for being a dad who never pushed us down roads but rather encouraged us to discover our own. You've always been a quiet influencer, always there to help us figure out our own solutions so that we became better problem-solvers and better human beings. In short, you've been what a dad is supposed to be—a true leader. You're also just a great dad.

Elizabeth. I can't think of a kinder and more authentically loving person than you. You are the best human out of all of us kids. Kind, caring, generous—I aspire to be the type of person you are. You are the best big sister that any of us could ever ask for, and I am proud to be your little brother.

B. Growing up, you and I never would have guessed that we'd live so close to each other for the bulk of our lives. Looking back, it seems like things just kind of worked out that way. I couldn't be more grateful that they did. It's been decades, and I still look forward to hanging out with you every weekend—and I feel it when we miss one. The joy that we experience when our families mesh together is indescribable. At the end of the day, I'm not sure who followed whom, but whichever one did is undeniably the smarter of the two of us (that's you, by the way).

And. You are my twin, so you already know how I feel. You've been there for me from the very first second of my life—literally—so thanks for that. So far, we've lived our lives vicariously through each other. I got to watch you live the dream of flying that we had since we were kids. You got to watch me do . . . well, all those SEAL things that I couldn't really tell you about. People always ask me, "What's it like to be a twin?" I think the more interesting question for us is, "What's it like *not* to be a twin?" But at the end of the day, I don't know and don't want to.

Josh. When you were born, you were big. Sure, in size, but as you grew up, we noticed that everything about you is big. Your personality, your laugh, your ideas, and most especially your heart. You are one of the most caring and big-hearted people I've ever met. You are the human expression of joy. Always default to that, kiddo—it will allow you to excel, and you'll help many people because of it. I love watching you grow up, and I'm grateful and proud that you are my son.

Connor. You've been my little swim buddy since birth. You've also had to watch me keep going away for long periods, and for much of that time not fully understanding why. Throughout it all, you've shown every single one of the grit attributes in spades—as well as a preponderance of most of the others. Now that you are a young man, I see you starting to look outward to the horizons that you might explore. I will always encourage you to find your own paths—and I'm excited to see which ones you do. Just know that wherever you go, regardless of whether we are together or apart, I will always be your swim buddy.

Kristen. We often comment to each other about how we won the familial lottery. When we look at our entire clan—immediate family, parents, in-laws, cousins, parents of in-laws, the list goes on—there is not a single person with whom we don't enjoy spending time. (Except the cat. He can sometimes be a jerk.) To think that we inadvertently collected such a beautiful, loving, caring, and fun group of people just proves that our decision to get hitched after only six months of a long-distance relationship was insanely perfect. At the end of each day, though, and the beginning of each new one, you are the person I most enjoy spending my time with. You are my favorite, and you always will be. Thank you for always pushing me to get out there, to discover, to find new edges, and to evolve. Thank you for being my wife, my best friend, my lover, my biggest fan, and my most trusted critic. Most important, though, thank you for being my lighthouse. When I'm lost or far away, when the fog rolls in and the rough seas of life begin to batter the boat, when I feel uncertain, alone, or even fearful, you have always been that beacon of light cutting through the dark. "I'm right here," you tell me. "Keep going. Come back if you need to but I'll always be right here." You have always been my lighthouse, and I will always strive to be yours. Thank you for the last twenty years, and for the next sixty or so. I love you.

LIFE PLOT

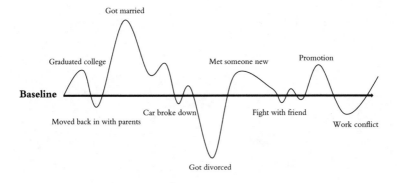

LIST OF VALUES

ABUNDANCE	COMMUNITY
ACCEPTANCE	COMPASSION
ACCOUNTABILITY	COMPETENCE
ACHIEVEMENT	CONFIDENCE
ADAPTABILITY	CONNECTION
ADVENTURE	CONTENTMENT
ALTRUISM	CONTRIBUTION
AMBITION	COOPERATION
APPRECIATION	COURAGE
AUTHENTICITY	COURTESY
BALANCE	CREATIVITY
BEAUTY	CURIOSITY
BEING THE BEST	DARING
BELONGING	DECISIVENESS
CAREER	DEDICATION
CARING	DETERMINATION
CHALLENGE	DEVOTION
CLARITY	DIGNITY
COLLABORATION	DILIGENCE
COMMITMENT	DISCERNMENT

DISCIPLINE	INCLUSION
DIVERSITY	INDEPENDENCE
EFFICIENCY	INFLUENCE
EMPATHY	INITIATIVE
EMPOWERMENT	INSIGHT
EQUALITY	INTEGRITY
ETHICS	INTELLECTUAL GROWTH
EXCELLENCE	INTELLIGENCE
EXCITEMENT	INTIMACY
EXPERTISE	INTUITION
EXPLORATION	JOY
FAIRNESS	JUSTICE
FAITH	KINDNESS
FAME	KNOWLEDGE
FAMILY	LEADERSHIP
FITNESS	LEARNING
FLEXIBILITY	LEGACY
FORGIVENESS	LEISURE
FREEDOM	LOVE
FRIENDSHIP	LOYALTY
FULFILLMENT	MASTERY
FUN	OPENNESS
GENEROSITY	OPTIMISM
GRACE	ORDER
GRATITUDE	PATIENCE
GROWTH	PATRIOTISM
HARD WORK	PEACE
HARMONY	PERSEVERANCE
HEALTH	POWER
HONESTY	PROSPERITY
HONOR	RECOGNITION
HOPE	RELATIONSHIPS
HUMILITY	RELIABILITY
HUMOR	REPUTATION
IMPACT	RESOURCEFULNESS

RESPECT

RESPONSIBILITY

RISK-TAKING

SACRIFICE

SAFETY

SECURITY

SELF-DISCIPLINE

SELF-EXPRESSION

SELF-RELIANCE

SERVICE

SHARING

SILENCE

SIMPLICITY

SPIRITUALITY

SPONTANEITY

STABILITY

STATUS

STEWARDSHIP

STRENGTH

SUCCESS

TEAM

TIME

TOLERANCE

TRADITION

TRANSPARENCY

TRUST

TRUTH

UNDERSTANDING

UNIQUENESS

UNITY

USEFULNESS

VISION

VULNERABILITY

WEALTH

WELL-BEING

WINNING

WISDOM

INDEX

A

accountability

  commitment and, 192

  described, 189–91, 195–96

  inability to control

    environment and,

    193–94

  learnability and, 193

  neutrality and, 191–92

  objectivity and, 193

  understanding actions and,

    192

acetylcholine, 79

Ackoff, Russell, 30

adaptability

  ability to increase or

    decrease levels of, 7

  decision-making and,

    184

  described, 65–66, 68,

    69, 70

  increasing one's, 71

  species survival and,

    67–68

  tactics and, 69

  using in real life, 14

adrenaline, 79, 80

adversity, 124–25

amygdala, 50–51, 54–55, 92

Antidotum Mithridatium, 34

anuras, adaptability and

  species survival, 67–68

arrogance, 218

assessments. *See also* self-

  assessments

  of attributes, 24

  compartmentalization and,

    96–98

assessments. *See also* self-
    assessments (*cont'd*):
of learnability in others,
    113–14
of skills, 22
attributes. *See also specific
    attribute types*
ability to learn skills and,
    14–15
assembling teams and, 6–7,
    28–31, 230–34, 258
brought out by stress, 38–39
core values and, 249
creating environments to
    discover, 233
described, 5–6, 23
developing new, 253–54
as difficult to measure, 24
diversity of, specific to
    mission or environment,
    230
dormant, 24–25
elemental nature of, 23–24
increasing or decreasing
    levels of, 7, 24, 37
as informing behavior, 23,
    24, 201
interplay of, 81
as necessary for survival,
    36–37, 67–68, 164–65
relationships and, 258
talent as dynamic
    synchronization of skills
    and, 38

as "the right stuff," 23
understanding, and
    unlocking potential,
    258–59
authenticity
consistency and, 177–78
described, 175
ever-present nature of, 6
as necessary for building
    trust, 177
personality and, 178–79
transparency and, 180
autonomic nervous system
fight, flight, and freeze
    responses, 52
parasympathetic nervous
    system and, 51–52,
    79, 80
set points for registering
    threats, 54–55
stress levels and, 35
sympathetic nervous
    system and, 51, 79, 80

B
Bandura, Albert, 180
Barry-Wehmiller, 161–62,
    167–68
behavior
attributes inform, 23, 24,
    201
core values and, 248–49
modeling, 180–81
skills direct, 22

Biggs, Tyrell, 65–66
Bobo doll experiment, 180
brain. *See also* dopamine
  amygdala, 50–51,
    54–55, 92
  courage circuit in,
    52–53, 55
  developing new attributes
    and, 253–54
  emotion and forebrain,
    165–66
  fear and, 50–51
  fight, flight, and freeze
    responses and, 52
  IT cortex, 91–93
  long-term memory in
    hippocampus, 87
  mirror neurons, 164–66,
    223
  nervous system, 51–52,
    79, 80
  patterns and, 87
  phases of fear and, 50
  plasticity, 108–11, 251–53
  task switching and
    forebrain, 104
  working memory in
    forebrain, 91
Brees, Drew, 21
Brown, James, 128

C
Candle Problem, 141–42
Carse, James P., 244

categories, described, 87
challenge coins, 176–77
Chapman, Bob, 162, 167–68
Churchill, Winston, 186
close-quarter combat (CQC)
  exercises, 8–9
commitment and
  accountability, 192
compartmentalization
  decision-making and,
    184
  described, 26, 95, 115
  effect on learnability, 115
  optimal performance
    and, 96
  practicing, 98–99
  process of, 96–97
  situational awareness
    and, 98
  stress and, 102
  task switching and, 101
competitiveness, 236–37,
  242–45
complex systems, versus
  complicated, 32–34
confidence
  attributes inspiring, 186
  as component of self-
    efficacy, 120
  described, 121
  humility and, 219
  as inert, 122
  leaders having and
    inspiring, 186

conscientiousness
　components of, 212
　described, 208, 209
　trust and, 211
consistency and authenticity,
　177–78
contexts
　described, 87–88
　integrity and, 204, 205,
　　206
　patience/impatience,
　　237–39
　recognition in IT
　　cortex, 91
　task switching and, 101–2,
　　104
core values, 248–50, 273–75
cortisol, 79–80
courage
　circuit in brain, 52–53, 55
　decision-making and, 184
　defining, 25, 47, 53
　developing, 55–56
　as dopamine trigger, 53
　fear and, 47, 48, 53, 225
　laughter and, 225
Coyle, Dan, 109, 216–17
creativity, 140, 141–43
The Culture Code (Coyle),
　216–17
cunning
　creativity and, 141–43
　described, 139
　narcissism and, 143

optimal performance and,
　144
curiosity, 137

D
decision-making, 183–85, 187
decisiveness
　described, 26–27, 182
　knowing purpose/goal
　　and, 187–88
　speed of decision-making
　　and, 185–86
　timeliness and, 183
Delaney, Joe, 173
DHEA, 80
discipline, 127, 128, 129
dopamine
　fear and, 225
　function of, 53
　increasing challenges
　　needed to receive, 54
　laughter and, 81–82, 223
　narcissism and, 150
　oxytocin and, 150–51
　seductive nature of, 153
　triggers of, 53
dream teams, assembling,
　30–31
Drive (Pink), 118
drive attributes
　basics, 117
　cunning. See cunning
　discipline, 127, 128, 129
　grit attributes and, 156–57

narcissism. *See* narcissism

open-mindedness. *See* open-mindedness

self-efficacy. *See* self-efficacy

drivers, described, 197

Duckworth, Angela, 46

Duncker, Karl, 141–42

dynamic subordination leadership model, 229–30

E

education, 36–38

emotional contagion, 163–64

empathy

  balance and leadership, 166–67

  described, 161, 163

  ever-present nature of, 6

  humans as wired for, 163–64

  listening and, 167–68

  as necessary for survival, 164–65

  neurologically, 165–66

  as partly matter of choice, 166

endocrine system, 79

endorphins, 223–24

environment(s)

  accountability and inability to control, 193–94

  creating different, to discover attributes, 233

  education and, 36

  integrity and, 207

  leadership and diversity of attributes specific to, 230

  level of stress and, 39

  not requiring leaders, 159–60

  optimal performance in, 40–41

  stress as physiological response to our environment, 50

  transferability of skills and predictability of, 32, 34–35

Everybody Matters (Chapman), 168

extrinsic vs. intrinsic needs, 117

F

fear

  brain and, 50–51

  courage and, 47, 48, 53, 225

  information from vision and, 49

  as necessary for courage, 53

  phases of, 50

  physical responses to, 18

  of rejection, 236–37, 239–42

  as subjective label put on response to stress, 50

fight, flight, and freeze
    responses, 52
finite games, 244–45
five-factor model of
    personality, 209
"flat" organizational model,
    228
focus
    choosing to, 111
    compartmentalization
        and, 97
    emotions and, 105
    task switching and, 101
    writing of scripts and, 110
Forbes, Malcolm, 171–72
forebrain, 91, 104, 165–66
formative memory and
    resilience, 78
fortitude
    described, 60–61
    developing, 63
    gauging, 62
Fosbury, Dick, 132–33
freefall jumps, 19
frogs, adaptability and species
    survival, 67–68
functional fixedness, 140

G
Gallipoli Campaign (1915),
    10–11
games, finite and infinite,
    244–45
generosity, 219

goals, as necessary for
    fortitude, 60–61
gratitude, 81
Greenleaf, Robert K., 173,
    228
Grit (Duckworth), 46
grit attributes
    adaptability. See adaptability
    basics, 45–46
    courage. See courage
    drive attributes and,
        156–57
    focusing on moment, 84
    interplay of, 85
    perseverance. See
        perseverance
    resilience. See resilience

H
Ham (space chimp), 22–23
Hell Week, 12–13
hierarchy in groups, 216,
    227–28
high altitude, high opening
    (HAHO) jumps, 19–21
hippocampus, 87
Hitler, Adolf, 130–31
The Honor Foundation,
    119
hormesis, 34
Hoyt, Edwin P., 183
Huberman, Andrew
    on amygdala, 92
    brain as source of fear, 50

on deliberately making
memories, 111
emotional contagion,
163–64
on emotion and forebrain,
165
neural circuits for fight,
flight, and freeze
responses, 52
study of neuroscience of
fear and, 48–50
on vigilance, 92
Hulse, Sir Edward, 219
humility
ability to increase or
decrease levels of, 7
described, 213, 215–16
generosity and, 219
vulnerability and, 215
humor
described, 221
neurological and
physiological effects of
laughter, 81–82, 222–23,
226
resilience and, 81–82
teams and, 226

I
impatience, 59, 236–39
inferior temporal (IT) cortex,
91–93
The Infinite Game (Sinek), 244
infinite games, 244–45

initiative
as component of self-
efficacy, 120
described, 121
as inert, 122
insouciance, 236–37, 239–42
integrity
context and, 204, 205,
206
defining right thing and,
205–6
described, 202
guideposts to, 204
teams and, 206–7
trust and, 206
intrinsic vs. extrinsic needs,
117

J
James, William, 223, 224

K
Kansas-Nebraska Act (1854),
170–71
Kauffman, Draper, 11–13,
144, 218
King, Martin Luther, Jr., 130,
131

L
Lao-tzu, 121, 173
laughter
bonding and, 226
courage and, 225

laughter (*cont'd*):
neurological and physiological effects of, 81–82, 222–23, 226
leaders
ability to inspire, 186, 197–98
environments not requiring, 159–60
of high-performing teams, 229–30
identifying and defining, 158
personalities of, 178, 179
skills of, 159, 186, 197–98
use of vulnerability loop, 217
leadership attributes
accountability. *See* accountability
authenticity. *See* authenticity
decisiveness. *See* decisiveness
empathy. *See* empathy
selflessness. *See* selflessness
speaking truth to power, 195
leadership models, 227–30
learnability
accountability and, 193
assessing in others, 113–14
decision-making and, 184

described, 27, 107, 108
effect of situational awareness, compartmentalization, and task switching on, 115
importance of, 107
increasing, 113
optimal performance and, 112
passion and, 112
sleep and, 115
using in real life, 14
Lemons, Chris, 33–34
Liddell, Chuck, 144–45
life plot, 74, 271
Lincoln, Abraham, 170–71
listening and empathy, 167–68
Louis, Joe, 66

M
Madoff, Bernie, 144
McCabe, Brian, 175–76, 177, 180, 181
McCallum, David, 227
meekness, 218–19
mental acuity attributes
basics, 86–88
compartmentalization. *See* compartmentalization
decision-making and, 184
learnability. *See* learnability
linkage of all, 115–16

situational awareness. *See*
  situational awareness
task switching. *See* task
  switching
Mithridates VI, 34
Moltke, Helmuth von, 66
motivation elements, 118
multitasking and
  performance, 100

N
narcissism
  cunning and, 143
  described, 148
  dopamine and, 150
  foundation of, 152
  keeping in check, 154, 155
  as motivator, 148
  myth of Narcissus, 149
  negative aspects, 149–50,
    152–53
Naval Combat Demolition
  Units (NCDUs),
  11–12, 13
nervous system, 51–52,
  79, 80
neuroplasticity, 108–11,
  251–53
neutrality and accountability,
  191–92
Nine Dot Puzzle, 139–40
non-competitiveness, 236–37,
  242–45
norepinephrine, 79

O
Obama, Barack, 188
objectivity and accountability,
  193
199 Days (Hoyt), 183
open-mindedness
  creativity and, 140
  described, 132, 133–34
  developing, 137–38
optimal performance
  ability to move up and
    down the active
    amygdala scale and, 55
  bidirectional attributes
    and, 237, 240–41,
    243–45
  compartmentalization
    for, 96
  cunning and, 144
  described, 40
  discipline and, 128
  environment and, 40–41
  learnability and, 112
  perseverance and, 40–41
  self-efficacy and, 122
  situational awareness
    and, 90
  understanding attributes
    and, 258–59
optimism
  as component of self-
    efficacy, 120
  described, 121
  as inert, 122

organizational charts, 227–30
oxytocin
    dopamine and, 150–51
    laughter and, 223, 226
    narcissism and, 152
    self-reinforcing nature of,
        153–54

P
parasympathetic nervous
    system, 51–52, 79, 80
Passport to Freedom (Travis),
    125
patience, 59, 236–39
patterns, 87, 102
peak performance, 40
Peale, Norman Vincent,
    78–79
perception, 61, 134–36
perseverance
    components of, 59–61
    described, 57–58, 61–62,
        63–64
    developing, 62–63
    optimal performance and,
        40–41
    tactics and, 69
persistence
    described, 59
    gauging, 62
    patience and, 59
    perseverance and, 60, 61
personality, 6, 178–79,
    209–10

Pink, Daniel H., 118
plans and adaptability, 66
positive attitude, 78–79,
    80–81
post-traumatic stress disorder
    (PTSD), 50
The Power of Positive Thinking
    (Peale), 78–79
predictability
    complicated systems and,
        32–33
    as preferred by humans to
        unpredictability, 34–35
    skill application and, 5,
        32, 38
prioritization, 97, 172–73

R
racing cars, 32–33, 37
realism and optimism, 120
reconnaissance by fire,
    187–88
rejection, fear of, 236–37,
    239–42
relationships and attributes,
    258
repetition, 109–10
resilience
    autonomic nervous system
        and, 79, 80
    described, 72
    elements of, 75, 76–77
    endocrine system and, 79
    ever-present nature of, 6

formative memory as root
of, 78
humor and, 81–82
positive attitude and,
78–79
two-minute rule and, 76
using in real life, 14
Riis, Jacob, 59
Rizzolatti, Giacomo, 164
Roosevelt, Theodore, 187

S
scenarios. *See* environment(s)
Schindler, Oskar, 144
scripts, 87, 110
Seinfeld, Jerry, 56
self-assessments
core values and, 248–50,
273–75
perspectives of others,
247–48
rankings on attributes, 251
tool for, 247
self-discipline, 128–29
self-efficacy
adversity and, 124–25
components, 120–21
decision-making and, 184
described, 119
developing, 125–26
ever-present nature of, 6
optimal performance and,
122
selfishness, 171–72

selflessness
described, 170
inspiration and, 178
prioritization and, 172–73
serotonin, 150–51, 152, 153
"The Servant as Leader"
(Greenleaf), 173
"servant-leader"
organizational model,
228
set points, 75–76
Shepard, Alan, 22
Shields, James, 170
Sinek, Simon, 244
situational awareness
compartmentalization
and, 98
decision-making and, 184
described, 26, 89, 115
developing, 93–94
effect of, on learnability,
115
evaluating efficacy of
solution, 27
IT cortex and, 91–93
optimal performance
and, 90
stress and, 102
using in real life, 14
using patterns, 90–91
vigilance and, 92, 93
skills
assembling teams and,
28–31

skills (*cont'd*):
assessing, 22
attributes as behind ability
to learn, 14–15
behavior as directed by, 22
decision-making as, 185
importance of, 234
of leaders, 159
learning, 12, 231
learning and, 21–22,
252–53
predictability and
application of, 5, 32, 38
talent as dynamic
synchronization of
attributes and, 38
transferability of, and
predictability of
environment, 32, 34–35
transferring to others,
31–32
skydiving, 18–21, 25–27
smartphones, 104–5
social relationships and
survival, 37
space exploration, 22–23
Stalin, Joseph, 182–83
static-line jumps, 18–19
Strayer, David, 101
stress
attributes brought out by,
38–39
autonomic nervous system
and levels of, 35

cortisol and, 79–80
courage and, 25
environment and level
of, 39
response to, 50, 102
situational awareness and,
102
subjective nature of, 39
sympathetic nervous system,
51, 79, 80
sympathy, 163

T
tactics, 69
talent, as dynamic
synchronization of
attributes and skills, 38
The Talent Code (Coyle), 109
task switching
calibrating levels, 105–6
contexts and, 101–2, 104
described, 100
effect of, on learnability,
115
energy requirements, 104
methods of, 101–2
stress and, 102
teamability attributes
basics, 199–201
conscientiousness. *See*
conscientiousness
humility. *See* humility
humor. *See* humor
integrity. *See* integrity

teams
  attributes and assembling,
    6–7, 28–31, 230–34,
    258
  attributes versus skills when
    assembling, 28–31
  conscientiousness and, 211
  defining, 199
  hierarchy in, 216
  high-performing, defined,
    199
  importance of humor, 226
  integrity and, 206–7
  leadership in high-
    performing, 229–30
  speaking truth to power in,
    195
  trust and, 200
  vulnerability loop, 216–17
tenacity, 59–60, 62
timeliness, 183
training, 36, 38
transparency and authenticity,
  180
Travis, Sandy, 119–20,
  123–25
Trumbull, Lyman, 171
trust
  attributes informing
    behaviors to encourage,
    201

  authenticity and, 177
  conscientiousness and, 211
  consistency and, 178
  dynamic subordination
    leadership model and,
    230
  as generative act, 215
  integrity and, 206
  teams and, 200
  vulnerability and, 215
  vulnerability loop and,
    216–17
Trust Factor (Zak), 151
two-minute rule, 76
Tyson, Mike, 65–66

V
vigilance, 92, 93
vision and fear, 49
vulnerability, 215
vulnerability loop, 216–17

W
Wolfe, Tom, 23
Wooden, John, 68
World War I, 10–11
World War II, 10, 11–13

Z
Zak, Paul, 151
Zuckerberg, Mark, 188

ABOUT THE AUTHOR

RICH DIVINEY is a retired Navy SEAL commander. In a career spanning more than twenty years, he completed more than thirteen overseas deployments—eleven of which were to Iraq and Afghanistan. As the officer in charge of training for a specialized command, Diviney spearheaded the creation of a directorate that fused physical, mental, and emotional disciplines. He led his small team to create the first-ever "Mind Gym," which helped special operators train their brains to perform faster, longer, and better in all environments—especially high-stress ones. Since his retirement in early 2017, Diviney has worked as a speaker, facilitator, and consultant with the Chapman & Co. Leadership Institute and Simon Sinek Inc. He's taught leadership and optimal performance to more than five thousand business, athletic, and military leaders from organizations such as American Airlines, Meijer Inc., the San Francisco 49ers, Pegasystems, Zoom, and Deloitte.

theattributes.com
Facebook.com/The-Attributes-110380034019335
Instagram: @theattributes

ABOUT THE TYPE

This book was set in Bembo, a typeface based on an old-style Roman face that was used for Cardinal Pietro Bembo's tract *De Aetna* in 1495. Bembo was cut by Francesco Griffo (1450–1518) in the early sixteenth century for Italian Renaissance printer and publisher Aldus Manutius (1449–1515). The Lanston Monotype Company of Philadelphia brought the well-proportioned letterforms of Bembo to the United States in the 1930s.